D0849414

# The Fate of Eloquence
in the Age of Hume

# Rhetoric and Society
General Editor: Wayne A. Rebhorn

---

# The Fate of Eloquence in the Age of Hume

ADAM POTKAY

CORNELL UNIVERSITY PRESS

ITHACA AND LONDON

*PR448*
*.R54*
*P68*
*1994*

Copyright © 1994 by Cornell University

All rights reserved. Except for brief quotations in a review, this book, or parts thereof, must not be reproduced in any form without permission in writing from the publisher. For information, address Cornell University Press, Sage House, 512 East State Street, Ithaca, New York 14850.

First published 1994 by Cornell University Press.


Printed in the United States of America

⊗ The paper in this book meets the minimum requirements of the American National Standard for Information Sciences— Permanence of Paper for Printed Library Materials. ANSI Z39.48-1984.

**Library of Congress Cataloging-in-Publication Data**

Potkay, Adam, b. 1961
    The fate of eloquence in the age of Hume / Adam Potkay.
        p.    cm.
    Based on the author's thesis (Rutgers University).
    Includes bibliographical references (p.    ) and index.
    ISBN 0-8014-3014-3
    1. English literature—18th century—History and criticism. 2. Rhetoric—1500–1800.  3. Literature and society—Great Britain—History—18th century. 4. Great Britain—Social life and customs—18th century.  5. Hume, David, 1711–1776—Contributions in rhetoric.  6. English language—18th century—Rhetoric.  7. Manners and customs in literature.  8. Courtesy in literature. 9. Virtue in literature.  10. Eloquence.  I. Title.
PR448.R54P68   1994
820.9'005—dc20
                                                            94-19001

# Contents

APR 27

# Foreword

Stated simply, the purpose of this series is to study rhetoric in all the varied forms it has taken in human civilizations by situating it in the social and political contexts to which it is inextricably bound. The series Rhetoric and Society rests on the assumption that rhetoric is both an important intellectual discipline and a necessary cultural practice and that it is profoundly implicated in a large array of other disciplines and practices, from politics to literature to religion. Interdisciplinary by definition and unrestricted in range either historically or geographically, the series investigates a wide variety of questions; among them, how rhetoric constitutes a response to historical developments in a given society, how it crystallizes cultural tensions and conflicts and defines key concepts, and how it affects and shapes the social order in its turn. The series includes books that approach rhetoric as a form of signification, as a discipline that makes meaning out of other cultural practices, and as a central and defining intellectual and social activity deeply rooted in its milieu. In essence, the books in the series seek to demonstrate just how important rhetoric really is to human beings in society.

By investigating the ambivalent response of the middling classes in Enlightenment Britain to classical eloquence, Adam Potkay's *Fate of Eloquence in the Age of Hume* offers an incisive analysis of one of the central tensions, perhaps *the* central tension, of the age. Potkay demonstrates how, on the one hand, those classes looked back nostalgically to the oratorical culture of Demosthenes and Cicero, admiring their eloquence because of its implication in the public domain, its direct association with republicanism, and its "masculine" force, a force thought to be the product of its characteristic figures of speech. On the other hand, the middling classes of Enlightenment Britain simultaneously distrusted classical eloquence: because it was associated with the lower orders and with the primitive and the vulgar, on whom figures of speech were supposed to be able to make particularly vivid impressions; because it was opposed to their standards of politeness and good manners, standards they identified as "feminine" in opposition to "masculine" political activity; and because it violated their behavioral norms of reserve and ironic detachment. After presenting this thesis in detail in the first two chapters, which focus on Hume as an exemplary or representative figure for the period, Potkay goes on in his third chapter to show how the tensions and contradictions he has mapped out inform some of the most important works of mid-eighteenth-century English literature, specifically Pope's *Dunciad*, Gray's *Elegy*, and Sterne's *Tristram Shandy* and *A Sentimental Journey*. Chapter 4 then turns to the question of religion and again focuses on Hume. Hume criticized religion as a form of rhetoric insofar as it used figures such as personification, apostrophe, and allegory to attribute powers—gods—to various aspects of the natural world, but he also sought to replace the community once produced by religion with a community of people brought together by their passions in a modern, internalized version of the classical polis once created by eloquence. Finally, in the last chapter of his wide-ranging and provocative study, Potkay examines Macpherson's Ossianic forgeries and shows how, in the imaginary realm of primitive Celtic society, those poems attempt to integrate the opposing tendencies of the Enlightenment. They do so through their heroes, who combine the force of classical eloquence with good manners and a refined sensibility, and who, though engaging in epic battles, simultaneously manifest the haunted consciousness characteristic of the modern world, a consciousness that may dismiss the superstitions of the ancients but still sees "ghosts," if only in the form of psychic projections.

WAYNE A. REBHORN

# Acknowledgments

This book grew out of ideas I first explored while I was still a graduate student, and I wish to thank all those who aided that exploration. I can scarcely imagine my higher education without the emotional and financial support of my parents and grandparents. My graduate career would have been neither so pleasant nor so fruitful were it not for the generous fellowships provided me by the Graduate School of Rutgers University, New Brunswick, and for the bonhomie of Rutgers English. I was first introduced to Hume in a provocative seminar of Jerome Christensen's. Early versions of several chapters benefited from the encouraging words of Cynthia Chase and Julia Sullivan. William C. Dowling, Thomas R. Edwards, William Galperin, and John Richetti provided instruction, example, and welcome advice as I developed my readings of Hume and Macpherson. My friends Steven Scherwatzky and William Walker kept me informed and entertained with many vivid discussions of eighteenth-century politics and epistemology. And Jonathan Reynolds had the most serendipitous habit of handing me little-known books before I knew I needed them.

In the years during which my ideas metamorphosed into the present book, I was assisted by a summer research grant from the College of William and Mary. My student Thomas Zadra spent a summer surveying a century's worth of Edinburgh magazines at the National Library of Scotland; his efforts were also supported by a William and Mary summer grant. On this side of the Atlantic, the offices of *Eighteenth-Century Life* proved an invaluable lending library, and I thank Robert Maccubbin and David Morrill for keeping me abreast of new books. John Lawrence of Swem Library, College of William and Mary, assisted me with microfilm research; and the staff of the Rare Book Room at Firestone Library, Princeton University, were most gracious during my visit there. Linda Dowling, whose stint among eighteenth-century periodicals in the Rare Book Room overlapped with my own, made reading through *Cato's Letters* and *The Craftsman* a less daunting experience than it might otherwise have been.

Parts of Chapters 1 and 2 have appeared in *Eighteenth-Century Studies*; part of Chapter 5 in *PMLA*. I am grateful to the editors for permission to reprint that material here.

At Cornell University Press I was fortunate to work with an editor as learned and sympathetic as Wayne Rebhorn; and Bernhard Kendler orchestrated my review process with remarkable speed and courtesy. I thank my anonymous Cornell University Press reader for impressing upon me the need for a new introduction; and thanks to Kim Wheatley for helping me draft one.

Above all I express my deepest gratitude to Monica Brzezinski Potkay for meticulously editing most all the prose I've written during the past four years and for making these years most wonderful.

ADAM POTKAY

*Williamsburg, Virginia*

# The Fate of Eloquence
in the Age of Hume

# Introduction

Tension between a nostalgia for ancient eloquence and an emerging ideology of polite style defines both the literary and political discourses of mid-eighteenth-century Britain; that this tension matters is the central claim of my book. Before pursuing this claim, however, I need to suggest what precisely was understood by *eloquence* and *polite style*, terms that for us may have acquired a deceptive film of familiarity. In the following pages I shall propose working definitions of these terms; in doing so, I shall also clarify how my book will trace the dialectic of eloquence and politeness from, roughly, 1730 to 1770, a period during which politeness, a social ideology in formation, gains ascendancy over, but never manages to silence, the renascent republican ideal of eloquence and its masculinist political assumptions.

## A Glossary of Terms

To avoid confusion, I shall distinguish between eloquence and a much more limited use of the term *rhetoric*. Technically, rhetoric is the prose art of describing, analyzing, and systematizing the eloquence of the past in order to guide the future orator; the rhetorician's main object, according to Longinus's introduction, should be to supply the aspiring speaker with practical help. Thus, in the terms of this study, Demosthenes has eloquence, whereas Longinus, however much he mimics, in Pope's phrase, "the great *Sublime* he draws," remains nonetheless a rhetorician.

Eloquence typically refers, in the eighteenth century, to the art of deliberative oratory. More specifically, eloquence serves as a metonymy for an imagined *scene* of ancient oratory in which the speaker moves the just passions of a civic assembly and implants a sense of community with his words. This scene of eloquence is most often set in Athens, where the orator is Demosthenes, evoking an esprit de corps as he opposes any compromise with the tyrannic Philip. Demosthenes' noble cause seized the political imagination of British citizens who sought a talisman to unify their interests and avert the putative threat of ministerial tyranny in Georgian England.

But Demosthenes' attraction was never wholly tied to his efficacy. Rather, his voice was valued as much as a means as for its ends—as much for the way in which he conveyed his meaning as for the meaning itself. That is, while men of letters savored through him a taste of self-transcendence, that flight hovered between aesthetic thrill and political commitment. Of course, for eighteenth-century readers Demosthenes' style derived much of its enrapturing power by being read through the magnifying lens of Longinus's *On the Sublime*. Thanks to Longinus, eloquence signified not only an ideal of secular community but an ideal effected by a numinous *manner* of speaking, a style marked by such vivid figures as apostrophe and prosopopoeia. And for Longinus this style was practically synonymous with the voice of Demosthenes.

For the eighteenth-century student of classical rhetoric—who was, typically, a devotee of Longinus—the preeminent home of impetuous oratory was Athens; Demosthenes' eloquence, however, proves to be a moveable feast. To some degree it recurs in Rome with Cicero's *Against Verres*, though British writers considered the judicial oratory of the Romans a dead end, agreeing that the eloquence of the bar had been superseded by an English legal system based on precedent and rule rather than on the disposition of the judge. David Hume—whose writings supply the point d'appui for my study—remarks in his essay "Of Eloquence" (1742), "I am ready to own, that . . . the multiplicity and intricacy of laws, is a discouragement to eloquence in modern times: But I assert, that it will not entirely account for the decline of that noble art. It may banish oratory from Westminster-Hall, but not from either house of parliament" (*Essays* 103). The British were attracted mainly to the eloquence of the ancient senate; and it was hoped, by some, that this eloquence could blossom anew, and in England.

In my first chapter, I examine the political context in which the ideal of eloquence was invoked from the 1720s through the 1740s. During this period, the *translatio* of ancient eloquence into the British Parliament—or, more broadly, into the new public sphere of print—was chiefly advocated by the "Country" or "Opposition" party, the political outsiders who, as Hume would say in 1741, "have been . . . long obliged to talk in the republican style" (*Essays* 72). They "talked" not only in coffeehouses and in Parliament but in the media of print: in Bolingbroke's journal *The Craftsman* (1726–36); in a body of verse that runs from Thomson's *Liberty* (1735–36) and Glover's *Leonidas* (1737) through Akenside's *An Epistle to Curio* (1744); and in pamphlets and books on the exemplary history of Greece, from Eustace Budgell's *Letter to . . . [the] Chief Minister of Sparta* (1731) to William Young's *History of Athens* (1786). In keeping with an assumption at least as old as Quintilian, the Country writers equate eloquence with "virtue," steadfastly maintaining that only the good citizen could be a good speaker. By virtue they mean the classical political virtues: courage, magnanimity, love of justice, civic participation, and, above all, a preference for the public above any merely private good. As Hume notes, "A man . . . without public spirit, or a regard to the community, is deficient in the most material part of virtue" (*Essays* 27). In theory, eloquence makes an inherently virtuous appeal to the civic passions; and it is, of course, aimed specifically at the civic sense of free *men*, for women were active citizens neither in Athens nor in London. As we shall see, from the fact that women *were* not full citizens in the governments of Europe, a number of male—or, more to the point, "masculinist"—writers, feeling more and more beleaguered by the clamor of feminizing sentiment as the century wore on, were increasingly liable to deduce that women *should* not have influence within a world that ought to remain political.

The British Opposition espoused its antique ideal of eloquence as a recipe for the orator of the future, the bold citizen who would arise in Parliament, in Thomson's phrase, "on some glorious day." At first glance Hume's "Of Eloquence" seems eager for this day to arrive. But although Hume endorses a renaissance of ancient eloquence with a great deal of cleverness, he does so with no more than half a heart. Nostalgia for Demosthenes, however far-reaching it may have been, engrossed neither Hume nor anyone else of his era. Indeed, although Hume laments the absence of eloquence from Hanoverian Britain, he nonetheless advances arguments against its revival. "Of Eloquence" effectively participates in the modern discourses that vied with a retrospective myth of eloquence for the hearts and minds of enlightened men of letters.

The essay nods, first of all, to the stylistic decorum of modern philosophy, a standard of taste and of truth defined by its objection to the animating figures of eloquence. From the beginnings of the Royal Society onward, figures were branded as signs of logical error and diagnosed as vestiges of primitive consciousness. According to the experimental ideal, procedural rigor and a transparent language of argumentation should supplant the deceptions of eloquence in all essays addressed to the understanding. And by an extension of that ideal into the political arena, Locke's liberal contractualism denies that eloquence has any place in the convocation or proper conduct of civil society.

But Hume, having first rejected Locke's contract theory of government, eventually deleted his Lockean censure of figures from "Of Eloquence." Indeed, as he time and again revised the essay between its initial publication in 1742 and its final version of 1770, he increasingly expressed his distrust of eloquence not in philosophic terms but rather in terms of the emerging discourse of manners or politeness. That is, he came to disapprove of eloquence not so much because it is deceptive or impolitic as because it is impolite. How the ideology of polite style emerged to challenge the ideal of eloquence is the subject of my second chapter. In charting the development of polite style I focus on writings by Addison, Shaftesbury, Swift, Hume, Adam Smith and the Scottish new rhetoricians, Johnson's *Rasselas* (1759), and Samuel Foote's *The Commissary* (1765). One of the aims of this book is indeed to determine what exactly eighteenth-century writers meant by the deceptively simple term *politeness*. I shall discuss this concept as both a literary and a social ideal: as a style that seeks to placate or stablilize rather than, as with eloquence, to make things happen; and as an ethos of concealment, entailing an aesthetic of invisibility—an ethos thought suitable to a sexually integrated public sphere and family circle. Apropos of its social function, politeness was implicated as well with the work of gender construction. Briefly, polite authors of both sexes held that the true template of politeness could be found in the particular notion of femininity that they themselves discursively created, and that femininity thus constituted could, by a recoiling energy, exert its polishing influence through the salon, parlor, or print on an audience of men.

Hume's essay "Of Eloquence" may ultimately be read as a *dialogue* between the assumptions of modern politeness and the claims of ancient eloquence, or, more precisely, a debate in which politeness is increasingly, though never conclusively, given the upper hand. This same dialogue is variously staged by other major authors of the period in which Hume wrote and revised his essay. My third chapter focuses on book 4 of Pope's *The Dunciad* (1742–43), Gray's "Elegy in a Country Churchyard" (1751), and the novels of Sterne (1760–68) as works that variously embody polite style while professing or implying the ideal of ancient eloquence—though Pope, Gray, and Sterne each profess that ideal with increasing irony. Still, discovering a tension between eloquence and politeness in their work argues that this dilemma is neither peculiar to Hume nor a ghettoized Edinburgh concern. Further, it demonstrates that this stylistic and political contradiction has inhabited our standard literature anthologies for some time now, although it does so in a language we have largely forgotten and that this study attempts to recall.

These three chapters, as a unit, delineate a gradual shift away from the ideal of eloquence and toward one of politeness; they are also an attempt to explain *why* that shift occurred. My argument is that this change in discursive models occurs as a corollary to shifting configurations of political power during the mid–eighteenth century. At the beginning of the period, the governing class was hardly unified in its aims or assumptions. I believe, as a student of Isaac Kramnick's *Bolingbroke and His Circle*, H. T. Dickinson's *Liberty and Property*, and the works of J. G. A. Pocock, that the eighteenth-century political arena did witness a real (though perhaps never disinterested) conflict of ideologies in the antagonism between Court and Country parties. These historians convincingly argue that the moralism of the Opposition to Walpole was more than merely ad hoc and opportunistic. While the rallying cry of the Country party was, as I maintain, "eloquence," the core of its ideology is what Pocock calls "civic humanism," with its dualistic vocabulary of "virtue" and "corruption." "Corruption," in England, has both a political aspect (the executive's subversion of the principles of representative government) and an ethical aspect (the degradation or "effeminization" of the political nation's former independence and martial complexion).

In this book I assume that the Country ideology maintains a certain recognizable consistency between *The Craftsman* and Frederick's Leicester House Opposition to Walpole's ministry, and the various Pittite agitations and extraparliamentary popular actions of the later 1750s and the early years of George III. During this span of time, however, the antagonism between Country and Court is gradually eclipsed by another conflict within the body politic: a struggle not between factions but between classes. W. A. Speck maintains that by the 1760s the rivalry between Court and Country elites gives way to the antagonism between a largely consolidated "ruling class" or Whig oligarchy and an increasingly vocal "mob." (On "the process by which the friction of two power elites was transformed into the rule of a governing class" between the years 1714 and 1760, see Speck 143–66.) As I shall argue, one of the chief ways in which the governing class sought to consolidate itself was through the ideology of politeness.

And professing politeness meant, for any writer (once) sympathetic to Country ideals, distancing oneself from the openly democratic ideal of ancient eloquence. As I have suggested in the précis of my first three chapters, Country shibboleths— eloquence foremost among them—become far less appealing to many men of letters, including Hume, in the years between Walpole and Wilkes; in their place one increasingly finds references to an evolving social norm concerning what "polite persons" say and do not say, do and do not do. As Pocock remarks, "Politeness and enlightenment were irenic, established, and oligarchic ideals, capable of being employed against Puritan, Tory, and republican alike and of making them look curiously similar" (*Virtue* 236). To some extent, my book's meditations on the meaning of politeness intend simply to unpack the wisdom of Pocock's compendious sentence.

Whereas my first three chapters establish the discordances between the ideals of eloquence and politeness, my fourth and fifth chapters concern two Scottish efforts to harmonize them—two distinct attempts to reimagine the scene of eloquence in order to make its communitarian assumptions palpable and effective for a new community of polite readers. Chapter 4 focuses on Hume's attempt, both in his early *Treatise of Human Nature* (1739–40) and, more elaborately, in *The Natural History of Religion* (1757), to establish a myth of community in which our common perceptions and mutual passions unite us in the manner of the ideal orator. Accordingly, perceptions that "strike" the mind in the *Treatise* do so with the same "force" and "vivacity" that classical and neoclassical rhetoricians attribute to Demosthenes. And Hume's *Natural History of Religion*—a work that traces vulgar religious belief to that species of perception called "passion"— resembles the *Treatise* in offering an enlivened account of how the force of passion "actuates" even the enlightened. Thus Hume styles both his epistemology and his historiography as allegories of eloquence, or stories in which personified perceptions assume the unifying power, and the very predicates, anciently attributed to the ideal orator—except that here they do so to consolidate not the polis but the polite.

My fifth and final chapter examines James Macpherson's extraordinarily popular *Poems of Ossian* (1760–63) as a crucial episode in the midcentury debate between a domesticated ideal of

politeness and an increasingly backward-looking cult of eloquence. British writers, *après* Rousseau, were apt to locate the
true scene of eloquence not among M.P.'s or Roman senators but
rather in the native American tribe or the ancient Scottish clan.
Macpherson capitalized on this archaizing of eloquence by paradoxically modernizing the ancient clan: that is, the Ossianic forgeries *reconcile* the age's nostalgia for sublime eloquence and political community with its taste for subdued manners and private
life. Thus, the Fingalian heroes possess fierce civic virtue but
feminized ties to home. And although they speak in rude apostrophes and prosopopoeias, effusively animating all nature and calling forth the dead, their figures of thought shade into Macpherson's distinctly modern depiction of "haunted consciousness," in
which the mind's private imagery—especially the speaking images of dead or absent loved ones—comes to seem more real than
a public reality we no longer trust. Macpherson thus achieves a
synthesis of modern self-absorption and primitive dispersal of
being; in the poems of Ossian, totem and trauma are one.

## The Age of Hume

The ongoing tension between the ideals of ancient eloquence
and modern manners informs not only a handful of canonical
authors but, as I hope to show throughout my book, a whole
constellation of rhetoricians, minor poets, popular playwrights,
magazine writers, political pamphleteers, and private correspon-
dents. I should note that most of these authors are men. I address
a number of women writers, major and minor—Mary Wortley
Montagu, Madame du Deffand, the Comtesse de Boufflers, Charlotte Lennox, Anna Seward, Mary Wollstonecraft—but these figures are somewhat less central to my concerns only because they
tend to champion the new ideology of politeness without the
ambivalence of their male contemporaries: for why should any
woman writer desire, even halfheartedly, a return to the rigidly
sexist communitarian assumptions of Demosthenes' Athens?

Because my study aims to re-create a sense of the conflicting demands of eloquence and politeness—and because I believe that Hume's prose serves as an extraordinarily sensitive register of that conflict—I have elected to designate the period under my consideration the "age of Hume." I do so warily, duly suspicious both of the prosopopoeic desire to give a face to an age and of the paternalistic habit of making that face a male one. I do so, however, less as a tribute to Hume's monumental ego or his centripetal force than in recognition of the extent to which he reflects and advances the several discourses with which my study is concerned: both the traditional languages of republican politics and Longinian aesthetics, and the emerging language of politeness. Moreover, it is with a greater self-consciousness than most that Hume expresses the predicament implicit in many authors of his time—namely, the sense of hanging between a neoclassical paradigm not wholly tenable and a modern ideology whose implications had yet to unfold. In general, this predicament was felt less keenly in England than in Hume's post-Union Scotland, a country in which, for complex political and economic reasons, zeal for improvement (and, among Scottish philosophers, theories of progress) coincided with a hearty regret for the independence and simplicity of the past.[1] In this book I consequently assume something of a Scots-centric perspective, one that is conveniently implied by labeling the era the "age of Hume."

I should mention that when I refer to Hume here I am thinking chiefly of the man of letters who most appealed to his contemporaries in Britain and France: Hume the Addisonian essayist, the critic of religion, and the historian of England. Although I do at times refer to the *Treatise of Human Nature* and to the *Enquiries* (1748–51), it should be noted that in Hume's own day the matter of these books—what Hume calls his "abstruse philosophy"— was mainly known through James Beattie's caricature of it in his *Essay on the Immutability of Truth* (1770). The *Treatise*, by Hume's own admission, "fell dead-born from the press" (*Essays*

---

1. On the historical and social factors that contributed to the distinctive nature of Scottish thought in the eighteenth century, see Nicholas Phillipson, "Towards a Definition of the Scottish Enlightenment," and the book-length studies by Anand Chitnis, Charles Camic, and Richard Sher.

xxxiv); but as Johnson wrote to Boswell (31 August 1772), "Beattie's book is, I believe, every day more liked; at least, I like it more, as I look more upon it."

But then, Johnson admired Beattie largely as an apologist for *Christian* truths. In the context of this book, Hume serves better as an exemplary figure than Johnson not least because of the resolutely secular cast of his neoclassicism. For Hume, as for most of the other authors addressed in this volume, an emphasis on religion constitutes "a blemish in any polite composition" (*Essays* 248). To quote Pope's *Epistle To Burlington*, the "soft Dean . . . never mentions Hell to ears polite" (149–50)—and, *pace* Aubrey Williams, neither does Pope.

Conversely, if hell is mentioned it is not attended to by ears polite: thus Benjamin Franklin, hearing George Whitefield preach on the streets of Philadelphia, seems to take no notice of the matter of Methodist oratory (notably, one of Whitefield's popular sermons was "The Eternity of Hell-Torments") but rather is fascinated by the acoustics of the scene:

> [Whitefield] preach'd one evening from the top of the Court House steps, which are in the middle of Market Street. . . . I had the curiosity to learn how far he could be heard, by retiring backwards down the street towards the river, and I found his voice distinct till I came near Front Street, when some noise in that street, obscur'd it. Imagining then a semicircle, of which my distance should be the radius, and that it were fill'd with auditors, to each of whom I allow'd two square feet, I computed that he might well be heard by more than thirty thousand. This reconcil'd me to the newspaper accounts of his having preach'd to 25,000 people in the fields, and to the ancient histories of generals haranguing whole armies, of which I had sometimes doubted. (90)

In computing the number of auditors that might hear a single voice, Franklin acts out of disinterested curiosity and for the sake of historical record: he would verify not only newspaper reports of Whitefield's audiences but the tales he has read in Herodotus of generals orating to their armies. For a fleeting moment Philadelphia becomes a shadow of Thermypolae, and Whitefield a reflection of Leonidas before his soldiers.

Indeed, in the age of Hume religion is often viewed as a mirage in a landscape deserted by the ancients. Confronted by Whitefield's fiery pulpit oratory, Franklin coolly thinks of the classics— a response that may derive, in part, from his youthful application to the works of Addison. Addison forged a literary world in which Cicero's *De Officiis*—a text that supplies fourteen *Spectator* mottoes—figures far more prominently than any work of devotional literature; and Hume professed, "I desire to take my catalogue of virtues from Cicero's *Offices*, not from the *Whole Duty of Man*" (*Letters* 1:34). Secularist polite culture thus opposes the more popular or middle-class eighteenth-century taste for works such as the *Whole Duty*, *The Pilgrim's Progress*, William Law's *Serious Call to a Devout and Holy Life*, or, indeed, Whitefield's *Sermons*. The latter quite pointedly denounces "polite" codes and diversions as a waste of "your precious time, which should be employed in working out your salvation with fear and trembling" (122). But polite deafness to such oratory is perhaps best expressed by the anonymous essayist who, writing "A Comparison of the Modern and Ancient Orators" in the *Edinburgh Magazine* (March 1785), defines "an orator" as "a political orator; for as to the eloquence of the pulpit, I leave it at present entirely out of the question" (227). It is precisely this sort of segregation or hurried dismissal of ecclesiastical oratory that accounts for its absence from my book.

Of course, should we concede J. C. D. Clark's contention that the Georgian era was fundamentally an Anglican, aristocratic, and monarchical "ancien régime," then my focus on an "age of Hume" admits a frankly countercultural bias. As Clark suggests, "theological heterodoxy" may have been no more than a speck in the eye of "the ordinary, the normal, the established" (6); that speck has, however, become a log in our own eyes, and one that this book does not attempt to remove.

## A Discourse on Method

By providing this broad summary of each of my chapters, I trust I have not exhausted the interest of a book that proceeds by minute steps as well as long strides. In my chapters I have tried to negotiate the hermeneutic circle, moving back and forth between fairly brisk synopsis and slow-motion readings of selected texts and passages; I have sought to observe both the history of literature and the literature of history, in the belief that one cannot stand without the other. However, if priority is to be granted, it is to be granted to close reading, the art of attending to the play and paradoxes of literary language. Indeed, the tensions and ironies that inhabit our very best efforts at getting something said are what make them, literarily speaking, our best efforts. They are what send us back time and again to texts we might otherwise just remember. In the words of Heinrich Zimmer, quoted in James Merrill's *The Book of Ephraim*, "The powers have to be consulted again directly—again, again and again. Our primary task is to learn, not so much what they are said to have said, as how to approach them, evoke fresh speech from them, and understand that speech."

At the present time, one prevalent way of evoking fresh speech from old texts is to adhere to a set of critical practices and thematic concerns sometimes organized under the rubric "the new historicism." Although I certainly have not been doctrinaire in following a program embodied in the pages of *Representations*, I do find that my own interests in examining eighteenth-century culture coincide with a number of those cultivated by the editorial board of that journal, and I would like here to assert those coincidences in the hope of drawing a wider audience of literary scholars than the field of eighteenth-century studies typically attracts. For while a wave of new historicist studies has stimulated a good deal of fresh interest in both the Renaissance and the Romantic period, the eighteenth century remains comparatively untouched by the movement's methodological and thematic concerns. The list of exceptions to that rule is, of course, steadily growing;[2] and I would like to situate my own work in relation to a

2. The student of eighteenth-century studies inevitably thinks of the work of Nancy Armstrong, John Bender, Jerome Christensen, Michael McKeon, and Felicity Nussbaum; and there are other, less certain candidates, among them critics of a British Marxist variety, such as Carole Fabricant and Donna Landry, and critics such as John Barrell and William C. Dowling—with whom my most immediate

hypothetical mainstream of new historicism and to suggest ways in which my book addresses some of the movement's signal concerns.

First of all, the discourses of eloquence and politeness participate in those "complex interactions of meaning in a given culture" that have, since Stephen Greenblatt's *Renaissance Self-Fashioning* (3), so intrigued literary and cultural critics. The ideal of eloquence affords a fairly obvious connection between literature (or the aesthetic) and political life, while politeness is evidently at once a social and a literary code. Neither ideal, in other words, is entirely textual, or if it is so it is only so in the broad sense that all cultural forms are "textual" or discursively created. Thus, in approaching the dialectic of eloquence and politeness, I modestly attempt here to demonstrate the situation of literature within, in Wittgenstein's phrase, a "form of life" as well as, conversely, to evince the literary moorings of any life at all.

Consequently, in canvassing eighteenth-century attitudes toward eloquence and politeness I have perforce studied the intersections among a wide range of "literary" and "nonliterary" texts (although this opposition is, generally, far more permeable in the eighteenth century—the once infamous "age of prose"—than it is in either the Renaissance or the Romantic era). In doing so, I have come to share something of the new historicists' sense that in a given slice of time all texts circulate more or less inseparably and that connections and consonances may profitably be found among seemingly disparate discourses and social practices. Such a vision of pantextuality (potentially a rather heady one) is quite soberly codified in a new historicist manifesto written by the eighteenth-century critic John Bender; note in particular the second and third points of his summary of the "three simultaneous postures" shared by those within the movement:

(1) an active awareness and employment of theory, including a certain self-reflexiveness; (2) a fairly pervasive use of original sources both literary and non-literary, with similar methods of analysis be-

---

affinities lie—who are engaged in working out the implications for literary studies of Pocock's political analysis of the period.

ing employed on both and with a minimum of the old-fashioned
background/foreground opposition; (3) a redefinition through re-
reading of some canonical work, or previously uncanonized work, as
a culturally operative text rather than as a strictly aesthetic object.
("A New History of the Enlightenment?" 65)

Although I have confined most of my own self-reflexiveness to
my Introduction here, I do, in the chapters that follow, engage a
heterogenous array of primary texts, and my book does culminate
in a sustained reading of the *Poems of Ossian* as a "culturally
operative" work—that is, one that derives its power not primarily
from aesthetic effect but rather through its ability to reconcile—
for eighteenth-century readers if not, presumably, for us—
contradictions between eloquence and politeness, or, more generally, between recollections of communal belonging and prospects
of societal loneliness.

Yet these shared methodological aims do not quite make me a
new historicist; for the movement, as I understand it, dictates not
only matters of procedure but also questions of content. New
historicists tend to be united by certain thematic concerns if not
(*tant mieux*) by shared professions of faith. And here is the third
and last area in which some of my interests coincide with those of
the new historicists: I too subscribe to Foucault's argument that,
as Bender puts it, "sexuality is constructed socially and operates
differently in each historical period" (12); and I too address the
theme par excellence of Greenblatt and his followers—the consolidation of group consciousness (here, "the polite") through opposition to a threatening Other (here, "the mob"). Allow me to
elaborate separately on each of these points.

The social construction of gender in eighteenth- and nineteenth-century literature is the theme of Nancy Armstrong's influential book *Desire and Domestic Fiction*. As her account of
the history of gendering is fairly well known, I will position my
own understanding of the matter in explicit relation to hers. Her
main contentions are these:

> To describe the history of domestic fiction . . . I will argue several
> points at once: first, that sexuality is a cultural construct and as
> such has a history; second, that written representations of the self

allowed the modern individual to become an economic and psychological reality; and third, that the modern individual was first and foremost a woman. . . . I will insist that one cannot distinguish the production of the new female ideal either from the rise of the novel or from the rise of the new middle classes in England. (8)

Although I agree with the first three points of Armstrong's thesis, my own argument is that the Anglo-American, gendered self was not created solely, or perhaps even primarily, by novels but—at least in the *mid*–eighteenth century—by the (loosely speaking) "middle-class" discourse of politeness, an ideology that was never confined to one literary genre.

Politeness, both as a style of social behavior and as well-behaved writing, is inculcated not only through novels or through the conduct books for women that Armstrong so thoroughly analyzes (60–95) but through essays, periodic and collected, from Addison to Hume (it is no small matter that the one book that Rousseau's Emile gives to his affianced Sophie is the collected *Spectator*); histories, especially those of Hume and Robertson; philosophical tales (preeminently, as I shall argue, Johnson's *Rasselas* as a fable of the ways in which polite women may socialize men); poetry from Pope to Gray and, above all, the poetry of Ossian, which represents the midcentury apex of the polite Addisonian ideal of the domestic woman, blended with the somewhat more innovative image of the woman of feeling. Novels, then, while surely making an important contribution to the cultural formation of "the new female ideal," had no monopoly on the process. And indeed, the only novelist I shall discuss at length is Sterne, an author whom Armstrong does not address and one who, unlike women writers of the period, expresses a residual tension in the novel between a reluctantly abandoned ideal of masculinist eloquence and an at least ironically accepted ideology of feminized polite style.

Thus, my sense of the *agency* of gender construction differs from Armstrong's: what she would attribute to the novel I would attribute to the more diffuse and more pervasive discourse of politeness. And as we differ in our account of the means of gendering, so too do we differ in our sense of its ends, or in precisely what constitutes "the new female ideal." Examining a wider range of texts within a more limited historical scope enables me to offer a more detailed description of what that ideal was like, at least in midcentury Britain. Certainly that ideal was, as Armstrong maintains, domestic—indeed, the criterion of domesticity became increasingly important as the century wore on. It was also, as she argues, both the effect and the spur of the middle ranks of society; and it entailed a representation of women as curiously *disembodied* creatures (75–76). Polite style is itself, as I shall argue, an essentially disembodying style from Pope onward. Armstrong notes that "the domestic woman executes her role in the household by regulating her own desire" (81): my own point will be that polite theorists often described the exemplary woman as lacking (and thereby prescribed the lack) of man's more volatile passions, especially sexual ones. Yet here we venture upon territory that Armstrong does not tread.

Advocates of politeness also described their feminine ideal as at once sensible, in keeping with an efflorescent cult of feeling, and commonsensical, in keeping with John Bull's (and the Scottish philosopher's) distrust of "metaphysics" or, more generally, impractical learning. Indeed, in rather startling contrast to the traditional Augustinian equation of women with fearful passion, during the age of Hume women were often attributed with an admirable purity of common sense, undefiled by the excesses of men's classical and clerical educations. The one aspect of male education that Hume, for one, exhorted women to cultivate is the study of history—for lessons in virtue, for matter in conversation, and in hope of removing the one rooted error of female judgment, a taste for "Books of Gallantry and Devotion" (*Essays* 537, 563–68). As Armstrong notes in passing, Hume's advice was propagated by later writers of conduct books for women (103–4), though not, presumably, by any self-respecting novelist.

Finally, I heartily agree with Armstrong's assertion that "conduct books transformed the female into the bearer of moral norms and socializer of men," specifically middle-class men, although I would insist that conduct books are but a part of the discursive field of politeness, and I would focus on precisely that historical period that is elided in Armstrong's account of educational treatises, the mid–eighteenth century (88–90). With Armstrong, I agree that the process of gender formation is inextricably linked to the history of class formation, though my own emphasis in discussing the latter will be not on the ideology of the "bourgeois" household but on the manner in which class formation is embedded in discursive practices, particularly in the language of politeness. For politeness, while participating in an economy of gendering, serves more fundamentally to distinguish those men and women under its aegis from those outside it—from the collective Other that polite persons deemed the vulgar or the mob.

Discussing the origins of class consciousness brings me to my second area of coincidence not only with Armstrong but, as I remarked previously, with the new historicism in perhaps its most general (and most leftist) aspect. And it is here that I would like to address, in a preliminary way, the status of eighteenth-century republicanism and politeness as *ideologies*. Republicanism functions as an ideology only in a weak sense, because its regressive vision is largely intended as a negative criticism of historical movements that it hardly aspires to control. Republican apologists, particularly in the age of Walpole, opposed the rise in Parliament of executive policy-making that was perceived as biased toward burgeoning commercial interests and against both the political prerogatives of gentlemen and (in some instances) the customary rights of common laborers; in Marxian terms, however, their protests seem oddly irrelevant to the progress of History, which, after all, demanded the rise of the middle class. Now, there was properly no "middle class" in the mid–eighteenth century, certainly no urban "bourgeoisie" in the nineteenth-century sense; so when I occasionally use these terms in the context of my study I do so advisedly, well aware that their presence is anachronistic and teleological, if useful as a kind of shorthand. Still, it is fair to say that politeness is an ideology in the classical Marxian sense because its proponents—especially in Scotland—conceiving of themselves as the restorers of a type of social equality found in the *places publiques* of Athens, disguised (perhaps even to themselves) their role as spokesmen for a rising class of gentry, professionals, well-to-do tradesmen, and moderate clerics who sought to confirm their identity and consolidate their power in contradistinction to a growing urban "mob." This mob refers to the smaller tradesmen, artisans, and workers of London and, to a much lesser degree, Edinburgh and Glasgow, insofar as they sought—as they increasingly did after 1760—to wrest political authority from its accustomed channels.

Politeness defines a "class" in Pierre Bourdieu's sense of that term, "a mode of vision and division." The theorist of politeness accepts and further propagates a divisiveness that the republican sought to avoid: indeed, the republican sought to envision the British body politic as *one* community, in the same way that, in theory, polis and community coincided in Athens or in early republican Rome. (Perhaps the greatest mystification involved in the Country Party's self-image was to see itself in the guise of the Greek popular assembly rather than as an elite corps united by the experience of having reading Demosthenes at school or university.) The polite, by contrast, perceived the workings of class in much the same way that Bourdieu does. As Richard Terdiman explains:

> What [class] asserts is achieved through an implicit but powerful negation: it forcefully excludes what it does not embrace. . . . To do so has required a considerable dose of what Bourdieu provocatively terms "symbolic violence" . . . [a phrase that] implies the forcible imposition of such principles of division, and more generally of any symbolic representations (languages, conceptualizations, portrayals). The speakers of a language have little choice about whether to accept or reject these: they are embedded in the medium itself. (227)

Indeed, at least since the eighteenth century, the medium has been the message. The mode of social reproduction for the middle class (*née* the polite class) remains—in Britain and, to an only somewhat lesser degree, America—the linguistic and social standards of a polite style.

My own interest is to analyze the historical origins of polite ideology, for the sake of both those whom it has commended and those whom it has excluded. I have no activist aspirations to hasten its demise and usher in a classless society, although I am sure that this book, as an exposé of the power relations that lie at the heart of politeness, might afford ammunition for those less comfortable with the class system than I am. But then, any unmasking that my book achieves might also be understood in a Straussian sense as a simple loss of innocence about the secret genesis of civilized values. I believe that none of us should lightly dismiss the notion of politeness because of its impure origins, its foundation—and perhaps continued basis—in symbolic violence; for once we begin to renounce value systems as merely superstructural in a vulgar Marxist sense, it is unclear if we shall ultimately be left with any values at all. And perhaps we may agree that some good might cling to the ethos of politeness, something we might salvage even were we to reject the history of superordination boldly inscribed in its origins. At least in America, the ideal if not the ideology of polite intercourse—the *politesse de coeur* appropriate to a concourse of people created equal—surely accords with our own constitutional sense of civic equality.

To understand politeness in yet another way, we might with Fredric Jameson invoke a Marxist hermeneutic that provides a positive as well as a negative evaluation of the varieties of human culture. That is, we may read politeness not only as the outward symptom of a process of fragmentation and alienation but also as a humane compensation for this very process, a social code that exists to answer, in Jameson's phrase, "the oldest Utopian longings of humankind." Jameson contends,

> If the function of the mass cultural text is meanwhile seen . . . as the production of false consciousness and the symbolic reaffirmation of this or that legitimizing strategy, even this process cannot be grasped as one of sheer violence (the theory of hegemony is explicitly distinguished from control by brute force) nor as one inscribing the appropriate attitudes on a blank slate, but must necessarily involve a complex strategy of rhetorical persuasion in which substantial incentives are offered for ideological adherence. We will say that such incentives . . . are necessarily Utopian in nature. (287)

Politeness expresses the type of utopian impulse that, as Jameson rightly insists, we need to take seriously as an ethical expression and longing for the good—whether or not we choose, with Jam-

eson, to interpret the good as the classless collective life projected
at the end of History (291).

This, then, is the extent of my allegiance to the new historicism; it hardly seems necessary here to rehearse my objections to
a number of its other tendencies—chiefly, its obscure invocations
of totalitarian "Power" and the dystopian view that any oppositional discourse is always already inscribed in a scenario dictated
by Power.[3] Instead of engaging in wayward polemic, let me close
with a comment on my final methodological interest in this
book.

I have sought in the following chapters not only to trace the
literary and political dialectic of eloquence and politeness but, as
an ancillary ambition, to sketch a history of the ways in which
eighteenth-century authors conceived of figural language, or "eloquence" as a taxonomy of tropes. I have, in short, attempted to
write a post–de Manian history of the ways in which Enlightenment writers variously theorized and engaged, in Paul de Man's
words, "the complex and philosophically challenging epistemology of the tropes" (*Allegories* 130). My interest lies not only in
what these writers thought about tropes but also in the inescapa-
bly figural nature of their own thought; in other words, I address
not only the philosophers' habit of thinking *in terms of* figures
but also their thinking *in* figures. In pursuing these intertwined
themes, I have come to historicize and thus to modify aspects of
de Man's pointedly ahistorical theory of figures, particularly his
late interest in prosopopoeia and apostrophe.[4]

In Chapter 1 I begin with Hume's Longinian invocation of these
figures, and some consideration of the tension in any eighteenth-
century assessment of figures between classical applause and Royal Society censure. Chapter 2 examines the alienation of figures
within the analytic art of rhetoric itself and proceeds to address
the ways in which this hoary philosophical opposition to elo-

3. For an incisive account of new historicism and "the councils of cynicism,"
see Frank Lentricchia, "Foucault's Legacy: A New Historicism?"
4. Although I address de Man's sense of prosopopeia in Chapter 5, the curious
reader is encouraged to seek out "Autobiography as De-Facement," in *Rhetoric of
Romanticism* 67–82, and, for a valuable commentary, Cynthia Chase's "Giving a
Face to a Name," in *Decomposing Figures* 82–112.

quence blends with a new social, polite bias against figuration as a vulgar or "Billingsgate" phenomenon. As Adam Smith characteristically pronounces, "There is nowhere more use made of figures than in the lowest and most vulgar conversation" (34); however, the excesses of low language find an echo in the equally untenable ornamentation of an outmoded aristocratic writing. Polite style will thereafter be marked, at least ideally, by the rejection or purely ironic admission of all passionate figures. Accordingly, Chapter 3 examines the ways in which Sterne opposes and ultimately sacrifices the traditional figures of apostrophe and prosopopoeia to the novel demands of a polite or sociable style.

Yet as the reader of Nietzsche or de Man knows all too well, figures are too deeply ingrained in language itself ever to be banished by an act of will. And indeed the last two chapters of this book represent two types of what we may call "figurative revival" in the age of Hume. First, there is Hume's recognition that (to quote the mythographer Thomas Blackwell) "there be no science unadorned by allegory" (285): that any science of man is bound to be fabulous, and that some fables, such as the labors of Demosthenes, are better than others. Hume's science dresses up the perceptions, and a fortiori the passions, with the traditional attributes and authority of the ideal orator, and it does so through a prosopopoeia that self-consciously mimics the constitutive figure of the religious imagination as Hume defines it in *The Natural History of Religion*. Thus, in a "deconstructive" turn, Hume inscribes his own prosopopoeia in the very act of demystifying the figure's sacral effects—a twist that at once acknowledges the figural conditions of any discourse and attempts to fill the moral vacuum left by the passing of the old gods.

The second and last figurative revival I address is Macpherson's copious, distinctive, and in his day famous use of prosopopoeia. I will argue that the *Poems of Ossian* inaugurates a peculiarly modern vision of prosopopoeia in which the figure suggests, psychologically, alienation from any living community and communion with remembered loved ones. Macpherson's prosopopoeia bridges the gap between the loss of a traditional belief in the ghosts or *manes* of the past, and the advent of a modern belief that nothing exists but the ghosts of the mind or—in de Man's still more spooky version—the spectral effects of sheer language.

Note, however, that even in teasing out the implications of Hume's "deconstructive" writing or Macpherson's "figural theory" I have attempted to draw my insights from a history of eighteenth-century reading and reception. Above all else, my aim has been to address the age of Hume *on its own terms.* Although I do not naively claim to be disinterested, I do object to the egoism of those who openly place an agenda above the text at hand. It seems to me that in our pluralistic world we need to allow other voices to speak in something at least resembling their own timbre, whether we ultimately concur with them or not. The reader of this study will find an array of voices that sometimes speak in terms of the critical concerns of our own moment, particularly our renewed fascination with rhetorical theory and our burgeoning interest in the social construction of class and gender. I have not, however, used these contemporary concerns as an a priori theoretical framework; to quote Pope, I have not taken "the high priori road." And I have avoided, as much as possible, "the jargon of a technical language and the impertinence of academical forms," long ago identified by Adam Ferguson as the bane of academic specialization (178). I hope to have written a book that may please any inquisitive reader but that will not prove uninstructive to those who have spent still more time with eighteenth-century texts than I have.

## Textual Note

In the body of my text, all translations from the French are my own unless otherwise noted. As a rule, I have left quotations from French authors untranslated in my endnotes but not, for ease of exposition, in the body of my text. I have tried to use published translations from the Greek and Latin that are both reputable and harmonious; at moments when I invoke the original languages my references are to the texts established in the Loeb Classical Library. In keeping with much current scholarship, I have modernized typographical conventions and orthography throughout;

however, I have through force of custom retained the first-letter capitalizations of the Twickenham Pope and the Lonsdale Gray. And I have very selectively retained an author's full capitalization or italics at moments when his or her emphasis accords with my own.

# 1 Ancient Eloquence and the Revival of Virtue

Hume's essay "Of Eloquence" is, apparently, an appeal for the revival of ancient eloquence in eighteenth-century Britain.[1] Hume asserts that modern eloquence, "calm, elegant, and subtle," pales in comparison to the "sublime and pathetic" eloquence of the great classical orators:

> Even a person, unacquainted with the noble remains of ancient orators, may judge, from a few strokes, that the style or species of their eloquence was infinitely more sublime than that which modern orators aspire to. How absurd would it appear, in our temperate and calm speakers, to make use of an *Apostrophe*, like that noble one of Demosthenes, so much celebrated by Quintilian and Longinus, when justifying the unsuccessful battle of Chaeronea, he breaks out, "No, my Fellow-Citizens, No: You have not erred. I swear by the *manes* of those heroes, who fought for the same cause in the plains

1. "Of Eloquence" was originally published in the second volume of Hume's *Essays: Political and Moral* in January 1742, the month before Walpole's resignation. The *Essays* were occasioned in part by the controversy between Walpole's administration and Bolingbroke's Opposition. In 1752, Hume published a new group of essays, the *Political Discourses*. These were soon combined with his earlier pieces, and an all but comprehensive collection, *Essays, Moral, Political, and Literary*, went through numerous editions in Hume's lifetime. Hume continued to supplement, withdraw, and revise the several essays in this collection until his death in 1776. For the details of publication history, see Eugene F. Miller's editor's note to the *Essays*, xi–xxvii.

of Marathon and Plataea." Who could now endure such a bold and poetical figure, as that which Cicero employs, after describing in the most tragical terms the crucifixion of a Roman citizen. "Should I paint the horrors of this scene, not to Roman citizens, not to the allies of our state, not to those who have ever heard of the Roman Name, not even to men, but to the brute-creatures; or, to go farther, should I lift up my voice in the most desolate solitude, to the rocks and mountains, yet should I surely see those rude and inanimate parts of nature moved with horror and indignation at the recital of so enormous an action." With what a blaze of eloquence must such a sentence be surrounded to give it grace, or cause it to make any impression on the hearers? And what noble art and sublime talents are requisite to arrive, by just degrees, at a sentiment so bold and excessive: To inflame the audience, so as to make them accompany the speaker in such violent passions, and such elevated conceptions: And to conceal, under a torrent of eloquence, the artifice, by which all this is effectuated! (*Essays* 100–101)

Hume's enthusiasm for apostrophe and prosopopoeia derives from Longinus, who had called Demosthenes' famous apostrophe from *On the Crown* "a passage of transcending sublimity." In it, Demosthenes "has deified his ancestors by suggesting that we ought to swear by men who died such deaths as we swear by gods" (*On the Sublime* chap. 16). Demosthenes, that is, gives an ear to dead heroes. Conversely, in the next sublime passage adduced by Hume, Cicero gives a voice to inanimate nature in his personi-fication of "rocks and mountains." Both Demosthenes' apostro-phe and Cicero's prosopopoeia must at first glance have appeared uncanny to Hume's polite audience: such figures bespeak a dark and superstitious passion, an animistic faith, a dispersion of self. Yet Hume quickly reassures us that these figures are purely artifi-cial, contrived by the ancient orators to "make an impression." Again following Longinus, Hume praises the artfulness with which the artifice of the figures is concealed: all that is apparent is the impression they do indeed make upon an audience.[2]

2. Hume's praise of sublime eloquence follows, I believe, the contours of Fén-elon's *Dialogues sur L'Eloquence* (1717): of Demosthenes, Fénelon writes, "C'est un raisonnement serré & pressant . . . c'est un enchaînment de figures hardies & touchantes: vous ne sauriez le lire sans voir qu'il porte la République dans le fond

It is an impression figured by Hume in terms of light and heat, the "blaze of eloquence," the "inflammation" of the audience. His description of the orator's mastery of his auditors relies on topoi familiar to classical and Renaissance rhetorics. For example, in the Port-Royalist *Art of Speaking* (1708 trans. of *L'Art de Parler* [1675]), prosopopeia is first considered a measure of madness (90), but the authors proceed to note that for the accomplished orator, the figure serves as an incendiary weapon. As the soldier "keeps his enemy in breath," so "an orator entertains the attention of his auditors; when their thoughts are straggling, reduces them by apostrophes. . . . When our proofs fail, or are insufficient, Nature herself must apostrophize; we make the stones speak, the dead to come forth of their graves, the heaven and earth are invok'd to fortify by their testimony the truth, for the establishment of which we speak with so much heat" (100–101). This heat fairly pervades earlier eighteenth-century discussions of eloquence: thus Thomas Gordon writes in *Cato's Letters* no. 104 (1722), "When the Orator . . . brings heaven and earth into his cause, and seems but to represent them, to speak their sense . . . his words lighten, and his breath is on fire; every word glows, and every image flames."

And, according to Hume, it is precisely this sense of heat that has passed from the modern assembly. As he attests in a temperately bold simile, "when compared with Demosthenes and Cicero," modern eloquence is "eclipsed like a taper when set in the rays of a meridian sun" (108). We are, perhaps, surprised to find Hume conjuring an image of a more ardent age, and regretting its passage. The Hume who is familiar to us is hardly a creature of the sun. Even his most favorably disposed reader will at least understand James Beattie when he belabors Hume for a lack of "warmth," "fire," "body and spirit" (quoted in Wind, 12).

Some recent critics have argued more sweepingly that the discourse of early modern liberalism (of which Hume is generally if

---

de son coeur; c'est la nature qui parle elle-même dans les transports; l'art y est si achevé, qu'il n'y paroît point; rien n'égala jamais sa rapidité & sa véhémence: N'avez vous pas vu ce qu'en dit Longin dans son Traité du Sublime?" (17–18).

misguidedly regarded as a spokesman) systematically denies, abstracts, or neuterizes the body; Michael Warner, for one, opposes "the reign of liberalism and its abstracted individual" to the recognition that "political systems are always inhabited by the body" (78). And Jerome Christensen declares at the outset of his literary biography of Hume, "The career of the [Enlightenment] man of letters begins with a radical abstraction of self" (6); throughout, Christensen contends that strategies such as symbolic self-castration and "the affectation of affectlessness" define Hume's conduct in his social as well as his literary affairs (228–29). Yet, to complicate all such assessments of Hume's Stoic restraint or simple cold-bloodedness, there remains the testimony of his essay "Of Eloquence." Surely part of what attracts Hume to ancient eloquence—beyond the burnishing effect of prior commentary, the illustrious mediations of the Longinian company— is an imaginative re-creation of the basic *scene* of oratory: the give and take of the orator and the assembled bodies he addresses; the emotional "heat" that ideally unites them. This is properly the scene of eloquence that Hume would resuscitate.

In the course of his essay, however, Hume anticipates evident objections to a renaissance of ancient eloquence. "Perhaps it may be acknowledged that our modern customs, or our superior good sense, if you will, should make our orators more cautious and reserved than the ancient, in attempting to inflame the passions, or elevate the imagination of their audience . . ." (104). The objection is plain: how is ancient eloquence suited to an age that does not want its passions inflamed? The objection is also prescient, anticipating the arguments that would be urged against the Humean position by Adam Smith and Joseph Priestley. As Smith would inform his students at Glasgow, "The behaviour which is reckoned polite in England is a calm, composed, unpassionate serenity noways ruffled by passion . . . floridity and splendor [have] always been disliked" (198–99). "Always" may not be historically accurate, but it is rhetorically pointed. In much the same vein, Priestley declared in England proper, "The English pulpit, the English bar, and the English senate, require an eloquence more addressed to the reason, and less directly to the passions, than the

harangues of a Roman pleader, or the speech of a Roman senator"
(113). Like Smith, Priestley is concerned with the demands of
current taste. And *de gustibus non disputandum est.*

Shrewdly, Hume does not attempt to answer an unanswerable
objection. The "answer" in his concluding clause is simply a
clever non sequitur. Modern orators might indeed have to be
"more cautious and reserved" in attempting to inflame us, "But, I
see no reason why [our superior good sense] should make them
despair absolutely of succeeding in that attempt." Hume's com-
pleted sentence is structured as a jeu d'esprit. The "reasonable"
objection to ancient eloquence has been sidestepped by a repartee
that is not an answer. However, once our smiling has stopped, we
recognize that an objection ridiculed is still an objection. The
question remains, How is a polite age to stomach a new Demosthenes? Hume draws us farther away from an answer by asking only that the modern orator not "despair absolutely" of moving the passions. The tone of this phrase (as ironically inflected as
it may be) does not bode well for the possibility of reviving ancient eloquence.

Nor does the evident bathos with which Hume ends his essay.
Directly after urging the modern orator to employ "the strongest
figures and expressions" in extemporaneous composition, Hume
stoops, quite unexpectedly, to conclude "that, even though our
modern orators should not elevate their style or aspire to a rival-
ship with the ancient, yet there is, in most of their speeches, a
material defect, which they might correct, without departing
from that composed air of argument and reasoning to which they
limit their ambition." In the same flattened tone, the essay's final
paragraph proceeds to recommend a greater regard for the "order
and method" of public discourse: "Observe a method, and make
that method conspicuous to the hearers, who will be infinitely
pleased to see the arguments rise naturally from one another"
(109–10). Ironically, Hume's ending call for expository cohesion
does not "rise naturally" from his earlier argument: rather, his
own ending seems curiously like a digression, an afterthought.
The sublime and pathetic force of Demosthenes that had so occu-
pied him has now vanished, unnoticed. Indeed, it seems that the
sublime "stroke" has here been sacrificed, according to a Longi-

nian ratio, to the "proper order and disposition of material" it ever opposes (*On the Sublime* chap. 1);[3] paradoxically, however, Hume prescribes this proper disposition by means of a flagrant discontinuity in his own argument.

What, finally, are we to make of "Of Eloquence"? To borrow a phrase from Hume's *Natural History of Religion,* "The whole is a riddle, an aenigma, an inexplicable mystery" (76). He seems at first to deplore the loss of sublime eloquence, and yet he offers no program for restoring it in Hanoverian Britain. Indeed, he jokes about the very possibility of such a restoration and appears, in the end, unruffled by the prospect of nothing much happening at all. Yet aside from its odd vacillations of tone, the essay contains a more evident paradox. The historian of rhetoric W. S. Howell, siding with Adam Smith and Joseph Priestley, calls Hume's position in "Of Eloquence" "curiously static, curiously unhistorical, and curiously antiquarian." Howell dismisses the essay as something of an aberration, since Hume's own modern style is not at all given to the reactionary figurative eloquence he advocates (616). Indeed, Hume attests to the loss of eloquence that he regrets in the very act of writing about it with analytic distance. Hume, unlike Longinus, is not the sublime he describes: "Of Eloquence" bespeaks at once a fascination with, and a distance from, the power of figurative eloquence it evokes.

Far from being a quandary peculiar to Hume, I shall argue that such an ambivalence toward eloquence characterizes the political and aesthetic discourses of midcentury Britain. According to the familiar hermeneutic circle, this wider discursive field may shed light on the paradoxes of Hume's particular essay, just as Hume's essay, in its exceptional comprehensiveness, may afford us a greater insight into the commonplaces of that field. In the remainder of this chapter and in the chapter that follows, I shall examine both the grounds on which the ideal of eloquence was

3. Longinus clearly distinguishes between the *chronos* of composition and the *kairos* of sublimity: "Inventive skill and the proper order and disposition of material are not manifested in a good touch here and there, but reveal themselves by slow degrees as they run through the whole texture of the composition; on the other hand, a well-timed stroke of sublimity scatters everything before it like a thunderbolt, and in a flash reveals the full power of the speaker." It is clear where Longinus's interest lies.

advanced and those on which it was opposed, not only in Hume's
*Essays* but in the age of Hume.


## The Demosthenic Moment

What was at stake in arguments for resuscitating classical eloquence? During the ministry of Robert Walpole, "eloquence"
served, above all, as an Opposition watchword "in the republican
style." Bolingbroke and his circle called for a revival of eloquence
as part of a return to the original republican principles of England's "ancient constitution." In so doing, they relied on the
classical notion that eloquence is proper to a popular form of
government. (In early Hanoverian England, "popular government" specifically meant stressing the claims of the commons
against the executive—that is, championing the republican elements of the constitution over the monarchic. Thus Hume in the
*Essays* interchangeably calls the Country party "the popular party" [496] and one "speaking in the republican style" [72].)

The vital tie between eloquence and popular government,
though expounded most fully in Tacitus's *Dialogue on Oratory*,[4]
derived much of its authority in the eighteenth century from
Longinus's *On the Sublime*. As Hugh Blair puts it, "It is an obser-

4. Tacitus's *Dialogue* was accessible to a wide range of eighteenth-century
British readers through William Melmoth's popular translation, appended to his
*Letters on Several Subjects* (1749), 2:244–336. Melmoth, presumably following
Dryden's lead in "Defence of the Epilogue" (*Essays* 164), incorrectly attributes the
*Dialogue* to Quintilian on the title page of his work, but he elsewhere maintains
that the authorship of the work remains uncertain. Hugh Blair remarks that the
dialogue—which he, like most of his contemporaries, refers to as *de Causis cor-
ruptae Eloquentiae*—"is attributed by some to Tacitus, by others, to Quintilian";
he is far more assured, however, about the intention of the work, which he reads as
an unambiguous condemnation of "arbitrary power" (2:34–35). In the *Dialogue*,
secs. 36–41, the character Maternus discusses how great eloquence is fostered by
the turbulence of democracies. Maternus professedly prefers the settled and peaceable nature of government under the autocratic Vespasian, "a monarch who is the
incarnation of wisdom," but it appears that Blair and his contemporaries took
Maternus's profession to be ironic. (On the eighteenth-century tendency to read
Tacitus as an ironist, see Gay 1:157–59.) Significantly, Maternus is described early
in the dialogue (sec. 2) as having written a play entitled *Cato*, which expresses
republican sentiments offensive to Court circles.

vation made by several writers, that Eloquence is to be looked for only in free states. Longinus, in particular, at the end of his treatise on the sublime, illustrates this observation with a great deal of beauty" (2:8). "The finest and most productive source of eloquence," writes Longinus in the dialogue that concludes his treatise, is "freedom." Longinus's first speaker accordingly attributes the decay of sublime eloquence in his own era to the loss of political liberty under the Roman Empire, whereas his second speaker inveighs against not only "slavery" but also "the love of money," "bribery," "corruption" and "luxury" (chap. 44). This litany comprises, of course, the very terms adopted by the Opposition to denounce the age of Walpole. Correspondingly, the Longinian nostalgia for an age of eloquence found an echo among the "patriots": haunted by their own anxieties about corruption and decline, they viewed Longinus as a companion in crisis.

The ideal of eloquence always refers back to the virtuous eloquence of a former age, and for both Longinus and his neoclassical admirers that age is typically Demosthenic Athens. But political virtue is, it seems, an ever-receding horizon. Demosthenes' own orations appeal to a still more ancient era, the days of Marathon and Plataea, when the polis was ideally intact and uncontaminated. Indeed, the fame of Demosthenes rests upon his ability to conjure a community of shared assumptions and beliefs at the very moment when that closed community had, in fact, arrived at its extinction. He sought to preserve Athens not only against the threat of tyrannic encroachment from without but above all from civic lassitude within: this, at least, is how his role was interpreted in the age of Hume. Thus, William Young writes in his *History of Athens* that in Demosthenes' day,

> The old compact and union of the democracy was . . . broken up into pretensions and pleas of individuals, and of their partisans; the people no longer held a collective self-regard; power, glory, and wealth, were no longer the boast and object to each as a citizen for the commonwealth, but to each as a selfish man for self: I read with feeling the words of Demosthenes, when he observes, "that in the good old times of the republic, it was not said that Militiades had conquered at Marathon, but the Athenians; nor that Themistocles had been victorious at Salamis, but the Athenians; now the lan-

guage is that Iphicrates has cut off a detachment, that Timotheus
has taken Corcyra, and that Chabrias beat the enemy at Naxos."
(231–32)

According to Young, the "palm of oratory" finally belongs to Demosthenes over Cicero because of his power to captivate and
thereby unite a "diversely affected" assembly. Young summarizes
his case with a quotation from Dionysius of Halicarnassus: "The
character I would give of [Demosthenes'] eloquence, is not that it
took in parts, but that it embraced the whole" (286–87). Demosthenes' achievement was to put the sundered selves of his
community back together again—if only for a moment. As Young
ruefully notes, the Philippics of Demosthenes could ultimately
effect but little "in times of general corruption" or, more vividly
phrased, *"in faece Solonis"* (279).

Young's interest in Demosthenic Athens is, of course, not simply antiquarian. As he writes in his introduction, the condition of
late republican Athens must prove "most interesting to a British
reader," especially in the views it affords of "the struggles and
intrigues of parties" and "the hasty increase of wealth and of
marine power from sources of trade, and thereon trade introducing a spirit of dissipation and self-interest to dissolve the very
strength and prosperity it gave birth to" (ix–x). Young clearly
associates Athens in the time of Demosthenes—politically con-
valescent after its wars with Sparta, though suffering from the
surfeits of luxury—with the England of his own day: an England
that prompts Young to lament, much as Demosthenes once lamented, *"Then* [i.e., in the early days of the ancient republics]
individuals formed a community; *now,* more properly it may be
said that a community consists of individuals. . . . the genius of
patriotism, which animated every breast, no longer exists; nay,
the very instances of its existence are questioned" (8).

Young's complaint is also a challenge to his compatriots, an
implicit appeal to a *ridurre ai principii.* Declaring the death of
community supplies a particularly vivid rallying cry for those
who would restore a sense of common enterprise—a truth that
holds for Demosthenes as for Young, for Cicero as for Bolingbroke, for Edmund Burke as for T. S. Eliot. These voices elo-

quently strive to counter or retard the centrifugal forces of commercial and imperial expansion or invasion; indeed they sound at moments when these forces are felt to accelerate. We may call this a "Demosthenic moment" in history, a recurrent motif in the political experience of Athens, Rome, and (to go no farther) eighteenth-century London.[5] The Demosthenic moment occurs whenever a moral community bestows "the palm of oratory" on a speaker for the very reason that he has addressed it with sufficient force to call it, however fleetingly, into being. The Demosthenic moment occurs with the celebration of a speaker able to invoke an affiliated past and to do so with the necessary strength to bring it, ephemerally, alive.

## Apostrophizing Eloquence in Opposition Verse

Apart from Bolingbroke's singular heights (to which I will be returning), the typical eloquence of Britain's Demosthenic moment occurs in its numerous eulogies on the lost civic eloquence of the past. It is thus an eloquence that paradoxically announces its own absence—or its relegation to *mere* poetry—in order to blame a government that has not allowed it to flourish in its proper, parliamentary sphere. For according to the Oppositional verse of the 1730s and 1740s, the ancient tradition of liberty and eloquence was all but submerged by the filthy tide of Walpole's ministry.

James Thomson's *Liberty* (1735–36), as it traces the progress of liberty from its origins in ancient Greece to its foundation and future prospects in Britain, firmly establishes the historical connection between liberty and eloquence. It is the liberty of Athens that gives rise to all of the "finer arts," of which "the power of eloquence" appears first:

5. My phrase alludes—and acknowledges my debt—both to J. G. A. Pocock's *The Machiavellian Moment* and to William C. Dowling's *The Epistolary Moment*. Indeed, the ideal of eloquence, as I understand it, arises from the same nisus that brings about, in Dowling's account, the verse epistle: "Epistolarity itself [is] a gesture toward community in a world where some preexisting order is threatened with decline or disintegration" (36).

> In thy full language, speaking mighty things;
> Like a clear torrent close, or else diffus'd
> A broad majestic stream, and rolling on
> Thro' all the winding harmony of sound—
> In it the power of ELOQUENCE at large
> Breath'd the persuasive or pathetic soul,
> Still'd by degrees the democratic storm,
> Or bad it threatening rise, and tyrants shook
> Flush'd at the head of their victorious troops.
>
> (2.252–65)

Such eloquence as Thomson imagined may, perhaps, be found in the many stately orations given by the Spartan hero of Richard Glover's popular *Leonidas* (1737). Leonidas, whose epithet is quite simply "the Patriot," proves anything but laconic in Glover's poem. He readily declaims on "the public cause," "virtue," and "liberty," and his eloquence is known by its effects. Leonidas is, in Bolingbroke's sense of the term, an incendiary, for "a person who makes it his business to excite the people to their duty, or even to inflame and blow up their passions against bad measures and wicked ministers, may be called an incendiary. . . . The two great orators of Greece and Rome . . . were incendiaries of this sort" (*The Craftsman* no. 221). Here, for example, is just one among several illustrations of Leonidas's power to inflame his soldiers:

> As in some torrid region, where the head
> Of Ceres bends beneath its golden load,
> If on the parching ground a fatal spark
> Fall from a burning brand; the sudden blaze
> Increas'd and aided by tumultuous winds
> In rapid torrents of involving flames
> Sweeps o'er the crackling plain, and mounting high
> In ruddy spires illumines half the skies:
> Not with less swiftness throught the glowing ranks
> The words of great Leonidas diffus'd
> A more than mortal fervour. Ev'ry heart
> Distends with great ideas, such as raise
> The patriot's virtue, and the soldier's fire,

> When danger in its most tremendous form
> Seems to their eyes most lovely.
>
> (2.167–81)

The flagrancy of Glover's simile appears less Homeric than pentecostal: Leonidas may as well be speaking here with "a cloven tongue like as of fire," with "a sound from heaven as of a rushing mighty wind" (Acts 2). Indeed, it is only such a translation that can make this scene at all credible, if only to those with a Christian upbringing. As Glover's audience would know, the flames that first united the apostolic community figure the gift of not only speech but of divine inspiration—and Leonidas's own eloquence scarcely seems less numinous, or the community he inspires less holy. The fact that this scene of eloquence is civic and secular is precisely the fact that is elided: Glover apotheosizes the orator, and sacralizes the civic. His fellow Opposition poets more or less do the same, rhapsodizing on the power of Greek eloquence and the civic ideals that authorized its refining fires.

Of course, Greece ceases to be of political interest to English poets after the Macedonian conquest. The next country to which Thomson turned in his panorama of *Liberty* and its voices is republican Rome, which for a while nurtured a transplanted eloquence:

> Rome in her glory see!
> Behold her demigods, in senate met;
> All head to counsel, and all heart to act:
> The commonweal inspiring every tongue
> With fervent Eloquence, unbrib'd, and bold,
> Ere tame corruption taught the servile herd
> To rank obedient to a master's voice.
>
> (1.75–81)

The loss of Rome's eloquence along with its liberty had earlier been remarked by the third earl of Shaftesbury: "With their liberty [the Romans] lost not only their force of eloquence, but even their style and language itself" (1:143). And as Thomson's patron George Lyttelton wrote in his *Life of Cicero* (1731), while poetry, "only proper for amusement," might flourish "under the smiles of an arbitrary prince . . . force and solidity of reasoning, or a sublime and commanding eloquence, are inconsistent with slavish restraint, or timorous dependency" (1:35; cf. Middleton's *Life of Cicero* 3:347). Thus, in *Liberty*, eloquence alone of all the arts proves inseparable from the parent soil of popular government. Other arts flourish under the petty tyrants of the Italian Renaissance (4.100–253), but eloquence, understandably, does not.

It is, however, more difficult to account for the absence of eloquence during the rise of liberty in Britain, a subject on which Thomson is discreetly silent. Although described as the destined heir of Roman "grandeur" and Greek "art" (5.573), Britain remains an apparent stranger to classical eloquence. Elsewhere, Thomson transforms this absence into an implicit criticism of Walpole's "junto" government. In his revised version of *Winter*, he envisions eloquence as the *potential* prerogative of the Opposition: apostrophizing the "patriot" earl of Chesterfield in 1744, Thomson conjures up a political scene in which a powerfully commanding eloquence is what the Opposition would have if it had a "listening senate." Although Chesterfield was noted for his parliamentary speeches, the true revival of eloquence remains for Thomson a political prophecy: Chesterfield's virtuous eloquence is destined to silence party strife and unite Parliament "on some glorious day" (679–83). Then will he impress his countrymen with a unifying sense of public virtue—or, as Thomson specifies them in *Liberty*, the "three virtues of British freedom": "independent life; / integrity in office; and o'er all / Supreme, a passion for the common-weal" (5.120–23).

Clearly, the Opposition presents eloquence as tantamount to liberty, civic virtue, and, in the tradition of Quintilian (and Acts), truth itself. The obvious objection that traitors or tyrants can be (and sometimes are) eloquent is nowhere acknowledged in the political debate of the period. Thus, in the second book of *Leonidas*, the traitorous orator Epialtes attempts "to deject the Spartan valour" but proves ineffective—and thus reveals himself to be not truly possessed of eloquence, which by its very nature is irresistible. Epialtes' specious eloquence serves, finally, only as a foil for the authenticity of Leonidas's. True eloquence, once heard, cannot be ignored; and thus the heroic orator cannot be rebutted but only silenced by death or, more effective still, by venality. As the messenger Alpheus informs Leonidas, in Thebes "A few corrupted by Persian gold, / Unjust dominion have usurp'd . . . / These in each bosom quell the gen'rous flame/ Of liberty. The eloquent they bribe" (1.479–82). And once bought off, the eloquent cease—by definition—to be eloquent, regardless of whether they continue to speak.

Accordingly, the Opposition depicted William Pulteney's desertion of the patriot cause as issuing, condignly, in silence. (Pulteney, a co-founder with Bolingbroke of the Opposition journal *The Craftsman*, accepted a peerage and a place in Carteret's cabinet upon the fall of Walpole.) In a negative image of Thomson's praise of Chesterfield, Mark Akenside's *An Epistle to Curio* (1744) figures Pulteney's new allegiance to the Court administration as a stifling alliance with "barbarous Grandeur":

> Thy powerful tongue with poisoned philters bound,
> That baffled reason straight indignant flew,
> And fair persuasion from her seat withdrew;
> For now no longer truth supports thy cause;
> No longer glory prompts thee to applause;
> No longer virtue, breathing in thy breast,
> With all her conscious majesty confest,
> Still bright and brighter wakes the almighty flame,
> To rouse the feeble, and the wilful tame . . .
>
> (244–52)

Akenside voices the common Opposition charge that Pulteney's flame of "fair persuasion"—formerly fanned by "reason," "truth," "virtue," and the desire for "glory"—has been snuffed by political dependency and mere personal ambition. Chesterfield himself would later note in his *Characters* that Pulteney, from having been "a most complete orator and debater in the house of commons," "turn[ed] courtier on a sudden. . . . The nation looked upon him as a deserter, and he shrunk into insignificancy and an earldom" (27–28).[6]

In the same volume, Chesterfield would look back on Robert Walpole as "the best parliament-man . . . that I believe ever lived." To be "a manager of parliament," however, is quite different from being a great orator in the classical mold. Indeed, Chesterfield calls him "an artful rather than an eloquent speaker; he saw, as by intuition, the disposition of the house, and pressed or receded accordingly" (31). By "artful," Chesterfield evidently means that Walpole was a temporizing speaker—one given to a cautious economy rather than a magnanimity of speech. Chesterfield's verdict, while elegantly balanced, does not differ in essentials from the far less gracious attacks leveled against Walpole by the Opposition hack Eustace Budgell. In *A Letter to . . . Mr. Ulrick D'Ypres* (1731) Budgell castigates, as an evident "type" of Walpole, Pericles of Athens, a "wicked minister" whose bribes and places "corrupted the Athenians with their own money" and whose supposed eloquence "was nothing more than what the French call, a *Flux de Bouche*, a prodigious volubility and flow of words, delivered with a most consummate assurance." Budgell concludes, "None of his speeches had any real strength or solidity, or would bear being read." In short, Pericles—or Walpole—is a "prating fellow" rather than a true orator (16–17; cf. *The Craftsman* nos. 324–26 [1732]).

For all their differences of temperament, Budgell and Chesterfield agree that real eloquence could never be attributed to a minister who reigns, in the latter's phrase, through "pecuniary temptation"; they agree that eloquence *is* virtue, and virtue eloquence. Walpole, for his part, possessed a more modern sensibility in dismissing all such "notions of public virtue, and . . . love of one's country" as "the chimerical school-boy flights of classical learning" (Chesterfield 32). Of course, Walpole was right to attribute the basic assumptions of the Country ideology to a classroom origin: translating Cicero's orations remained a principal university exercise, and we may suppose that Latin declamations in

6. Vincent Carretta canvasses Opposition attacks on Pulteney during the period 1741–47 (158–59, 177–84).

praise of Demosthenes were not uncommon (the *Dictionary of National Biography* notes an extant example by William Murray, later Lord Mansfield). And there is evidence that such exercises— at least at Edinburgh—were imbued with political spirit. In "The Scottish Professoriate and the Polite Academy, 1720–1746," Peter Jones argues that although Edinburgh students read such standard rhetoricians from the medieval and Renaissance curricula as Cicero and Quintilian, their professors "played down the *ars dicendi* in favor of the dependence of liberty on the right acquisition of philosophy and eloquence" (100). Edinburgh professors, it seems, were as steeped in the discourse of classical republicanism as were Bolingbroke and the Country party in England.

Born in the inkhorn and fostered in partisan polemics, the Opposition's guiding dream of classical eloquence came closest to coming true during the debate over Walpole's conciliatory stance with Spain in 1737–39. As Voltaire remarked in his *Encyclopédie* entry on "Eloquence," "We have several speeches which were given [in the English Parliament] in 1739, when it was preparing to declare war against Spain. The spirit of Demosthenes and Cicero seem to have dictated several strokes of these orations" (*Oeuvres* 24:494). Indeed, when the Opposition spoke in favor of a patriotic war, they explicitly invoked the Demosthenic moment. Philip V of Spain, they argued, threatened Britain's safety no less than Philip of Macedon had imperiled Athens; and the British, no less than the Athenians, would be fit to repel foreign invasion only after they had been rescued from their own moral decline into avarice and luxury. They thus conceived war against Spain— at least ideally—as a doubly indemnifying war, the war Athens should have waged against Philip at the first signs of his imperial ambitions.

As Henry Knight Miller notes in his edition of Fielding's *Miscellanies*, the Opposition habit of applying the orations of Demosthenes to current affairs was by 1738 sufficiently noisome to the Court to prompt a response in the administration paper, the *Daily Gazetteer* (xlii). Among these applications we must count Fielding's translation of Demosthenes' *First Olynthiac*: "Good Gods! is there any of you so infatuated, that he can be ignorant that the war will come home to us, if we neglect it? And if this should happen, I fear, O Athenians, that we shall imitate those who borrow money at great usury, who for a short affluence of present wealth, are afterwards turned out of their original patrimony" (*Miscellanies* 208). The monthly magazines offer similar sentiments in great abundance. *The Craftsman* no. 523 (July 1736) contains "Demosthenes's Exhortation to Publick Spirit" (reprinted in the *Gentleman's Magazine*), an interlacing of the *Third Olynthiac* with a running commentary on its contemporary applications. And the *Gentleman's Magazine* first published Akenside's *British Philippic* (August 1738), a poem that invokes "the various powers of forceful speech, / All that can move, awaken, fire, transport"—"the arousing thunder of the patriot Greek," Anglicized—to "fire each British heart with British wrongs" (13, 29–32). In the *Scots Magazine* (June 1739), Aaron Hill's poem "The Northern Star" prophesies that "Athens shall teach once more" and "Spartan breasts re-glow with martial fire" (quoted in Dwyer, "Enlightened Spectators" 101). Thus, although the Opposition poets typically present themselves as orators *manqué*, Walpole's temporizing policy with Spain supplied them with their best occasion to attain to the oratorical strain they apostrophized. The specter of Philip V gave them an opportunity to steal something of the Demosthenic fire.

## Hume's Opposition Voice

Hume, a close observer of English politics in the years leading up to the *Essays*—as well as a former student at Edinburgh and evidently an attentive reader of Longinus—was entirely aware of the political implications of eloquence. Indeed, the "science of politics" that Hume would outline in the *Essays* incorporates the maxim that "eloquence certainly springs up more naturally in popular governments" ("Of the Rise and Progress of the Arts and Sciences" 119). That he tacitly assumes this maxim throughout "Of Eloquence" is strongly suggested in his remarks on the English Interregnum:

There is certainly something accidental in the first rise and the progress of the arts in any nation. . . . Had such a cultivated genius for oratory, as Waller's for poetry, arisen, during the civil wars, when liberty began to be fully established, and popular assemblies to enter into all the most material points of government; I am persuaded so illustrious an example would have given a quite different turn to British eloquence, and made us reach the perfection of the ancient model. Our orators would then have done honour to their country, as well as our poets, geometers, and philosophers, and British Ciceros have appeared, as well as British Archimedeses and Virgils. (106–7)

It is with the full establishment of "liberty" in the Commonwealth era that a truly sublime eloquence might have been expected to spring up in Britain. That popular government produced no British Ciceros is written off as an "accident," an exception to the general Longinian rule of Hume's political science. It is, however, no accident that the autocratic Cromwell was possessed of an "elocution homely, tedious, obscure, and embarrassed" (*History of England* 6:57). According to Plutarch, Demosthenes affirmed that as eloquence is "a kind of respect to the people," so "to slight and take no care how what is said is likely to be received by the audience shows something of an oligarchic temper" (*Lives* 1026). Tyrants stand in no need of eloquence.

Yet, as Hume argued in his *History*, the constitutional monarchy established at the Glorious Revolution gave rise to "the most entire system of liberty that was ever known among mankind" (6:531). Why, then, did early Hanoverian Britain produce no great orator in the classical republican mold? Michael Meehan argues that "Of Eloquence" was written precisely to disprove the Longinian principle that liberty entails eloquence (84–85). And, on the surface, the essay indeed presents a Britain that enjoys liberty without enjoying eloquence. But Hume's *Essays* are situated in a context of political controversy that supplies a proper Longinian explanation for the absence of eloquence in Walpole's Britain: as Hume laments in his "Character of Sir Robert Walpole," "During his time . . . liberty [has] declined, and learning gone to ruin" (576). That Walpole had endangered liberty and letters was indeed the Opposition's major claim. For, as *The Craftsman* no. 201 explained, "Men of letters . . . may at least be called the second bulwarks of the state," next to great statesmen and generals. The labors of the learned supply "living lesson and instruction against tyranny and arbitrary power . . . [to] many succeeding ages. . . . For this reason, tyrannical princes and wicked politicians have always been enemies to men of letters." In conjuring up this Opposition keystone, Hume self-consciously assumes a "republican style."

Indeed, the *Essays* largely side with the Country party in censuring Walpole's encroachment upon British liberty. In "Of the Independency of Parliament" (1741), Hume cautions that Parliament's dependence on Walpole has become "dangerous to liberty"; in a later essay, "Of Public Credit" (1752), Walpole's ghost is once again brought to the bar for having threatened British liberty with the burden of national debt. At these moments Hume seems inspirited with the strains of *The Craftsman*. And, although Hume's stated aim in his 1752 *Essays* volume is to moderate impartially between Court and Country,[7] such moderation is, perhaps, already weighted in favor of one side. As John Barrell argues, an "impartial" or panoramic perspective is itself an ideal of the Country party (intro. and chap. 1). Accordingly, "Of Eloquence" may be read as an Opposition comment on the decline of liberty under Walpole. The failure of Hanoverian Britain to produce a sublime orator is, at least in part, a confession of its antirepublican nature.

Elaborating on this assumption some years later, John Quincy Adams lectured,

> [The assemblies of Athens and Rome] were held for the purpose of real deliberation. The fate of measures was not decided before they were proposed. Eloquence produced a powerful effect, not only upon the minds of the hearers, but upon the issues of the deliberation. In

7. See, particularly, Hume's *Essays*, part 2, essays nos. 12–15. In essay no. 14, "Of the Coalition of Parties," first added to some copies of the 1758 edition of the *Essays*, Hume openly declares his self-appointed task "to encourage moderate opinions, to find the proper medium in all disputes, to persuade each that its antagonist may possibly be sometimes in the right, and to keep a balance in the praise and blame, which we bestow on either side" (494).

the only countries in modern Europe, where the semblance of deliberative assemblies has been preserved, *corruption*, here in the form of executive influence, there in the guise of party spirit, by introducing a more compendious mode of securing decisions, has crippled the sublimest efforts of oratory, and the votes upon questions of magnitude to the interest of nations are all told, long before the questions themselves are submitted to discussion. (19)

While Adams speaks in a familiar republican manner, he does so with the peculiar comprehension of one whom—to think of Hegel's owl of Minerva—the twilight of a passing age affords a clearer view. Adams comments on the failure of eighteenth-century efforts, in Britain and France, to revive deliberative eloquence, noting that oratory will never flourish in governments that possess only "the semblance" of popular rule. Adams concludes by exhorting his Harvard students to cultivate oratory anew in the "purely republican" government of America; for "under governments purely republican . . . the voice of eloquence will not be heard in vain" (27).

Not possessing Adams's faith in pure republicanism, however, British men of letters might seem more ready to temper or even compromise their enthusiasm for ancient eloquence. Hume, for one, turns, at the end of "Of Eloquence," toward an unruffled acceptance of the deficiencies of British oratory. Although this may come as a surprise in the essay at hand, it does accord with his detached observation, elsewhere in the *Essays*, that the "tide" of British government has begun "to turn towards [absolute] monarchy" ("Whether the British Government Inclines More to Absolute Monarchy, or to a Republic" 51). But although he wore his philosophical detachment well, "Of Eloquence" implies a less disengaged perspective, and a more impassioned politics.

Not only is "eloquence" itself an Opposition shibboleth but Hume's illustrative examples of ancient eloquence are rife with implications for the political scene of the early 1740s. Discounting their many differences, both Demosthenes' *On the Crown* and Cicero's *Against Verres* defend republican values against the encroachments of tyrannic or corrupt power, and both thus ask to be read as installments in the cosmic struggle between autocrat and heroic orator. The villains of the speeches are, respectively, the emperor Philip of Macedon and the Roman governor Verres of Sicily, wicked governors who take their place in Opposition mythology alongside Xerxes, corrupted Theban oligarchs, Pericles, Catiline, and Antony. The central concerns of both Demosthenes and Cicero are liberty and the forces ranged against it. In his celebrated apostrophe, Demosthenes swore by the souls of the dead at Marathon that "no, my countrymen, it cannot be that you have acted wrong in encountering danger bravely for the liberty and the safety of all Greece" (416). And Cicero predicted that the very rocks and mountains would be horrified by Verres' unlawful crucifixion of the Roman citizen Gavius: "It was not Gavius against whom your hate was then displayed: you declared war upon the whole principle of the rights of the Roman citizen body . . . [and] the common liberties of all" (*The Verrine Orations*, Loeb trans., ed. Greenwood, 5.66). The orations of Demosthenes and Cicero draw clear and unpassable boundaries between virtue and corrupt rule; and Hume consciously evokes the same black and white world when he asks in "Of Eloquence," "It would be easy to find a Philip in modern times, but where shall we find a Demosthenes?" (106).

   This question, even if intended to be rhetorical, is partially answered in the remainder of the essay. Any contemporary reader would have recognized the denunciatory vigor of republican eloquence in Bolingbroke's writings against Walpole. And, indeed, Hume concedes as much in speaking of modern "attempts for the revival of ancient eloquence": "Lord Bolingbroke's productions contain a force and energy which our orators scarcely ever aim at" (108; I have here omitted Hume's 1754 addition to this sentence). Significantly, the "force and energy" that British orators scarcely aim at is not simply that of ancient eloquence in general but more specifically the *vis* and *impetus* of Demosthenes. In ancient as well as neoclassical rhetorics, "force"—in Greek, *ischus* or *bia*; in Latin, *vis*—serves to distinguish Demosthenes from all other famous orators.[8] Drawing on a tradition he presumably knew

8. See Cicero, *De Oratore* 3.7.28; Quintilian 12.10.23; Dionysius of Halicar-

well, Bolingbroke himself remarked, "Force . . . [is what] Demosthenes had in an eminent degree" (*Works* 3.26). Hume's essay,
in turn, grants some degree of Demosthenic force to the works of
Bolingbroke.

## The Sentimental Politics of Oratory

But Bolingbroke's productions, precisely because they are written, cannot attain the "force and energy" of oral eloquence. Hume
continues his assessment of Bolingbroke by noting, "It is evident,
that such an elevated style has much better grace in a speaker
than in a writer, and is assured of more prompt and astonishing
success. It is there seconded by the graces of voice and action: The
movements are mutually communicated between the orator and
the audience: And the very aspect of a large assembly, attentive to
the discourse of one man, must inspire him with a peculiar eleva-
tion, sufficient to give a propriety to the strongest figures and
expressions" (108–9). The orator's "voice and action" supplement and ultimately vindicate ("give propriety to") his passionate eloquence. (*Action* is the rhetorical term for the manner
in which the orator speaks as well as the physical gestures he uses
to accompany his words; Hume, however, uses the term mainly to
mean emphatic gestures such as stamping one's foot or bringing
tears to one's eyes.) According to Hume, figurative expression and
oratorical action mutually validate each other, and both are ultimately validated by the large and presumably democratic assembly in which the orator acts.

Hume's interest in eloquence as a political institution here

---

nassus, *Demosthenes* 21; Longinus chap. 12 (and John Holmes's adaptation of
Longinus in *The Art of Rhetoric Made Easy*, 2:12). The eighteenth century's
enduring fascination with Demosthenes' force and energy is evidenced in two of
its great commonplace books, the *Encyclopaedia Britannica* (1771) and Hugh
Blair's *Lectures*. The *Encyclopaedia* entry on "Language" describes Demosthenes'
"genius" as "irresistible force and overwhelming impetuosity" (2:873). Blair ex-
patiates on Demosthenes' "admirable and masterly force of masculine eloquence," 2:22–32.

shades into a psychological analysis of the "mutually communicated movements" between orator and audience. He interprets both figurative expression and oratorical action as evidence of the sympathetic circuit that connects the orator, whose passion is enabled by the "elevating" presence of auditors, and the audience, which is, in turn, elevated by the passion of the orator. Eloquence thus becomes a vivid illustration—if not the literary origin—of the doctrine of sympathy at the heart of Hume's moral philosophy. In book 3 of the *Treatise* Hume writes,

> The minds of all men are similar in their feelings and operations, nor can any one be actuated by any affection, of which all others are not, in some degree, susceptible. As in strings equally wound up, the motion of one readily communicates itself to all the rest; so all the affections readily pass from one person to another, and beget correspondent movements in every human creature. When I see the *effects* of passion in the voice and gesture of any person, my mind immediately passes from these effects to their causes, and forms such a lively idea of the passion, as is presently converted into the passion itself. (575–76)

I would suggest that Hume's doctrine of sympathy derives rather directly from classical rhetorical descriptions of "action" or "delivery." In Cicero's *De Oratore*, Crassus maintains that "action, which by its own powers displays the movements of the soul, affects all mankind; for the minds of all men are excited by the same emotions which they recognize in others, and indicate in themselves by the same tokens." And as Crassus also notes, of all orators Demosthenes is preeminently committed to action (3.56–59). The Ciceronian-Demosthenic ideal of sympathetic identification between orator and audience is a commonplace of eighteenth-century rhetoric, which we may see not ungracefully expressed by John "Orator" Henley: "Passions are wonderfully conveyed from one person's eyes to another's; the tears of one melting the heart of the other, and making a visible sympathy between their imaginations and aspects" (*Art of Speaking* [1727], 188). According to Thomas Gordon's "Of Eloquence, considered philosophically" (*Cato's Letters* no. 104), "Sound and action . . . constitute the mechanical power of eloquence," for they "strike the animal spirits sympathetically." Because of "the human sympathy in our souls," the orator may play upon his auditors as upon "musical instruments."

It is no far cry from Gordon's to Hume's model of sympathetic exchange. In "Of Eloquence," sympathy explains how the audience "accompanies" the orator in his "bold and excessive" passions. But the orator, for his part, cannot merely feign his passions but rather must be an adept method actor. Despite Hume's nod to the Horatian (and Longinian) dictum that the greatest art is to conceal art, the orator is ultimately represented less as an artist manipulating his audience's sympathy than as a man feeling with men: "The ancient orators . . . hurried away with such a torrent of sublime and pathetic, that they left their hearers no leisure to perceive the artifice, by which they were deceived. Nay, to consider the matter aright, they were not deceived by any artifice. The orator, by the force of his own genius and eloquence, first inflamed himself with anger, indignation, pity, sorrow; and then communicated those impetuous movements to his audience" (104).[9] The "impetuous movements" between orator and audience are properly "the movements of the heart" of Hume's sentimentalist psychology, the sympathetic impulses that connect individuals and provide the basis for social morality—which is, for Hume, the only meaningful morality.

"Reduce a person to solitude," wrote Hume in his second *Enquiry*, "and he loses all enjoyment . . . because the movements of his heart are not forwarded by correspondent movements in his fellow creatures" (43). This notion gained a widespread currency in the later eighteenth century. Adam Ferguson, for example, considers the sympathetic "movements of the heart" as the basis of everything that is considered worthy in society (33–34). And these same "movements" appear in the well-known "Snuff-Box" episode of Sterne's *A Sentimental Journey*: when Yorick offers Father Lorenzo his snuff-box, "The poor monk blushed as red as scarlet. . . . I blushed in my turn; but from what movements, I

---

9. Compare Shaftesbury's "Letter concerning Enthusiasm" (1:6): "The appearance of reality is necessary to make any passion agreeably represented; and to be able to move others we must first be moved ourselves, or at least seem to be so, upon some probable grounds."

leave to the few who feel to analyze" (43). Here, as with the orator and his audience, the movements of the heart are necessarily reciprocal. Lorenzo blushes, and Yorick blushes "in turn."

As Hume's *Enquiry* proceeds to argue, the "sympathetic movements" that we feel "wherever we go" are at once demonstrated and intensified by our experience of the theater. We there become a part of an audience that responds in unison to the passions of an actor who, in turn, responds to our responsive presence. The movements are mutual: "A man, who enters the theatre, is immediately struck with the view of so great a multitude participating of one common amusement; and experiences, from their very aspect, a superior sensibility or disposition of being affected with every sentiment, which he shares with his fellow creatures. He observes the actors to be animated by the appearance of a full audience, and raised to a degree of enthusiasm, which they cannot command in any solitary or calm moment" (44). Evidently, the passional dynamics of the theater harken back to Hume's earlier description of the ancient assembly in "Of Eloquence." There, his remarks on rhetorical action clearly suggest the theater's proximity to democratic politics: "The *supplosio pedis*, or stamping of the foot, was one of the most usual and moderate gestures which [the ancient orators] made use of; though that is now esteemed too violent, either for the senate, bar, or pulpit, and is only admitted into the theatre, to accompany the most violent passions, which are there represented" (101–2). In the ancient assembly as in the modern theater, the success of the orator or actor depends chiefly on a sympathetic exchange of passions with the audience: action, along with boldly figurative speech, serves to initiate as well as indicate this circuit.

Accordingly, the politics of eloquence, like the ethics of sympathy on which it relies, is fundamentally arational. Hume's ideal democracy relies upon an intercourse of hearts. It is thus fitting that Samuel Johnson, anxious to assert the guiding role of reason in politics (as well as the theater), should censure an oratory of action. Boswell recounts:

At Mr. Thrale's, in the evening, [Johnson] repeated his usual paradoxical declamation against action in public speaking. "Action can have no effect upon reasonable minds. It may augment noise, but it can never enforce argument. If you speak to a dog, you use action; you hold up your hand thus, because he is a brute; and in proportion as men are removed from brutes, action will have the less influence upon them." MRS. THRALE. "What then, Sir, becomes of Demosthenes's saying? 'Action, action, action!'" JOHNSON. "Demosthenes, Madam, spoke to an assembly of brutes; to a barbarous people." I thought it extraordinary, that he should deny the power of rhetorical action upon human nature, when it is proved by innumerable facts in all stages of society. Reasonable beings are not solely reasonable. (*Life of Johnson* 3 April 1773)

Boswell, in accord with Scottish moral sense philosophy, had much more faith than Johnson in the rectitude of a popular and passionate response. His friend Hume was even less inclined to overestimate the role of reason, in politics or elsewhere. Indeed, Hume's most celebrated sentence asserts that "reason is, and ought only to be the slave of the passions, and can never pretend to any other office than to serve and obey them" (*Treatise* 415).[10] In overturning the classical faculty psychology that places reason above passion, Hume elevates eloquence from a subrational to a suprarational art. To one who generally believes in the benevolence of natural impulses, the politics of eloquence will always be prepossessing.

If the first consequence of political eloquence is to naturalize truth, the second consequence is to give truth a more or less *local* habitation. Rhetoric, as Stanley Fish aptly defines it, is indeed "the skill which produces belief and therefore establishes what, in a particular time and particular place, is true" (*Doing What Comes Naturally* 480). A degree of relativism clings to the very notion of eloquence, particularly of a sublime variety. Socrates, of course, objected to rhetoric precisely because it neglected any type of transcendent truth (*aletheia*) (*Phaedrus* 267a–b); and in

10. As Peter Jones points out, Hume's sentence derives from Pierre Bayle's praise of Cicero for remarking upon "la servitude de l'âme [or "l'esclavage de la raison"] sous l'empire des passions" (*Hume's Sentiments* 5). Hume's high estimate of the "sentiments of the heart" is expressed more popularly in "Of Moral Prejudices," *Essays* 538–44. See Norman K. Smith for an assessment of Hume's optimistic naturalism (131–32); but also note Smith's important qualifications of Hume's "antirationalism" (539–40).

the early eighteenth century, Fénelon—as both a student of Plato and a Catholic archbishop—found it necessary to temper his admiration for Longinian aesthetics with an admonition against a sheerly instrumental eloquence: "We must admit that [Longinus] applies himself more to the admirable than to the useful, and that he scarcely refers eloquence to morality" (19–20). Fénelon's verdict on Longinus might equally be applied to the Hume who discusses Athenian oratory in book 2 of the *Treatise*: "Nothing is more capable of infusing any passion into the mind, than eloquence, by which objects are represented in their strongest and most lively colours. We may of ourselves acknowledge, that such an object is valuable, and such another odious; but 'till an orator excites the imagination, and gives force to these ideas, they may have but a feeble influence either on the will or the affections" (426–27). Hume attends to the technical force of eloquence, with only implied reference to its ethical aims; indeed, he approves its purely practical end of stirring a limited audience who *already* share certain values and aversions. Eloquence, we may say, operates only within a given community of sympathetic hearts.

Conversely, Hume attributes the differences between one community and another to the effects of sympathy. As Duncan Forbes argues, Hume's doctrine of sympathy accounts for the "socially plastic and variable" quality of human nature (108). Sympathetic exchange explains the peculiarities of both a "club or knot of companions" and "a common or national character" (*Essays* 202–3). The bonds of sympathy hold us together in groups that are smaller and more homogenous than universal human nature. Sympathy is thus belonging, in some more or less delimited way, and as such may be seen as a modern remnant of the ideally close community of the ancients. Indeed, Hume models his dynamics of sympathy not merely on the idea of "spectatorship" but, I would argue, on the specific experience of an ancient assembly that heard its own voice and saw its own face in the gestures and words of the orator.[11] Sympathy argues a social commonality

---

11. John Mullan (18–56) argues that between the *Treatise* and the *Enquiry concerning Morals* Hume transforms sympathy from a doctrine of unlimited mutuality into the principle of "spectatorial aloofness," which is later elaborated in Smith's *Theory of Moral Sentiments*. However, Mullan's distinction is subsumed

equivalent to, though less visible than, the old sense of community associated with the polis; in a commercial age, sympathy becomes a vestigal myth of passionate solidarity. It is a myth endorsed by those who, like Hume, feel at ease in an imaginary scene of oratory. But for philosophers less sanguine about the justness of our untutored responses, the passionate appeal of oratory provides a perennial source of anxiety.

## Arguments against Rousing Eloquence

Johnson's distrust of political eloquence accords with a well-known Royal Society tradition that includes, most famously, Thomas Sprat and John Locke. Having lived through the civil wars, both Sprat and Locke had opportunities to see oratory in action, and both came to equate it with a vicious demagogy. They would have applauded Samuel Butler's satire in *Hudibras* of the age of "civil Fury," "When Gospel-Trumpeter, surrounded / With long-ear'd rout, to Battel sounded, / And pulpit, Drum Ecclesiastick, / Was beat with fist, instead of a stick" (1.9–12). As for Sir Hudibras, "He could not ope / His mouth, but out there flew a Trope" (1.81–82).

After the strife of the Interregnum—and during the continued civic and religious turbulence of Charles II's reign—most writers of the late seventeenth century desired, in Dryden's phrase, "common quiet" (*Religio Laici* 450). Even Milton, whose "acrimonious and surly republican[ism]" Johnson famously deplored (*Lives* 1:156), wrote at the end of his career:

> [Greek] orators thou then extoll'st, as those
> The top of eloquence, statists indeed,
> And lovers of their country, as may seem;
> But herein to our prophets far beneath,
> As men divinely taught, and better teaching

by the larger dialectic of oratory upon which Hume consistently models the dynamic of sympathetic exchange. The scene of oratory contains *both* spectatorial division (between audience and orator) and the negation of that division (in their mutual reflection).

The solid rules of civil government
In their majestic unaffected style
Than all the orators of Greece and Rome.
                    (*Paradise Regained* 4.354–60)

The Bible proves a better statesman's manual than ancient oratory precisely because it tends more toward the stability of the
state. Thus Cromwell's late secretary, no less than Dryden's country kinsman, found himself "studying peace, and shunning civil
rage" ("To my Honoured Kinsman, John Driden" 1.3).

Accordingly, the Royal Society was understood by Johnson to
have been "instituted soon after the Restoration, to divert the
attention of people from public discontent" (*Lives* 2:94–95).
Sprat's *History of the Royal Society* (1667) indeed proposes that
the dispassionate pursuit of science will heal "our civil differences, and religious distractions." Sprat continues, "The most
effectual remedy to be us'd is, first to assemble about some calm,
indifferent things, especially experiments" (426). Experimental
science is conciliatory both because it involves a collaborative
effort and because it entails a dispassionate, pacifying prose style.
Sprat offers the Royal Society's "close, naked, natural way of
speaking" as an antidote to the civic turmoil stirred up by passionate eloquence. As an ardent Royalist, he distrusts an eloquence traditionally associated with "commonwealths, where
the greatest affairs are manag'd by the violence of popular assemblies, and those govern'd by the most plausible speakers." And
although he admits that eloquence was once "an admirable instrument in the hands of wise men," he quickly asserts that in his
own "degenerated" times "eloquence ought to be banished from
all civil societies, as a thing fatal to peace and good manners" (15–
22, 111–15).

For Sprat, the only justifiable motive for eloquence has become
self-defense, using the "ornaments of speaking" as a weapon
against the "wicked" eloquence of the times. Thus Sprat is su-
perbly eloquent in his denunciation of figurative eloquence: "[Or-
naments of speaking] are in open defiance against reason; professing, not to hold much correspondence with that; but with its
slaves, the passions: they give the mind a motion too changeable,

and bewitching, to consist with right practice." Following closely upon his accusation that eloquence is factious ("fatal to peace and good manners"), Sprat here accuses figurative eloquence of casting "mists and uncertainties . . . on our knowledge" (111–12). Eloquence, that is, is not simply "wicked" according to an absolute standard of virtue; it is also "specious" according to empirical criteria of knowledge. Sprat, like all foes of rhetoric, moves easily between political and epistemological registers, demonizing eloquence for being dangerous as well as, and often by dint of, being deceptive. Eloquence must accordingly be banished so that rational discourse might facilitate both peace in the political arena and true knowledge in the field of the "profitable and difficult arts."

Philosophy is surely one such art, and we hardly need to rehearse here the hoary feud between rhetoric (as the taste for *copia*) and philosophy (the preference for things over words), though the curious might want to turn again to George Williamson's classic study of seventeenth-century prose style.[12] But the eighteenth-century reader would, I think, have considered English *law* as another strenuous and useful art that proves more or less incompatible with sublime eloquence. The English legal system was widely thought to preclude an English Cicero because of its more-than-Roman formality and dependence on legal precedent: as George Mackenzie, a chief legal figure under Charles II and Anne, put it, "The definition which Cato of old gave of an orator was that an orator is an honest man who has eloquence to express his thoughts. But now the body of law is increased to so great a bulk, we must add that a [forensic] orator is an honest and *learned* man, who is master of a handsome way of speaking" (22).

12. See especially chap. 6, "Bacon and Stoic Rhetoric," 150–85. Williamson's work has recently been contested by Richard Kroll, who argues against the notion that seventeenth-century philosophers aimed at transparent referentiality: Kroll's philosophers rather assumed that the mind works within the "narrow confines" of language, accepting its "metaphorical constraints" (16); thus, for example, he asserts that Sprat "resists . . . not figuration as such, but its false application" (278). Although Kroll's argument is persuasive, it need not obscure the extent to which, as Jay Tribby reminds us, the stylistic procedure of the Royal Society represents a decisive break from the "metaphorical witticisms" of a *civil conversatione* model of scientific inquiry.

And indeed, the bulk of Mackenzie's *Idea of the Modern Eloquence of the Bar* consists of sample speeches drawn from the various bodies of law that the British lawyer must master: the law of nature, the law of nations, the civil law, the municipal law, the feudal law.

Such training and exactness hardly allow for the liberties or bravura of a Cicero, let alone a Demosthenes: as Adam Smith remarks, the Athenian courts were "in very little better order than the mob in the pit of an ill regulated play house," and although "the courts at Rome were much more regular" they still allowed Cicero ample room to "fool the judges" with vivid but circumstantial narrations, confirmations drawn from the "topics" without regard for the truth of the case, and so forth (178–82). English law had curtailed these irregularities—and with them the occasion for sublime eloquence. Hume himself owns, in "Of Eloquence," that "the multiplicity and intricacy of laws, is a discouragement to eloquence in modern times" (103); indeed, he thereupon dismisses the very possibility of reviving forensic eloquence in Britain and proceeds to address the possibilities for importing Athenian oratory of "the deliberative kind." (Hume, incidentally, was himself early intended for the law but soon "found an insurmountable aversion to everything but the pursuits of philosophy and general learning" ["My Own Life," *Essays* xxxiii].)

For eighteenth-century authors this anatagonism between eloquence and the law was no less real, and probably more pressing, than the relatively arcane debate between rhetoric and philosophy. Hume explains in "On the Rise and Progress of the Arts and Sciences" that eloquence arises before the law: "Men may have made some advances, even in the sublime arts of poetry and eloquence, where a rapidity of genius and imagination assist their progress, before they have arrived at any great refinement in their municipal laws" (116). Stamped with such origins, eloquence ever seems not simply prior to but distinctly outside the law—indeed, it appears little less than illicit to some independent Whig writers in the early years of Walpole's ministry. Thus, Gordon's "Of Eloquence, considered politically" (*Cato's Letters* no. 103) proceeds with evident ambivalence as it moves from neo-Longinian praise of Demosthenes' "dictatorial force of speaking" in the service of "glory and liberty," to a cooler appreciation of an English legal system that affords no such latitude for oratory: "The [English] judge is tied to the rigid letter of the law, and [is] not to be moved from it by pity or resentment." Gordon finally concludes that all in all "rhetoric, though (as Plato says) a bad art," is a necessary evil: "I do not think it possible to destroy it, without destroying with it most other good arts; for it almost always flourishes and decays with them." The "good art" most evident in Gordon's essay is quite simply the law.[13]

Similarly, despite Lyttelton's popular reputation in the mid-1730s as the parliamentary Demosthenes of the Opposition (Davis 79–80), he too casts a cold glance at eloquence in his *Letters from a Persian in England.* Amid the volume's predictable Opposition squibs against luxury, corruption, credit, and the novel office of prime minister, letters 43 and 44 surprisingly present "an Englishman" who vigorously denounces eloquence—the Opposition ideal—as "the most pernicious of all our refinements, and the most to be dreaded in a free country." The ancient Romans were happy in their commonwealth only "before Greece had infected them with rhetoric," which "is less the talent of enforcing truth, than of imposing falsehood." He continues: "Good laws have been established by wise men, who were far from being eloquent; and eloquent men, who were far from being wise, have everywhere destroyed or corrupted them. Look into history, [and] you will find that the same period which carried eloquence to its perfection, was almost always mortal to liberty. . . . I maintain that it would be just as proper for us to decide a question of right or wrong, after a debauch of wine, or a dose of opium, as after being heated or cooled, to the degree we often are, by the address of one of these skilful speakers." Although the Englishman finally concedes that eloquence may be beneficial in the hands of a heroic orator such as Demosthenes or Cicero, he nonetheless concludes that it is at best a dangerous supplement

---

13. Gordon's ambiguous or conflicted attitude toward Demosthenic eloquence may be a result or an extension of the broader dialectic in *Cato's Letters*— detected by Shelley Burtt (64–86)—between an abiding republican ideal of civic virtue and a Lockean liberalism in which eloquence (as I argue presently) plays no part.

to "the truth" (*Works* 273–80). His voice is nowhere ironized by Lyttelton, who apparently advocates a calm and wholly legal method of government.

Lyttelton's ideal of government—and of "truth"—may of course be traced back to Locke. Locke's well-known animus against eloquence, as expressed in the *Essay concerning Human Understanding* (1689), indeed comprises both political and philosophical objections:

> Since wit and fancy finds easier entertainment in the world than dry truth and real knowledge, figurative speeches, and allusion in language, will hardly be admitted, as an imperfection or abuse of it. . . . But yet, if we would speak of things as they are, we must allow, that all the art of rhetoric, besides order and clearness, all the artificial and figurative application of words eloquence hath invented, are for nothing else but to insinuate wrong ideas, move the passions, and thereby mislead the judgment; and so indeed are perfect cheat: and therefore however laudable or allowable oratory may render them in harangues and popular addresses, they are certainly, in all discourses that pretend to inform or instruct, wholly to be avoided; and where truth and knowledge are concerned, cannot but be thought a great fault, either of the language or person that makes use of them. . . . 'Tis evident how much men love to deceive, and be deceived, since rhetoric, that powerful instrument of error and deceit, has its established professors, is publicly taught, and has always been had in great reputation; and, I doubt not, but it will be thought great boldness, if not brutality in me, to have said thus much against it. Eloquence, like the fair sex, has too prevailing beauties in it, to suffer itself ever to be spoken against. And 'tis in vain to find fault with those arts of deceiving, wherein men find pleasure to be deceived. (508)[14]

Of all the discourses in which men find deceit pleasurable, Locke significantly specifies only one—declamation. He satirizes the

14. The "wit and fancy" of Locke's final flourish—"eloquence [is] like the fair sex"—was duly observed in the eighteenth century; as Thomas Leland puts it, "Even Mr. Locke, that enemy to figurative speech, slides imperceptibly into those paths, from whence he is so solicitous to divert mankind" (18). The casual misogyny of the passage derives from the convention of personifying eloquence as a woman, particularly an overdressed woman. Plato feminizes eloquence in the *Phaedrus*, 260–61, as does Quintilian in the *Instiutio Oratoria*, 8.Pr.21–22 and 8.3.7; see also Puttenham 3.1.

politics of oratory with curt sarcasm: eloquence is deemed a "perfect cheat," and hence "laudable or allowable" in "harangues and
popular addresses." Locke is clearly not, like Sprat, a Royalist
who would silence popular assemblies on principle; he is, however, a political theorist who conceived of government in strictly
rational terms. And thus, in his *Letter concerning Toleration*
(1689), "strong arguments and good reason" constitute the only
type of eloquence Locke will abide. Inverting the common con-
ceit of the orator's fire, Locke's speaker would indeed "allay and
temper all that heat, and unreasonable averseness of mind" (33–
34).

Conveniently, the social contract theory of Locke's *Second
Treatise of Government* (1690) has no place for the passionate
appeal of harangues and addresses. According to Locke, government originates in, and depends on the continuing consent of, a
union of largely self-sufficient and remarkably sober individuals
who have convened for a limited purpose, chiefly the mutual
protection of private property. The main purpose of politics in
this "liberal" model of society—or what Pocock would call, more
broadly, a "civil jurisprudential" model—is thus the allocation
and preservation of rights, especially property rights. These
rights, natural and self-evident, antedate the political arrange-
ments that are instituted to uphold them; accordingly, a stable
idea of justice transcends the arena of political debate. We may
here recall Socrates' objection in the *Gorgias* that eloquence is a
technique designed to achieve success rather than implement justice.

In contrast to Locke, Hume, inasmuch as he supports democratic oratory, advocates a political arena without a fixed or rational standard of justice that could transcend the contingencies of
custom and prejudice, persuasion and force. The politics of oratory pragmatically vindicate that which has succeeded. And, as
we learn from reading the classical orators, nothing succeeds like
excess. Hume revives the Ciceronian argument that the force of
eloquence alone has the power to civilize mankind; in Cicero's
*De Oratore*, Crassus asks, "What other power [*vis*] could either
have assembled mankind, when dispersed, into one place, or have
brought them from the wild and savage life to the present hu-

mane and civilized state of society?" (1.8). Hume, in his essay "Of
the Original Contract," similarly argues that people need to be
"persuaded" (presumably with vehement action and bold figures)
and sometimes "forced" into political society (468).

Cicero's story of the origins of civil society serves Hume in his
campaign against Locke's rationalist fiction of the social contract.
To refute the contract theory as a historical proposition, Hume
maintains that all known governments are originally founded on
force and conquest, not voluntary consent. To refute it as a sanc-
tioning argument for established government, he observes that
the authority of a government commonly rests upon no more
than its antiquity and the acquiescence of popular prejudice.
Hume thus concurs with Bolingbroke, who, as Kramnick argues,
grounds the polity on the persuasive ties of "duty and honor"
rather than on "rationally conceived laws" (*Bolingbroke* 79). In
this light, Hume's advocacy of classical eloquence may be read as
a skeptical and conservative critique of Locke's liberalism.

These speculations are offered, however, as if Hume wholeheartedly advocated a revival of ancient eloquence. But reading "Of
Eloquence" has dispelled the misconception that Hume's en-
dorsement is so simple. In the following chapter, I shall examine
the grounds on which Hume and other writers of his age opposed
or disabled the ideal of classical oratory.

# 2 Eloquence versus Polite Style

Hume's advocacy of eloquence is limited in a number of ways—as we shall see, he had important social or "polite" reservations concerning the desirability of importing sublime oratory into Britain. We may begin, however, by noting his early conceived (and fairly de rigueur) distrust of figures as instruments of, in Locke's phrase, "error and deceit." This philosophic topos of eloquence as error first appears in the introduction to *A Treatise of Human Nature*, where Hume complains that in the learned world, "'tis not reason, which carries the prize, but eloquence; and no man needs ever despair of gaining proselytes to the most extravagant hypothesis, who has art enough to represent it in any favourable colours. The victory is not gained by the men at arms, who manage the pike and the sword; but by the trumpeters, drummers, and musicians of the army" (xiv).

Writing these lines at the outset of his career, Hume pledges his allegiance to the plain style of philosophical prose adopted by British empiricism. His parable of how the public regrettably rewards the sound of an argument over its sense echoes Sprat's earlier complaint, "How many rewards, which are due to more profitable, and difficult Arts, have been snatched away by the easy vanitie of fine speaking?" (112). Moreover, Hume's depiction of eloquence as the "musician" of an army is analogous to Locke's more traditional image of eloquence as a deceptive beauty. Military music and the painting of "the fair sex" are equally cosmetic, applied to the corps to distract from its underlying character. According to either metaphor, eloquence masks even as it supplements the body of the philosophic text.

The philosophical suspicion of eloquence reappears throughout Hume's work. In his *Enquiry concerning Human Understanding*, a recasting of the first book of the *Treatise*, Hume appears particularly concerned to keep the understanding uncontaminated by undue appeals to the passions: thus, in "Of Miracles," he writes, "Eloquence, when at its highest pitch, leaves little room for reason or reflection, but addressing itself entirely to the fancy or the affections, captivates the willing hearers, and subdues their understanding. Happily, this pitch it seldom attains." Hume's judgment here—poised in tone between complacency and relief—would seem to align him with those who reprove eloquence as an instrument of irrationality. However, as his next sentence reveals, his immediate target is not eloquence per se but contemporary pulpit orations on prodigies and supernatural events: "But what a Tully or a Demosthenes could scarcely effect over a Roman or Athenian audience, every Capuchin, every itinerant or stationary teacher can perform over the generality of mankind, and in a higher degree, by touching such gross and vulgar passions" (125–26). Still, even the eloquence of a Demosthenes offers a technique for subverting the calm understanding, and his being less efficient than a common Capuchin hardly makes him less culpable. Although Hume later tempers this criticism of the scene of oratory by wishfully doubting that Athens, "that ancient and polite city," even had, properly speaking, an unphilosophic "mob" (144), he cannot utterly retract his one quite Lockean moment.

"Of Eloquence" is more openly—even systematically—ambivalent toward a passionate eloquence. In a passsage that he deleted from the 1770 edition of the *Essays*—perhaps because of its own impolite egoisms—Hume acknowledges both the deceptiveness and (introducing a category that Locke does not) the "immodesty" of sublime expression, even as he admires its aesthetic appeal.

The English are conspicuous for good-sense, which makes them very jealous of any attempts to deceive them by the flowers of rhetoric and elocution. They are also particularly modest; which makes them consider it as a piece of arrogance to offer any thing but reason to public assemblies, or attempt to guide them by passion or fancy. I may, perhaps, be allowed to add, that the people in general are not remarkable for delicacy of taste, or for sensibility to the charms of the muses. Their musical parts, to use the expression of a noble author, are but indifferent. Hence their comic poets, to move them, must have recourse to obscenity; their tragic poets to blood and slaughter: And hence their orators, being deprived of any such resource, have abandoned altogether the hopes of moving them, and have confined themselves to plain argument and reasoning. (622)

For Hume, the orator's "flowers" are rationally deceitful and socially "arrogant," but they are also the test of an audience's "sensibility" and "delicacy of taste." His complaint seems to be that the English cannot sustain his own complex attitude toward eloquence. Given the lamentable dissociation of sense and sensibility in the English character, their oratory is reduced to plain reasoning, while their theater is reduced to "obscenity" and "blood and slaughter." As Hume makes clear, there was no such sharp division between oratory and theater in the classical era. For the classical orator the ideal public assembly would be composed of citizens who were neither conspicuously rational nor bluntly insensible, neither British philosophers nor John Bulls.

But such an assembly would seem to exclude Hume, whose ear for deceit appears to be too finely trained by British philosophy. While his appreciation of eloquence draws variously upon the tenets of civic virtue, sublime aesthetics, and his own sentimentalist psychology, his suspicion of eloquence has a no less impressive lineage, which may be traced back, ultimately, to the art of rhetoric itself. I shall now turn to consider that art, and its politely condescending sense of the archaic or "vulgar" nature of figural language.

## The Progress of Language from Vivacity to Accuracy

Rhetoric's relation to eloquence is essentially the relation of theory to practice. Rhetoric analyzes and codifies the oratorical performances that a culture considers pleasing and effective. Given our usual reverence for past performances, the analytic description of "canonical" orations typically becomes a prescription for future orations; thus, the study of rhetoric is deemed the proper education for the aspiring orator. For an eighteenth-century account of this scenario, we may turn to Shaftesbury's "Soliloquy, or Advice to an Author" (1710). Shaftesbury begins with the familiar topos that eloquence develops organically in popular governments: "Free nations . . . from the nature of their government, as from a proper soil, produced the generous plants." Whereas eloquence develops with the ease and naturalness of a plant, rhetoric, as eloquence's proper reflection upon itself, requires an intellectual exertion. Once eloquence has "grown into repute, and the power of moving the affections becomes the study and emulation of the forward wits and aspiring geniuses of the times, it would necessarily happen that many geniuses of equal size and strength, though less covetous of public applause, of power, or of influence over mankind, would content themselves with the contemplation merely of these enchanting arts." These contemplative men are the Greek Sophists, "who by their example taught the public to discover what was just and excellent in each [oratorical] performance." The Sophists, as the first rhetoricians, taught the public to appreciate, imitate, and perhaps even surpass the excellence of selected oratorical models (1:155–57).

But rhetoric and eloquence are not always conceived as mutually beneficial allies. In our own time, both Walter Ong and Eric A. Havelock have argued that rhetoric, as an embodiment of written culture, fundamentally opposes the oral phenomenon of eloquence. They attribute to oral culture a figurative or "poetic" criterion for the transmission of knowledge, while holding that written culture employs the antithetical criteria of rationality, abstraction, and logic. Thus the cultural shift that produces rhetoric specifically archaizes the figures of oral eloquence. A general sense of this historical process dates back (at least) to Shaftesbury, who maintains that of all the styles of discourse,

> the easiest attained and earliest practiced was the miraculous, the pompous, or what we generally call the sublime. Astonishment is of

all other passions the easiest raised in raw and unexperienced mankind. . . . This the prince of critics [Aristotle] assures us to have
been the manner of the earliest poets, before the age of Homer, or
till such time as this father-poet came into repute, who disposed
that spurious race and gave rise to a legitimate and genuine kind. He
retained only what was decent of the figurative or metaphorical
style, introduced the natural and simple, and turned his thoughts
towards the real beauty of composition, the unity of design, the
truth of characters, and the just imitation of Nature in each particular. (1:157–58)

In Shaftesbury's thumbnail history of eloquence, men in their
developmental infancy spoke in sublime, astonishing figures. (We
may imagine the unrepresented speech of the primitive as a torrent of fiery apostrophes, prosopopoeias, and hyperboles). Emerging from humanity's nonage, Homer introduced (anachronis-
tically) the Aristotelian virtues of rationally unified composition,
a "simple" style, and mimetic intent. The taming of the figurative style thus marks the birth of modern consciousness. Rhetoricians agree that the tropes and figures, born of passion or necessity in some dark prerhetorical past, are reduced to discursive
ornaments in the age of rhetoric.[1]

Rhetorics from Aristotle onward exhibit a fascination with,
and distance from, the figurative eloquence they codify. This
much is common to all rhetorics, *qua* rhetoric. But the novelty of
the so-called new rhetoric of the eighteenth century lies in the
degree to which it submits both oral and written composition to
the standards of written culture—rationality, abstraction, logic.
In the era of Bacon and Locke, these standards were referred to as

---

1. From another point of view, of course, the art of rhetoric invents the very
*concept* of figurative speech. The terms of stylistic rhetoric—metaphor,
metonymy, prosopopoeia—are the produce of philosophical discrimination, not
spontaneous passion. As Jacques Derrida contends in "White Mythology," "A
philosophical thesis, one might even say the sole thesis of philosophy, [is] the
thesis which constitutes the concept of metaphor, [that is,] the opposition between what is proper and what is not, between essence and accident . . . between
the intelligible and the sensible, and so forth" (28–29). To illustrate Derrida's
contention, we may say that Demosthenes' apostrophe to his dead forefathers
becomes a "figurative" speech only in opposition to what we posit as proper
speech according to an Aristotelian ideal of mimesis and perspicuity.

"science." The scientism or, more broadly, the "graphocentrism" of the new rhetoric explains what Howell describes as its two distinguishing features: its advocacy of inductively probable arguments (over classical rhetoric's reliance on enthymemes) and its redoubled emphasis on a plain or perspicuous style (441–47). But although the age may have wished to write a plain style, its fascination with the ornaments of the old eloquence was far from extinguished.

Both within and without the new rhetoric, the study of tropes and figures flourished as never before. First of all, technical manuals of tropes and figures, also known as "stylistic rhetorics," continued to be included in school curricula and gentlemen's libraries, and thus educated persons still experienced literature in terms of tropes and figures. Critics of eighteenth century literature sometimes mistakenly assume that, given the pretensions of the new rhetoric, interest in the traditional study of tropes and figures all but disappears in the eighteenth-century; thus, a scholar as astute as Graham Petrie remarks, "Sterne's intense interest in, and mastery of, the 'figures' of rhetoric was of course rather exceptional for his time" (481). However, stylistic rhetorics proliferated in the period. In precollege curricula, slender stylistic manuals, using memorable distichs to define the tropes and figures, remained popular throughout the eighteenth century: Thomas Farnaby's Latin *Troposchematologia* (1648) reached a fifteenth edition by 1767, and John Stirling's *A System of Rhetoric . . . for the Use of Schools* (1733) was reprinted fourteen times. This indoctrination in the tropes and figures did not cease with one's school days but extended into college lectures and private reading. John Holmes includes an extensive listing of tropes and figures in *The Art of Rhetoric Made Easy* (London, 1755). John Ward's *A System of Oratory Delivered in a Course of Lectures Publicly Read at Gresham College* (1759)—lectures that he began to give in 1720—devotes twenty-seven of its fifty-four lectures to stylistic rhetoric. And in 1767 Thomas Gibbons wrote a five-hundred-page exposition entitled *Rhetoric: or, A View of Its Principle Tropes and Figures, in Their Origins and Powers*.

Second, and more important, the rhetoricians and philosophers of Hume's generation analyzed the tropes and figures with a philosophical rigor unparalleled since their original elaboration and division in the Hellenistic era. Roman rhetoricians conceived of the tropes pragmatically, that is, in terms of how they might persuade or delight an audience: tropes were to be cultivated for their effects. This pragmatic study of trope was revived, with proselytizing exuberance, by Renaissance rhetoricians such as Sherry, Peacham, Fraunce, and Puttenham. While eighteenth-century rhetoricians never lost sight of the classical conception of trope as persuasion, they added to tropology a new dimension: an inquiry into the *psychological causes* of tropes.

Aristotle wrote on the purely logical relations that constitute metaphor, which he listed as a transference of properties from genus to species, species to genus, species to species, and according to analogy (*Poetics* 21; *Rhetoric* 3.2–4). But the characteristic Enlightenment question was, What psychological or "passional" principles cause us to think metaphorically? What motivates "tropical" thinking? George Campbell writes that tropes

> are so far from being the inventions of art, that, on the contrary, they result from the original and essential principles of the human mind;—that accordingly they are the same *upon the main*, in all nations, barbarous and civilized;—that the simplest and most ancient tongues do most abound with them, the natural effect of improvement in science and language, which commonly go together, being to regulate the fancy, and to restrain the passions;—that the sole business of art in this subject is to range the several tropes and figures into classes, to distinguish them by names, and to trace the principles in the mind which gave them birth. (316)

To derive the tropes from "the original principles of the mind" became a flourishing field of speculation in the eighteenth century; indeed, after the new rhetoric, figures of speech may more properly be called figures of thought. Authors on both sides of the channel sought to diagnose the cognitive foundations of eloquence. In keeping with the Enlightenment's methodological imperative to investigate origins, they would establish an *etiology* of figures.

They begin, of course, by wholly or partially rejecting traditional accounts of the origin of tropes. In Judeo-Christian tradition,

God originally endowed Adam and Eve with an accurate language, a word-thing correspondence that was lost in the confusion of Babel. The excrescence of figuration that has since corrupted language thus signifies no less than our fallen state (Fish, *Surprised by Sin* 113; cf. Foucault 34–44). Even eighteenth-century theorists who perfunctorily acknowledge orthodox Adamic language theory—such as Vico, Condillac, Warburton, and Blair—evidence their real interest in the natural ("Gentile," "postdiluvian") history of language and trope. And Cicero's account of tropes, although overtly naturalistic in maintaining that tropes are necessitated by a deficiency of proper terms in early languages (*De Oratore* 3.38), was considered insufficient because it stops short of analyzing the root psychological causes of tropes.[2] Eighteenth-century authors sought to trace figurative thinking back either to the trunk (so to speak) of experiential trauma—primal scenes of "fear," terror, and so on—or to the root of more fundamental psychological processes such as the association of ideas. To risk a generalization, we may say that the British (excepting Hume) tended to deduce figures from these deeper processes of mind, whereas the French were more interested in the anthropological dramas that first gave rise to figurative thinking.

British associationism, from Hobbes onward, routinely located the origins of tropes in associative human nature. Bolingbroke, for example, wrote, "What is the juxta-position of ideas? What is that chain which connects, by intermediate ideas, that are links of it, ideas that are remote, but figurative style?" (quoted in Kallich, 23–24). Tropes may be explained by reference to the universal associational laws of resemblance and cause-and-effect that govern all our thought processes. The associationist doctrine thereby domesticates tropes, making them a necessary part of our workaday imagination. The innovative implication, however, is that because tropes are a function of thought (the "juxtaposition" or association of ideas), and because thought, in the tradition of

2. With Cicero, see also Quintilian 8.6.4–6. In a paradox characteristic of the Enlightenment temper, eighteenth-century rhetoricians and linguistic philosophers readily cite the Ciceronian theory as authoritative, even while advancing their own heterodox theories. See, for example, Warburton, *Divine Legation* 2:57; Monboddo 4:16–17; and Witherspoon 3:404–5.

Hobbes and Locke, precedes speech, tropes become a properly *prelinguistic* phenomenon. This is also the implication of Adam Smith's remark that language develops from a collection of proper names (which cannot properly be called a language) into a system of common nouns through a process "which the grammarians call an *Antonomasia*" (204). Without figurative thinking, language itself could not come into being. (Later philosophers such as Priestley [182] and Monboddo [1:577] cite Smith on this point). Yet by a further twist—which I examine presently—a culture arrives at truly "polite" language use only through renouncing its heritage of figurative expression.

While the British thus situated tropical thought (if not expression) within an orderly scheme of human nature, the French traced it to primal scenes of fear and irrationality. The rhetorician Dumarsais (1729) asserted that figurative language originates not according to rational necessity but under the pressure of the imagination (1:36); his assertion became axiomatic during the French Enlightenment. Voltaire writes in his *Encyclopédie* entry on "Eloquence" (1751), "Nature renders men eloquent in great concerns and in great passions. Whoever is vividly moved sees things with a different eye than other men. . . . A strong passion, a pressing danger, suddenly calls forth the imagination" (24:491). At roughly the same time, Rousseau renders such a scene of "pressing danger" with pictorial vividness:

> Upon meeting others, a savage man will initially be frightened. Because of his fear he sees the others as bigger and stronger than himself. He calls them *giants*. After many experiences, he recognizes these so-called giants are neither bigger nor stronger than he. Their stature does not approach the idea he had initially attached to the word giant. So he invents another name common to them and to him, such as the name *man*, for example, and leaves *giant* to the fictitious object that had impressed him during his illusion. That is how the figurative word is born before the literal word, when our gaze is held in passionate fascination; and how it is that the first idea it conveys to us is not that of the truth.

Rousseau "paradoxically"—and famously—concludes that "figurative language" precedes "proper" language. He explains this apparent paradox by referring to the current notion that figurative language transposes primarily ideas, not words. The savage man of his example thinks figuratively (that is, improperly) before he arrives at the proper or "true" name for that which he sees ("Essay on the Origin of Languages," trans. Moran 12–13).[3]

The British certainly agreed with Rousseau that figures, however natural or ubiquitous, have a distinctive history; that not only do they derive from a hypothetical moment in mankind's psychological development but indeed they originate in full blossom, for the earliest "stages" of mankind are most passionately attached to them. Oliver Goldsmith merely states a commonplace when he writes that "barbarous nations speak in a style more affecting and figurative than others; they feel with passions unabated by judgment, and tropes and figures are the natural result of their sensations" (1:169). Of course, no origin hunting is ever disinterested; one typically tells stories about ultimate causes in order to explain—and often to justify—the way things are now. Thus the historicizing of figures also politicizes them, for the contemporary speech of the "vulgar," as well as that of children and the insane, was thought to abound in bold figures. Enlightenment authors eagerly sought out the "savage man" who walks among us—precisely for the purpose of excluding him from mature, rational discourse.

In arguing that ontogeny repeats phylogeny, Freud simply gives twentieth-century expression to the eighteenth-century belief that children are the primitives in our midst. Freud calls children "the primitives of our times," with reference not only to their atavistic Oedipal anxieties but also to their archaic capacity for "speech symbolism" (*Moses and Monotheism* 103, 125–26; cf. *Future of an Illusion* 18); similarly, for eighteenth-century writers the child's propensity to speak in astonishing figures affiliates him with an earlier period of human development. Shaftesbury remarks that the sublime or "miraculous" style of the earliest

---

3. Although Rousseau's essay was not published until 1781, it was probably written around the time of Rousseau's *Discourse on the Origin and Bases of the Inequality among Men* (1754), which alludes to Rousseau's basic argument on the origin of language. See Charles Porset's Introduction to *Essai sur l'origine des langues*, 8–15.

pre-Homeric poets can now appeal only to the imagination of "children in their earliest infancy" (1:157). Hugh Blair equates the speech of children and primitives still more directly in his *Critical Dissertation upon the Poems of Ossian* (1762). As the experience of the primitive was believed to parallel that of the contemporary child, Blair concludes that "the progress of the world [in respect to language] resembles the progress of age in man. The powers of imagination are most vigorous and predominant in youth; those of the understanding ripen more slowly, and often attain not to their maturity, till the imagination begins to flag." In adulthood, "style becomes more chaste, but less animated" (*Poems of Ossian* 63–64).

The mentality and attendant expressions of the primitive were thought to recur as a stage in our normal development. The child may thus speak like Shaftesbury's pre-Homeric poet or Blair's Ossian without fear of reproach. The proof of enlightened maturity, however, is an accurate and cool style of expression: as Alexander Jamieson phrased it, the progress of language is "from vivacity to accuracy; from the fire of poetic enthusiasm, to the coolness of philosophical precision" (31). If an adult allows his imagination and passions to influence his expression unduly, he betrays arrested development. Eighteenth-century parlance occasionally denominates rhetorically immature adults "mad": thus the Port-Royalists' *Art of Speaking* explains that a violent passion "renders [them] *mad* in some measure that are possessed with it. In that case we entertain ourselves with Rocks, and with dead Men, as if they were living, and make them speak as if they had souls" (90). But while persons with flammable fancies might at times be designated "mad," the British increasingly relegated them to the social category of the "vulgar."

"The vulgar" has two distinct but not mutually exclusive meanings. First and most generally, the vulgar are all but the enlightened few. The vulgar are those who fail or refuse to acknowledge the secular achievements of the new physical and human sciences. From the standpoint of the Scottish Enlightenment, the vulgar in this broad sense includes not only superstitious peasants but the Evangelical or "Highflying" party of the Church of Scotland, Anglican polemicists such as Warburton and Hurd, and whoever else opposed or neglected advances in secular knowledge. As A. C. MacIntyre points out, Hume, for one, commonly uses the expression "the vulgar" interchangeably with "the generality of mankind" (258–59); similarly, Goldsmith defines "the vulgar" as "the bulk of mankind" (1:482).

The unenlightened vulgar are allegedly led into conceptual errors by the palpably rhetorical or poetic style of discourse that they favor; thus Lord Monboddo proudly distinguishes his own Aristotelian or scientific prose from the type of writing some benighted readers might expect. As he announces in the introduction to *Of the Origin and Progress of Language* (vol. 1, 1774), his style "will not . . . have that mixture of the rhetorical and poetical . . . which pleases the vulgar so much: for, as I do not write for the vulgar, I will not adapt my style, any more than my matter, to their taste." Monboddo's antirhetorical stance may claim the immediate lineage of Locke's *Essay* and Hume's introduction to the *Treatise*; the odd petulance of his tone, however, alerts us that the problem of vulgar taste has taken on new significance during the course of the century.

As Monboddo proceeds, he makes clear that the rhetorical and poetical do not simply "please" the vulgar but inevitably color their understanding of reality. Invoking the Platonism that informs most attacks against figures, he distinguishes the abstract "forms" from the sensual "matter" of language. The "form" is a pure idea, whereas the "matter" is the sound, sign, or figurative vehicle of its conveyance. Monboddo complains that "the vulgar among us . . . make this abstraction of the matter from the form very clumsily, and, if I may be allowed to use the expression, leave always something of the matter sticking to the form." In an attempt to peel the matter from the form, Monboddo later argues that the vulgar, naturalistic metaphor of aesthetic "taste" should be replaced by reference to a "science" of style and composition. Even a metaphor as tame and presumably understood as "taste" encourages subjectivism and error (1:4, 162, 3:6–9).

Yet matter also clings to form in the phrase "the vulgar," which shades from signifying one's intellectual opponents to simply meaning the lower ranks of society. Adam Smith evidences this etymologically prior sense of the term in his lectures on rhetoric:

"There is nowhere more use made of figures than in the lowest and most vulgar conversation. The Billingsgate language is full of it" (34). And, as Goldsmith again chimes in, "It has been remarked, that the lower parts of mankind generally express themselves most figuratively, and that the tropes are found in the most ordinary forms of conversation" (1:477). Smith, alternatively, recommends the beauty and efficiency—presupposing the prestige— of a plain, unadorned style. Such a recommendation is at all necessary because, as George Campbell attests, tropical "vulgarisms" ever threaten to encroach upon proper language use. He writes, "We always associate with [the use of vulgarisms] such notions of meanness, as suit those orders of men among whom chiefly the use is found. Hence it is that many, who have contracted a habit of employing such idioms, do not approve them; and though, through negligence, they frequently fall into them in conversation, they carefully avoid them in writing, or even in a solemn speech on any important occasion" (142–43).[4]

Because vulgarisms are contagious and liable to contaminate the speech, if not the writing, of those who should know better, it is necessary to establish criteria for reputable language use. Campbell immediately concludes that such use can be established only by persons of liberal education, with reference to the standards set by "authors of reputation." Campbell extricates himself from the apparent circularity of this argument by specifying that a reputable prose style may be derived "neither from living authors, nor those who wrote before the Revolution; not from the first, because an author's fame is not so firmly established in his lifetime; nor from the last, that there may be no suspicion that the style is superannuated" (144, 150–51). Campbell's sweeping exclusions leave, in effect, the generation of Swift and Addison to serve as the model of linguistic propriety. And of all writers who had both written and died between the Glorious

---

4. The social and political ramifications of Campbell's position on language are addressed by John Barrell, 132–37. Carey McIntosh provides a commendable description of the actual style (insofar as we can determine it) of lower-class speakers in the eighteenth century (12–68). For a sense of the extent and peculiar depth of eighteenth-century "vulgarisms," see also Captain Francis Grose's compendious *Classical Dictionary of the Vulgar Tongue* (1785).

and American Revolutions, Swift was the stylist most celebrated by the new rhetoricians. Smith, who devotes four lectures to the excellence of Swift's style, remarks that he "is the plainest as well as the most proper and precise of all the English writers" (42). Earlier, Hume wrote of Swift, "The first polite prose we have, was writ by a man who is still alive" ("Of Liberty and Despotism" [1741], *Essays* 91). Hume considers his verdict self-evident, but those of us who would like to see some elaboration may turn to Johnson: "[Swift's] delight was in simplicity. That he has in his works no metaphor, as has been said, is not true; but his few metaphors seem to be received rather by necessity than choice" (*Lives* 3:51). If, as Johnson asserted, Swift's language "rather trickles than flows," then a trickling style is what the age demanded; Johnson's own essay style, which in a more sympathetic era might have been praised for its *copia*, was to Hume's mind only "diverting from [its] peculiarity and enormity" (*Letters* 2:240).

In effect, then, what complicates the age's ideal of classical eloquence is an ambivalence toward its actual *style*. Longinus melds politics and aesthetics: sublime eloquence accords at once with civic liberty and with the impact of figures such as apostrophe and prosopopeia. But in mid–eighteenth-century Britain, a chief problem for any attempted revival of classical eloquence was the putative irrelevance of figures to the polite or enlightened mind. Philosophical circles considered them too vehement for rational speech, analyzing them instead as the effect of passionate error in a savage past. The polite world held figures to be either too high or too low for decorous speech, disparaging them as affected or "vulgar." Though the response to figures may be thus divided into its social and its philosophical aspects, the polite and the enlightened were not distinct audiences in midcentury Britain: the philosophers were eager to gain a polite readership, and the polite were not unresponsive. Because of the merging of polite and more strictly philosophic criteria, the categories of vulgarity and error overlapped in the assessment of figures. If used vulgarly, figures are erroneous; if affected by orators, poets, or priests, figures are deceitful, and deleterious to the extent that they are imposed as truth upon an audience.

In short, as authors invoked the power of eloquence in defense of the republican values of liberty and virtue, they simultaneously understood that the republican style of eloquence was at best problematic. Politically, eloquence aligned with virtue, but philosophically it derived from error; and socially, it was beyond the pale. The ambiguous status of eloquence is perhaps nowhere more apparent than in Hume's acutely perplexed essay "Of Eloquence."

## Polite Style and the Question of Audience

As Hume revised "Of Eloquence" between 1753 and 1770, he increasingly treated the figures of classical eloquence as an embarrassment. And increasingly, the criterion by which he criticizes figuration turns out to be social etiquette rather than philosophical rigor. Figures are not simply deceptive but also impolite. In a passage that Hume added to "Of Eloquence" in the 1753–54 edition of the *Essays*, he disparages Ciceronian copiousness not for being misrepresentative but for being too showy:

> Some objections, I own, notwithstanding his vast success, may lie against some passages of the Roman orator. He is too florid and rhetorical: His figures are too striking and palpable: The divisions of his discourse are drawn chiefly from the rules of the schools: And his wit disdains not always the artifice even of a pun, rhyme, or jingle of words. The Grecian [Demosthenes] addressed himself to an audience much less refined than the Roman senate or judges. The lowest vulgar of Athens were his sovereigns, and the arbiters of his eloquence. [*Hume's note*: The orators formed the taste of the Athenian people, not the people of the orators . . . ] Yet is his manner more chaste and austere than that of the other. (105)

Hume, in effect, chastises Cicero's style for its exhibitionism. Unlike Locke's more philosophical complaint that the adornments of eloquence mask underlying questions of truth and error, Hume's concern is apparently with surfaces. Cicero's figures may or may not be "instruments of error and deceit"—Hume faults them simply for being gross. They are "too striking and palpable" for an audience accustomed to elegant prose. Indeed, Johnson's

*Dictionary* defines "elegance" as a quality that is "rather sooth-ing than striking." An "elegant"—or, synonymously, "polite"—work of art is "pleasing with minuter beauties"; it is "nice, not coarse, not gross." According to this standard, Cicero appears vulgar in his orations before the elegant Roman senate and judici-ary, whereas Demosthenes' stylistic achievement consists of hav-ing elevated a vulgar, democratic taste with his "chaste and aus-tere" manner.

Moreover, in the wake of Demosthenes' chastity, there is some-thing unmistakably obscene about Cicero's "striking and palpa-ble" use of figures. Hume heightens this suggestion in a sentence that he added to the 1768 edition of the essay: following his quotation and praise of the "bold and poetical figure" of pros-opopoeia in Cicero's *Against Verres*, he remarks, "Should this sentiment even appear to us excessive, as perhaps it justly may, it will at least serve to give an idea of the style of ancient eloquence, where such swelling expressions were not rejected as wholly monstrous and gigantic" (101). Hume's earlier enthusiasm for the assembly's sympathetic fire is here superseded by a tone of wry detachment. He draws back from his empathetic identification with the classical orator's "blaze of eloquence" and situates him-self instead among his own polite audience: Cicero's sentiment may justly "appear *to us* excessive."

## In the Company of Modest Women

Of whom does this supposed audience consist? In "Of Essay Writing" (1742), Hume envisions his audience as "the elegant Part of Mankind, who are not immers'd in the animal Life, but employ themselves in the Operations of the mind" (533). Like Addison, whose ambition in *The Spectator* was to bring philoso-phy "out of closets and libraries . . . to dwell in clubs and assem-blies, at tea-tables and in coffee houses" (no. 10), Hume consid-ered his role in the *Essays* "as a kind of ambassador from the dominions of learning to those of conversation," whose "constant duty [is] to promote a good correspondence betwixt these two states, which have so great a dependence on each other." In his capacity as ambassador, Hume addresses himself "with a particular respect, to the fair sex, who are the sovereigns of the empire of conversation" (535). Within this *doux commerce*, the figures of classical eloquence are entirely too priapic—too "swelling . . . monstrous and gigantic"—to be admitted. Hume qualifies his intent in having addressed the quotation from Cicero in the first place: his is merely the antiquarian's concern "to give an idea of the style of ancient eloquence."

We might say of that style what Camille Paglia has said of Greek male nudes and Blake's composite art—it too is "a psychic gigantism, a compulsive externalization." We may also add her observation that "gigantism is distinctively masculine, as in Michelangelo and Goethe" (294). If, as I suggest in Chapter 1, classical republicanism entails the recognition that all political systems are inhabited by the body, then we must also acknowledge that it is distinctly a male body. Quintilian, for one, considered the ancient assembly as analogous to the Greek gymnasium, as places where—literally or figuratively—men exercise naked: swelling expressions evoke "swelling thews," whereas a more austere eloquence corresponds to "wiry sinews" (10.1.33). The culture of eloquence, with its insistent force and rapture, its assertiveness and indeed its invasiveness, is a male culture, homosocial if not homosexual in nature. Joan Landes indeed argues that, in general, "the early modern classical revival"—which, for her, culminates in the "modern republican" discourse of the French Revolution—"invested public action with a decidedly masculinst ethos," an ethos that tended to silence the public voice aristocratic women had attained during the ancien régime (2–3). To support the notion that the call to ancient principles is always a "masculinist" appeal, I would adduce Bolingbroke's passing remark in his *Patriot King* that "women, by nature and education, [are little fitted] to be harkened to, in the great affairs of government" (85)—except, of course, for Queen Elizabeth, who is, despite biology, staunchly masculine to Bolingbroke and his Opposition cohorts.

The masculinism and attendant misogyny of ancient virtue troubled Hume. Hume's gambit as a man of letters was that women were fit to listen and even (at times) to be listened to; in this, he imitates the "fair-sexing" vein of Mr. Spectator. "I have always had an easy and familiar admittance to the fair sex," boasts Steele—who adds, "I shall take it for the greatest glory of my work, if among reasonable women this paper may furnish tea-table talk" (*The Spectator* no. 4). In no. 10, Addison concurs that "there are none to whom this paper will be more useful, than to the female world." Hume, in turn, offers as his signal social achievement in "My Own Life": "As I took a particular pleasure in the company of modest women, I had no reason to be displeased with the reception I met with from them" (xl–xli).

As the century wore on, the polite codes that increasingly governed conversation between the sexes—especially, as I argue below, among the rising classes—comprehended a growing list of what could not be said (and perhaps not thought) about sexuality or the body in general. J. H. Plumb remarks on the sharp contrast between "the rustic obscenities of Walpole and Queen Caroline" in the 1720s and Malmesbury's shock in 1795 at the scurrilous Caroline of Brunswick (168–69). In the midst of this transition, what mainly ruffles Hume's admiration for ancient Greece is his recognition of the unsuitedness of much ancient literature, in its obscenity and arrogance, for "mixed company." Polite speech may be defined as a thoroughly conventional code of self-censorship about one's physical or passional desires or aversions, whether in speech or in writing, in jest or in discussion. Casual misogyny became one such aversion that dare not speak its name. Hume's "Of Moral Prejudices," a proto-Burkean defense of natural or inveterate sentiments against rationalist innovators, recounts the following anecdote: "My learned reader will here easily recollect the reason, which an ancient philosopher gave, why he would not be reconciled to his brother, who solicited his friendship. He was too much a philosopher to think, that the connection of having sprung from the same parent, ought to have any influence on a reasonable mind, and expressed his sentiment after such a manner as I think not proper to repeat" (539–40). The anecdote comes, I believe, from Plutarch by way of Montaigne's "Of Friendship"; and the Greek philosopher's unmentionable sentiment runs, "I do not value him any more highly for having come out of the same hole" (Montaigne 93).

Montaigne endorses the sentiment, arguing that true friendship has nothing to do with familial or biological ties, and adding that it is in any event a bond of which women (whether mothers or not) are incapable. He is thus entirely too Greek—and hence too impolite—for Hume's more Addisonian tastes, according to which one is to speak no more of "holes" than of the adult Greek's penchant for receptive boys, which Hume simply refers to as "something else [in the Athenian man of merit] too abominable to be named" (*An Enquiry concerning the Principles of Morals* 110). What accounts for this Athenian grossness of deed and word? In "Of the Rise and Progress of the Arts and Sciences," Hume comments upon a certain "want of politeness" in republics both ancient and modern, noting in particular that "the scurrility of the ancient orators, in many instances, is quite shocking, and exceeds all belief. Vanity too is often not a little offensive in authors of those ages" (*Essays* 127). Hume attributes the vanity and obscenity of ancient authors—their "coarse railleries and cold jests"—precisely to the fact that "among the ancients, the character of the fair-sex was considered as altogether domestic; nor were they regarded as part of the polite world or of good company" (134). Women, it seems, are instrumental in polishing men's otherwise coarse manners; in transforming them, so to speak, from orators to conversationalists.

Thus Hume roundly asserts, "If the superiority in politeness should be allowed to modern times, the modern notions of *gallantry*, the natural produce of courts and monarchies, will probably be assigned as the causes of this refinement" (131). Hume defines gallantry as "a studied deference and complaisance for all [a woman's] inclinations and opinions," an attention demanded precisely to "alleviate [man's natural] superiority" (133). Gallantry's objective, as Hume describes it, is precisely (if superficially) social equality—a "society," in Arendtian terms, that seeks precisely to exclude the type of outstanding individual achievement encouraged by the polis (*The Human Condition* 40–41). The polite world—the world of manners—is a scene of self-effacement, of cheerfully bland conformity.

Hume recognizes that the polite concept of gallantry, antithetical to the spirit of the ancients, derives from the economy of courts—which are, of course, a medieval institution. That the presence of women at court serves to polish the manners of men indeed belongs to the notion that the nineteenth century would label "courtly love." And though Hume in a schoolboy essay may have derided the "extravagances" of the chivalric code (Mossner, Life 46–48), his mature conception of women and politeness comes right out of the tradition of Andreas Capellanus. "Love," declares Hume, "when properly managed, is the source of all politeness and refinement" (Essays 215); according to Andreas, "Love causes a rough and uncouth man to be distinguished for his handsomeness; it can endow a man of even the humblest birth with nobility of character; it blesses the proud with humility; and the man in love becomes accustomed to performing many services gracefully for everyone" (31). We may fairly neglect the gap between this sentence and Hume's jubilant query toward the end of "The Rise and Progress of the Arts and Sciences": "What better school for manners, than the company of virtuous women; where the mutual endeavour to please must insensibly polish the mind, where the example of the female softness and modesty must communicate itself to their admirers, and where the delicacy of that sex puts every one on his guard, lest he give offense by any breach of decency?" (Essays 134).

Several of Hume's contemporaries address more openly the debt owed by modern manners to the chivalric code. William Robertson, in the prefatory essay to his History of Charles V (1769), adduces three historical causes for the rise of modern manners from the twelfth century onward: chivalry, the revival of learning, and, above all, the renascence of commerce (12:79–94). But even though commerce may be the most emphatic cause of European manners, it is chivalry that gives them their distinctive coloring. Thus Robertson describes "the political and permanent effects of the spirit of chivalry": "Perhaps the humanity which accompanies all the operations of war, the refinements of gallantry, and the point of honor, the three chief circumstances which distinguish modern from ancient manners, may be ascribed in a great measure to this institution" (19:81–82).

Twenty years later, when the specter of populist revolution (and of eloquence) threatened European politeness, Burke would declaim with greater urgency upon "the ancient chivalry": "It was this, which, without confounding ranks had produced a noble equality, and handed it down through all the gradations of social life." Significantly, Burke saw the death of chivalry portended in the insults offered Marie Antoinette, for the heart of chivalry is ever a "generous loyalty to rank and sex" (*Reflections* 170). Yet he concludes, defiantly, that the British majority—those "thousands of great cattle . . . [who] chew the cud and are silent"—"have not (as I conceive) lost the generosity and dignity of thinking of the fourteenth century" (181). And lest we conceive that Burke spoke in desperation or too soon, witness no less a radical than Shelley pronounce upon the fourteenth century, "If the error which [in antiquity] confounded diversity with inequality of the power of the two sexes has been partially recognized in the opinions and institutions of modern Europe, we owe this great benefit to the worship of which chivalry was the law, and poets the prophets" (*Defence of Poetry* 289).

The worship of love—or, in the eighteenth century's less rapturous terms, a due regard for the refining social presence of women—informs a wide range of enlightened reflections on sociability. Addison, not surprisingly, announces that "women were formed to temper mankind, and soothe them into tenderness and compassion" (*The Spectator* no. 57). Somewhat less expectably, perhaps, Swift advances the same opinion, noting "the highest period of politeness in England (and it is of the same date in France) to have been the peaceable part of King Charles the First's Reign," for only then did "women . . . share in our society":

> Several ladies, whom we find celebrated by the poets of that age, had assemblies at their houses, where persons of the best understanding, and of both sexes, met to pass the evenings in discoursing upon whatever agreeable subjects were occasionally started; and, although we are apt to ridicule the sublime platonic notions they had, or personated, in love and friendship, I conceive their refinements were grounded upon reason, and that a little grain of romance is no ill ingredient to preserve and exalt the dignity of human nature, without which it is apt to degenerate into every thing that is sordid, vicious and low. If there were no other use in the conversation of

ladies, it is sufficient that it would lay a restraint upon those topics
of immodesties and indecencies, into which the rudeness of our
northern genius is so apt to fall. ("Essay on Conversation," *Prose
Works* 4:94–95)

Indeed, in the *querelle* between conversation and eloquence—
that is, between postchivalric politeness and ancient virtue—
Swift, much less ambivalently than Burke, sides with the moderns. Indeed, besides recommending modest conversation in
mixed assemblies, Swift repeatedly ironizes the lofty pretensions
of oratory: thus in the first chapter of "A Voyage to Lilliput,"
Gulliver's first sight is of the Lilliputian Hurgo (or great lord)
who, mounted on a stage "erected about a foot and a half from the
ground," "acted every part of an orator, and I could observe many
periods of threatenings, and others of promises, pity and kind-
ness." Gulliver responds to this dumb show of vehemence and
action with a simple sign, the inelegant efficiency of which belies
the orator's more elaborate "action": he puts his finger to his
mouth, "to signify that I wanted food" (*Gulliver* 18–19). In a way
that he had not understood the Hurgo, the Hurgo immediately
understands him. Gulliver's sign quietly undermines the sphere
of broad-gesturing political action—the scene of Demosthenes, or
of ancient generals, men who spoke to tens of thousands (and, as
Ben Franklin with some surprise inferred from hearing Whitefield
preach in Philadelphia, could actually be heard). It affirms instead
the social world, the world of small-scale (though in Swift ironically large) signs and simple (if not always simply gustatory)
needs: the world, in other words, of the emergent novel.

Of course, Swift's own conversational ideal more closely ap-
proximates the ancien régime salon than the bourgeois novel.
Swift complains that England has not had a proper or extensive
salon culture since Charles I's reign; but in France (to paraphrase
Sterne) they ordered the matter better. Not only did salons flourish in France but, as Peter France notes, the "one constant feature
of politeness discourse in France . . . is the place it gives to wom-
en": according to the Abbé Trublet and others, *le commerce des
femmes* improves men because women, naturally polite, provide
exemplary models; because the desire to please women forces

men to act and talk in more polished ways; and because women, as indoor creatures, "woo [men] away from the brutality that goes with their outdoor—and often military—pursuits" (56). Hume had of course been to France, first as a young man at work on the *Treatise* in the mid-1730s and finally as the celebrated *bon David*, feted in the salons of the 1760s. As he wrote to the Comtesse de Boufflers shortly after his return from France in 1766, "The method of living is not near so agreeable in London as in Paris. The best company are usually, and more so at present, in a flame of politics: the men of letters are few, and not very sociable: the women are not in general very conversible. Many a sigh escapes me for your sweet and amiable conversation" (*Letters* 2:10–11).

Clearly, Hume considers the flame of politics as fundamentally opposed to the feminized social sphere. Women, Hume implies, do not allow the potential ferocity of politics to disrupt their equable tenor of conversation: and in his letter he at least impersonates someone who does not, either. Society seems the reserve of "sweetness" and "amiability," of a mild deportment, of quiet and refined passions. The conversible woman that Hume dreamily sketches seems to be in no way ruffled by any rude passions, nor are her appetites (if she is granted to have any) at all visible.[5] She mollifies the discovery that reason is and ought only be the slave of the passions by evidencing just how gentle a master passion can be. Indeed, insofar as Hume abides by the conventional couplings of maculinity with reason and femininity with passion (see, e.g., *Essays* 593), it follows that both his antirationalism and his passional optimism would entail an idealized regard for women. Alive to the wisdom of the heart, and improved, Hume hoped, by belles lettres and the study of history, "the fair sex," as Kant would say, "can leave Descartes's vortices to whirl forever with-

5. Hume's image of the sexually passionless woman neatly accords with Thomas Laqueur's contention that mid-eighteenth-century medical literature, decisively breaking with Galenic tradition, "ceased to regard the female orgasm as relevant to generation." Consequently, modern science represents "the precise inversion of pre-Enlightenment notions that, extending back to antiquity, equated friendship with men and fleshliness with women. Women, whose desires knew no bounds in the old scheme of things . . . became in some accounts creatures whose whole reproductive life might be spent anaesthetized to the pleasures of the flesh" (4–5).

out troubling itself about them" (quoted in Schiebinger, 271). But Hume, much more than Kant, would be glad to see any such rationalist impertinence forevermore disregarded. As Schiebinger notes, "Both Hume and Diderot . . . considered women of the salons their best allies against the impotent philosophy of the scholastics" (152). The company of women, it was hoped, would tether learning to what the heart approves, as well as render learned style conversational and accessible.

In his famous conclusion to book 1 of the *Treatise*, Hume offers his own life as an instance of how social commerce—presumably with the modest women he boasted of having known—can redeem the uncouth rationalist. This first book is the piece of Hume's writing made notorious in his own lifetime by Beattie's attack upon it: it is the book in which Hume demonstrates that by the exercise of reason alone the closeted philosopher can be assured neither of causality nor of the inductive principle upon which it is based; neither can he uphold the principle of personal identity or the stability of others. Hume concludes these meditations by dramatizing, with a good dash of theatrical zest, the aporia to which they have led him: "I am first affrighted and confounded with that forelorn solitude, in which I am plac'd in my philosophy, and fancy myself some strange uncouth monster, who not being able to mingle and unite in society, has been expell'd all human commerce, and left utterly abandon'd and disconsolate" (264).

After canvassing the dolors of reason for several pages, Hume rises to this operatic pitch: "Where am I, or what? From what causes do I derive my existence, and to what condition shall I return? Whose favour shall I court, and whose anger must I dread? What beings surround me? and on whom have I any influence, or who have any influence on me?" This vertiginous moment of existential doubt is, however, ultimately just a setup, a prelude to the comedic reconstitution of the social sphere. Hume continues, in a much quieter tone, "Most fortunately it happens, that since reason is incapable of dispelling these clouds, nature herself suffices to that purpose, and cures me of this philosophical melancholy and delirium. . . . I dine, I play a game of back-gammon, I converse, and am merry with my friends; and when after three or four hour's amusement, I wou'd return to these speculations, they appear so cold, and strain'd, and ridiculous, that I cannot find it in my heart to enter into them any farther" (269).

The scenario here orchestrated by Hume finds its sequel in Samuel Johnson's *Rasselas*. The episode of the mad astronomer (chaps. 40–47) serves as a veritable exemplum of how the company of conversible women may cure the ills of chronic rationalism. At the outset, the solitary astronomer explains to Imlac that for five years he has regulated the weather and distributed the seasons; he recognizes that although he may have assumed his office through a logical error—the *post hoc ergo propter hoc* fallacy of commanding the rain to fall, and relating its subsequent fall back to one's will—he continues in it, in Humean fashion, because he "feels" he possesses such causative power (146–47). (Hume had written "that all our reasonings concerning causes and effects are deriv'd from nothing but custom; and that belief is more properly an act of the sensitive, than of the cogitative parts of our natures" [*Treatise* 183].) The astronomer persists in his conviction, however, only as long as he remains sequestered from society. Consequently, he is brought around to commonsense views about the weather—and his place in the cosmos, generally—by talking with other people: because people routinely talk, of course, about the weather. (This is just one such moment in Johnson—and in eighteenth-century literature generally—when the banal becomes salvational, and the commonplace happily conquers all.)

The astronomer is saved, moreover, not simply by conversation but specifically by the *commerce des femmes*: it is the princess and Pekuah who, with their "European liberty" and beautiful understandings, succeed in reintegrating the astronomer into society—bringing him, so to speak, out of the closet and into the salon. Upon their first meeting, the "ease and elegance" of Pekuah's conversation "took possession of his heart"; the women thereafter receive him at Imlac's house, where "he began gradually to delight in sublunary pleasures . . . [and] laboured to recommend himself by assiduity and compliance." In the presence of Nekayah and Pekuah he becomes not only social but positively polite: smooth, deferent, eager to please. He ends by admitting to the folly of his former ways: "I have purchased knowledge at the

expense of all the common comforts of life: I have missed the
endearing elegance of female friendship, and the happy commerce
of domestic tenderness" (158–61). Biographically, Johnson must
have earned these lines—one recalls his own loneliness, his own
fear of madness; and then (how prescient the astronomer's fate
seems!) one pictures him buoyed from the deeps by Mrs. Thrale's
companionship at Streatham Park. More broadly, however, the
episode of the astronomer's voyage from solitude to society may
indeed be read as an allegory of Western philosophy from Descartes to Hume.

Predictably, not everyone approved of the means by which men
of letters descended from their metaphysical clouds—or awoke
from their Demosthenic daydreams—to court a female audience.
Critics of Hume have perenially looked askance at his increasing
concern with polite style after the *Treatise*, by his own account,
"fell dead-born from the press . . . more from the manner than
the matter" (*Essays* xxxiv–xxxv). Early detractors such as Bishop
Hurd attributed Hume's "fair-sexing" to arrant careerism:
"[Hume] thought fit to come out of the clouds, and to attempt a
popular vein of writing, as the more likely to get himself read and
talked of in the world" ("Life of Warburton" [1794], reprinted in
*Divine Legation*, 1:41). Whereas Warburton and Hurd represent
the indignation of orthodox Anglicanism, John Brown develops
their critique of polite free-thinking into a full-blown jeremiad
against the times (see Chapter 5): along the way, he contemptu-
ously remarks that Hume gained an audience through writing
"under the inviting shape of Essays . . . [which] come under the
compass of a Breakfast-reading" (33–34).[6]

Hume's polite wager is not, as his opponents suggest, mere
cynicism, but it does indeed prove a timely career move. And
Hume, while never pandering to his audience, does possess a pragmatic faith in success. There is more than mere modesty in

6. The eighteenth-century charge against Hume is echoed by T. H. Huxley (11)
and J. H. Randall (1:629–35). More recently, critics such as James Noxon have
defended the philosophical integrity of Hume's later work, while John Sitter (40)
and John Richetti (*Philosophical Writing* 254–63) have variously argued that
Hume's increasing concern with *effective* style follows naturally from his epistemology, in which persuasion and belief are equated.

Hume's advertisment to book 1 of the *Treatise*: "The approbation of the public I consider as the greatest reward of my labours; but am determin'd to regard its judgement, whatever it be, as my best instruction" (xii). As Vindling Kruse said of Hume, "He was consistently led to regard the judgement of the public as his supreme court, his only guide in his literary work" (quoted in N. K. Smith, 11). Although it overstates the case, Kruse's sentence does alert us to a peculiarly *oratorical* anxiety in Hume's life of writing: for, to a much greater extent than authors (who may always dream of posterity), orators depend upon the approbation, and fear the blame, of their audiences. An assembly always has the power to validate or invalidate that which is presented to it, even if that means no more than passively registering what degree of force and vivacity will suffice to enforce its conviction. Demosthenes himself declared, "What is called the power of eloquence depends for the most part on the hearers" (432). Thus Hume asserts in "Of Eloquence" that "the lowest vulgar of Athens were [Demosthenes'] sovereigns, and the arbiters of his eloquence," concluding that "whoever, upon comparison, is deemed by a common audience the greatest orator, ought most certainly to be pronounced such, by men of science and erudition" (105–7).

The aesthetics of oratory—which, despite his nods to connoisseurship, Hume never quite relinquishes—entails a fundamental democratization of taste. Hume is quite explicit about this: "The principles of every passion, and of every sentiment, [are] in every man; and when touched properly, they rise to life, and warm the heart, and convey that satisfaction, by which a work of genius is distinguished from the adulterate beauties of a capricious wit and fancy" (107). Anciently, the orator sought to confirm his genius in the satisfaction of everyman; but in Hume's day, the glory of the assembly had been translated into the merely figurative applause of a reading public. Thus Thomas Parnell addresses Bolingbroke, "Sublime in eloquence, where loud applause / Hath styl'd thee patron of a nation's cause" ("Essay on the Different Styles of Poetry" 439–40). Applause proves the sublimity of its cause: one might say of eloquence, by its fruits shall you know it. Indeed, it is Bolingbroke's success no less than his vehemence that prompted Hume to dub him the Demosthenes of the hour.

But Hume himself was attempting both to transform and to expand the audience that had crowned Bolingbroke. Hume would speak to women as well as men; to rising professionals as well as landed proprietors; to the Scottish and French nations as well as the English; to citizens of the world as well as compatriots. He would call into being a new community of polite consensus.[7] Doing so requires a greater finesse than that found in the voice of Demosthenes or Bolingbroke: Hume's style is avowedly less passionate than the classical orator's, because in the polite world less is always more. Just how well a restrained force and liveliness could succeed is evinced in a letter that the Comtesse de Boufflers wrote to Hume: "The clarity, the majesty, the touching simplicty of your style, ravishes me" (Hume, *Letters* 2.367). This is, perhaps, the applause that Hume most wanted, this the success of his crossover dream. He had cultivated an audience in which gender circulates and simplicity is felt—a "general" audience, in some sense, though this is not to say that Hume was ever indiscriminate. Certainly, as indeed he made increasingly clear, he did not want the applause of just anybody.

## Consolidating Polite Society

Any social formation is, of course, defined as much by its exclusions as by whom it includes. By the time that Hume came to revise "Of Eloquence," the governing elite had, it seems, acquired an ear for the voice of "the mob"—and it promptly wished to discredit that voice. Accordingly, politeness is an eighteenth-century ideology in formation, intended to consolidate the members of the gentry and professional orders and to differentiate this group from a "vulgar" class of laborers, servants and "cits" (a "cit," according to Johnson's *Dictionary*, is "a pert low towns-

7. As Leo Damrosch argues, nonfiction writers in the age of Hume and Johnson consciously strove to forge a sense of community among their readership: "Their texts seek both to elicit and to create the consensus to which they appeal" (5). V. M. Hope cogently argues for the centrality of "consensus" in the moral theory of Hutcheson, Hume, and Smith; I would add only that their literary and political judgments, no less than their moral philosophy, appeal to "intersubjective truths" (7–8).

man; a pragmatical trader"). Notably, Hume's most decisive emendation of his essay, in which he remarks that Demosthenic sentiments may "appear *to us* excessive," was made in 1768: in a year that witnessed the rise of Wilkite radicalism and Priestley's early political tracts, the better sort evidently felt the need to protect their distinctive linguistic privileges against popular encroachment.

Hume censures the ancient orator's "excessive" figures in the interest of politeness: figures, as the language of the passions, are clearly incompatible with a social ethos that applauds restraint. And to possess polished manners means, in word and in deed, precisely to restrain one's passions; whereas polite taste is the corresponding ability to appreciate restraint in social and aesthetic expression. Pocock, rather than refer to this polite ethos with the familiar and misleading appellation "bourgeois," speaks of an "ideology of manners" or "Addisonian morality" arising in mid-century Britain—especially in Scotland. In an increasingly commercial, mobile, and variegated society, politeness vies with the traditional aristocratic prerogatives of birth and land for being that which sets the gentleperson apart from the lower orders.[8]

To meet the needs of old land and new money alike, the rhetorics of the mid– to late eighteenth century engage in an implicit "Emily Post–ism." Revived commitment to rhetorical training combines with a novel interest in polite style, and both are explicitly situated within the politics of emergent class society. Adam Smith bluntly informs his students at Glasgow that a restrained manner of expression is the sure sign of distinction between the gentleperson (or the would-be gentleperson) and the mob: "The behaviour which is reckoned polite in England is a calm, composed, unpassionate serenity noways ruffled by passion. . . . The

---

8. For Pocock's suggestive remarks on "the ideology of manners," see especially *Virtue, Commerce, and History* 48–50, and "Cambridge Paradigms and Scotch Philosophers." Norma Landau speculates that it was the professional class and "the retirees from trade and commerce" who "most insisted upon adoption of manners as the hallmark of the civilized citizen" (217). Landau also suggests that manners were largely adopted by the rural elite "rather than the urban bourgeoisie"; while this may or may not be true of eighteenth-century England, it is clearly not true of Scotland, where the major advocates of manners were, like Hume and Smith, urban men of letters.

most polite persons are those only who go to the operas and any emotion would there be reckoned altogether indecent. And we see that when the same persons go out of frolick to a beargarden or such like ungentlemanly entertainment they preserve the same composure as before at the opera, while the rabble about express all the various passions by their gestures and behaviour" (198). As Smith observes in an earlier lecture, the passionate behavior of the rabble includes their knack for figurative expression (34), which is presumably as evident at the beargarden as it is in Billingsgate. Because the figures and action of the ancient orator have been debased among the "gestures and behaviour" of the lower orders, the gentleman will cultivate a new demeanor and standard of speech. This standard is apparently determined by sheerly negative criteria: Smith offers his students no reason for self-restraint other than the casual observation that the rabble have not acquired it.

Of course, the paradox here is that if politeness can be taught, then the rabble *could* conceivably acquire it. This possibility, however real or looming, is neatly curtailed in the novels of the period. As John Richetti argues, the early novelists generally represent "plebeians" (servants, husbandmen, etc.) as irrevocably tied to their social origins. Thus, though Smollett's Peregrine Pickle can temporarily pass off a rural laborer as a polite lady, her "linguistic social identity" soon proves insuppressible: "Her dialect, [Smollett] makes clear, is a gutter eloquence such 'as would have intitled her to a considerable share of reputation, even among the nymphs of Billingsgate'" ("Class Struggle" 204–5). One might add to Richetti's example an equally colorful episode from Charlotte Lennox's The Female Quixote, in which the quixotic Arabella mistakes a young gardener, who had acquired "a great deal of *secondhand* politeness" in London, for "a person of *sublime quality*, who submits to this disguise only to have an opportunity of seeing me every day." Expectably, this romantic gardener is soon caught in the act of stealing carp and sneaks off "with an air very different from [the romance hero] Oroondates" (22–25). Our smile here comes primarily at Arabella's expense, for her belief in romances better left unread—as Hume remarked, modern politeness hardly consorts with the "ridiculous passions" of "an Artamenes, an Oroondates" (*Letters* 1:110). But Lennox's joke also asks us to laugh at gardeners who assume airs, assuring us that their unrestraint will out.

But even if the polite thus indemnified themselves (at least ideologically) from plebeian apings, there remained the problem of direct assault. There remained, quite specifically, the threat of a truly "bourgeois" attack upon the very notion of hierarchy and its political apparatus—the disinterested patriot, virtual representation, analogies with Rome. As Isaac Kramnick points out, the radicalism "that began to emerge during the 1760s . . . had a new dimension, the conviction that the people now excluded— the urban and commercial interests—wanted in, wanted to be represented in Parliament and wanted their MPs to be their spokesmen, serving their interests, not serving as wise men independent of both court and the people who elected them" (*Republicanism* 172). Thus, in the 1760s—a decade in which, as Hume reported to the Comtesse de Boufflers, even the best company was in a flame of politics—Hume's increasing distrust of eloquence derived, in part, from his fear that it was being used by men like Wilkes and Pitt to inflame the inferior sort. In other words, Hume became increasingly concerned that the eloquence that had at last arrived in Georgian England was classical demagoguery, the roiling of hoi polloi. The "eloquence" ideally suited to Commons had unexpectedly stooped to the streets.

Indeed, to authors of Hume's generation who had, like Hume, even half-believed in the Demosthenic trappings of Bolingbroke's Opposition, the 1760s served as quite an eye-opener: the final proof that London was not Athens and that popular English orators (or essayists) were not likely to form the taste of the people in any beneficial way. Hume, for his part, was appalled first by Wilkes's "low, vulgar, and ungenerous" anti-Scottish campaign, then by the "noise" of "the Wilkites and the Bill of Right-men" (*Letters* 1:383, 2:235);[9] next there appears Pitt, "creep[ing] out

9. On Wilkes and the political atmosphere of the 1760s, see the seminal works of George Rudé and John Brewer (esp. 163–200). Hume's animus against "Wilkes and Liberty" is well analyzed by Pocock (*Virtue* 125–41) and by Donald Livingston (269–71); see also David Raynor's "Hume on Wilkes and Liberty" for a possible addition to the Humean canon.

from his retreat": "This villain is to thunder against the violation of the Bill of Rights, in not allowing the county of Middlesex the choice of its member. Think of the impudence of that fellow; and his quackery; and his cunning; and his audaciousness; and judge of the influence he will have over such a deluded multitude" (2:197–98). Popular success no longer seems a happy criterion of merit. Instead, Hume's letters relentlessly decry the politics of oratory, as well as its aesthetic: "What other talent indeed has [Pitt], but that of reciting with tolerable action and great impudence, a long discourse in which there is neither argument, order, instruction, propriety, or even grammar?" (2:242). Hume could well have answered his own question by observing that Pitt's "other talent" was a force and energy unsurpassed among eighteenth-century parliamentary orators. But his enthusiasm for sublimity had ostensibly cooled. Hume now judges Pitt's oratory by the standards of a plain or polite style, according to which he finds it wanting.

Of course, in the classical tradition eloquence lives not by its aesthetic appeal alone but by the strenuous moralism of the Demosthenic stance. For Hume, however, Pitt appears the very antithesis of Demosthenes, an orator who fosters and reflects the narrow self-interest, bigotry, and jingoism of "the despicable London mob" (Letters 2:234). Thus Pitt threatened to expand Britain's national debt with the expense of an "idle war" over the Falkland Islands (2:237)—an act of aggression far removed from the noble self-defense urged by Demosthenes and echoed by the Opposition poets of the 1730s. And thus Pitt threatens the balance of Britain's mixed constitution with an excess of popular liberty, while Demosthenes, as William Young pictures him, is no populist but rather a stalwart defender of the mixed republic originally established by Solon's constitution. Young's Demosthenes speaks against popular encroachment from within as well as tyrannic invasion from without (39–40, 256–57). On the contrary, Hume's Pitt plays the leveler: "Pitt and his myrmidons . . . will, no doubt, chain the king for ever, and render him a mere cypher. Our government has become an absolute chimera: so much liberty is incompatible with human society: and it will be happy, if we can escape from it, without falling into a military government, such as Algiers or Tunis" (2:210).

The fate that Hume fears is the *dominatio plebis* that Swift warned of, the popular insurrection that according to classical wisdom ever eventuates in dictatorship ("Contests and Dissensions between Nobles and Commons," *Works* 1:217). If during Walpole's ministry the Polybian balance of Britain's government had weighed too heavily toward the executive—so much so that Hume felt "the people must be rouzed" to the threat of arbitrary power (*Essays* 12)—by the 1760s this situation had been reversed, the constitution no longer needing protection against ministerial encroachment but against, in Hume's phrase, "this inundation of the rabble" (*Letters* 2:245). Accordingly, in a 1770 addition to his essay "Of Public Credit," Hume warned of "democratical frenzy" in London (355); and, some years later, a final revision in "Of the Liberty of the Press" calls an "unbounded liberty . . . one of the evils, attending those mixt forms of government" (13). This hardly seems an atmosphere in which Hume would advocate a revival of a passionate and in any way popular eloquence.

But not everyone of Hume's ilk responded to the critical early years of George III's reign with such anxiety—indeed, such acrimony. Equally telling is an entry from Boswell's private papers, dated 29 March 1768: upon hearing of Wilkes's victory at the Middlesex elections, Boswell muses, "So fascinating is success that I began to quit the determinations of my own reason, and to imagine him really a patriot and like a Roman whom 'The crowd of fickle voters strives to exalt to the highest honours' [trans. of Horace *Odes* 1.1.7–8]. But a little reflection soon cured me of this. After breakfast I was joined by a jolly London justice who had lands in the neighborhood. He and I were very hearty" (*Boswell in Search of a Wife* 156–57). Boswell here affords us a neat digest of the alternate dread and complacency that blended in the gentleperson's response to bourgeois radicalism: the giddy suspicion that Wilkes somehow symbolized change in the political nation, and the complementary assurance that in a world of jolly hunting justices no real change was, after all, possible.[10]

10. To situate Boswell's quandary in terms of current historiography: though his nervous awe of Wilkes would seem to vindicate "Whiggish" or Marxist historians who read the eighteenth century as an era of unrest, social change, and the intense promise of more change to come, his hearty complacency informs "neo-

Of course, Boswell in any mood would probably admit to if not change then at least the shifting valencies that held among the strata of his society. He would recognize the quiet shift in sensibility that allowed for a growing consensus, in Roy Porter's phrase, "among the affluent and the aspirant" (3)—a consensus represented by an emphasis on polite behavior that not only stigmatized the passions of the crowd but eschewed the excesses of aristocratic culture.

## The Bathetic End of Oratorical Culture

Indeed, the polite world would separate itself not only from the speech of Billingsgate but from an antiquated aristocratic ideal of commanding eloquence—from the Greco-Roman oratorical culture of which Wilkes and Pitt, in their demagogic ways, seemed to be the last gasp. One might, perhaps, adduce Richardson's *Pamela* as an example of how the spoiled aristocrat, given to ruse and to command, is brought into the fold of polite conversation by a patient bourgeois: as Mr. Martin remarks to Mr. B. toward the novel's end, "Gad, sir, you are a happy man; and I think your lady's example has made you more polite, and handsome too, than I ever knew you before" (401). But the most salient (and in some ways unaccountable) transformation of the period occurs not to Mr. B. but to the reputation of the third earl of Shaftesbury. And whereas Mr. B. is redeemed from his aristocratic insensibility, Shaftesbury, on the contrary, is made to seem *more* arrogant than he had either appeared to his contemporaries or appears to us today. Smollett's *Peregrine Pickle* (1751) dubs him "that frothy writer" (232) and proceeds, through a satiric portrait of a republican doctor (shades of Akenside!) who appears as his disciple, to associate his Grecian "zeal for community" with a hypocritically selfish disregard for "particular friendship" (256). But

---

Tory" historians, like J. C. D. Clark, who are prompt to assure us of the social stability of the period.

the more comprehensive case against Shaftesbury comes a decade later in the works of Scottish rhetoricians curiously eager to disparage his putatively "pompous" style.[11]

Although Hume never explicitly condemns Shaftesbury's style, he fails to mention it when he attributes "the first polite prose" to Swift. Smith works Hume's implications into an argument. He insistently criticizes Shaftesbury's prose style—in all its varied moods, from analytic to rhapsodic—for its pretentious aloofness from common usage: "It is plain this author had it greatly in view to go out of the common road in his writing, and to dignify his style by never using common phrases or even names for things, and we hardly see any expression in his works but what would appear absurd in common conversation" (8). Smith leaves no doubt that Shaftesbury, whom he consistently refers to as "this nobleman," represents the sins of his elevated rank: the man, like the style, is "puny," deficient in real passion, and removed from the common transactions of life (56–60). His studious avoidance of common language frequently leads him, however, "into a dungeon of metaphorical obscurity" (8) that is ironically equivalent to the figurative exuberance of Billingsgate. Thus vulgar speech and aristocratic writing fly equally wide of a temperate, polite language, which is common without being (to quote Johnson's diacritical phrase from the *Dictionary*) "low or bad."[12]

11. For recent cultural and stylistic analyses of Shaftesbury's *Characteristics*, see the essays of Lawrence Klein and Robert Markley. Curiously, neither critic acknowledges the ironic midcentury fate of Shaftesbury's attempt to pioneer a polite style. We remain in need of a detailed historical and political explanation of how and why Shaftesbury's "well-bred" prose is perceived by the Scottish new rhetoricians as a model of stylistic *hauteur*. The irony of this attack on Shaftesbury—and perhaps its deep or Oedipal reason—is that Scottish philosophy, from Hutcheson to Hume and Smith, owes a fundamental debt to Shaftesbury's main tenets—his critique of religious enthusiasm; his rejection of Hobbes's thorough, as well as Locke's more circumspect, egoism; his alternative view that we instinctively desire the public good. Further, Shaftesbury anticipated the new rhetoricians in his appreciation of the "familiar" language of Athens. His unpublished papers include notes toward an essay in praise of the superior "politeness" of Attic Greek to modern English; he attributes that superiority to the freedom and equality of the *places publiques* that are absent from London (Klein 211).

12. The politics of Johnson's *Dictionary* is currently a much debated topic. Elizabeth Hedrick, fundamentally in agreement with John Barrell (chap. 2), argues for Johnson's conservatism in "establishing genteel, metropolitan speech as the

Blair's *Lectures* conveniently summarize the later eighteenth century's case against Shaftesbury:

> His lordship can express nothing with simplicity. He seems to have considered it as vulgar, and beneath the dignity of a man of quality, to speak like other men. Hence he is ever in buskins; full of circumlocutions and artificial elegance. In every sentence, we see the marks of labour and art; nothing of that ease, which expresses a sentiment coming natural and warm from the heart. Of figures and ornament of every kind, he is exceedingly fond; sometimes happy in them; but his fondness for them is too visible; and having once laid hold of some metaphor or allusion that pleased him, he knows not how to part with it. (1:396–97)

The charges consistently leveled against Shaftesbury—inkhorn terms, excessive contrivance—may remind us of Hume's criticism of Cicero: "He is too florid and rhetorical: His figures are too striking and palpable: The divisions of his discourse are drawn chiefly from the rules of the schools." Smith's lectures serve to reinforce this parallel. According to him, Cicero's "pompous and ornate" style derives from his status as a "Nobleman of Rome": "As he spoke generally to his inferiors he would talk in a manner becoming to one in that station. Respect and deference would be what he thought his due as one of superior dignity and his behaviour would aim at approving himself to be such." Cicero (like Shaftesbury) thus "abounds with all those figures of speech which are thought to give dignity to language." Demosthenes, on the contrary, "has no such affectation." Living in democratic Athens, he talks "with the ease of an equal" (158–59). To further unravel Smith's implied analogies, if Shaftesbury is the age's Cicero, then its Demosthenes is Swift—on account not only of his easy and familiar style but also of his savage indignation. As Smith concludes of Demosthenes, "The florid and splendid [do] not appear in his works[;] a more easy and familiar [style] was more esteemed in his time. The passion which animates him in all his orations is indignation" (194).

---

linguistic standard." Recent critics who view Johnson's *Dictionary* as a more democratizing project include Donald T. Siebert and Robert DeMaria.

Thus, by midcentury even the mild floridity and splendor of a Shaftesbury could not be brooked; indeed, in an ironic meeting of extremes, the high Ciceronian eloquence traditionally associated with the nobility comes to be seen not as a token of superiority but as a sign of vulgarity. This is evidenced not only in Scottish rhetorics but on the London stage. With superb compression, Samuel Foote's *The Commissary* (1765) at once illustrates the disrepute into which high eloquence had fallen and satirizes cits who misguidedly aim at true politeness. The title character of the play is Mr. Zac Fungus, a person of obscure origins who has acquired a considerable fortune through "pretty pickings abroad" (1.1), presumably during the Seven Years' War. The play centers around Zac's misguided efforts to become a gentleman, chiefly through instruction in the arts of fencing, dancing, riding, and, most important, oratory. From a polite point of view, however, Foote's piece represents nothing less than the bathetic finale of oratorical culture.

Zac would naturally seek instruction in oratory from one of the so-called "elocutionists" who abounded at midcentury; their teaching stressed proper utterance and action, the aspects of rhetoric that the Romans included under the heading *pronuntiatio*. The elocutionary movement effectively begins with John "Orator" Henley's *The Art of Speaking in Public; or, An Essay on the Action of an Orator* (1727); its most famous text is ultimately Thomas Sheridan's *Courses of Lectures on Elocution* (1762). The lectures delivered and published by the elocutionists were addressed largely to a rising class of small tradesmen, many of whom were not born in England and all of whom wished to become reputable members of the metropolitan language community. Unlike most of them, however, Zac can afford to hire an elocutionist, one "Mr. Gruel," as his private tutor. The introduction of Gruel on the stage interrupts Zac's conversation with his commonsensical and plain-speaking brother, Mr. Isaac Fungus, chandler.

> *Zac.* Mr. Gruel, your servant; I have been holding forth in your praise.
> *Gruel.* I make no doubt, Mr. Fungus, but to your declamation, or recitation, (as Quintilian more properly terms it) I shall be in

debted for much future praise, in as much as the reputation of the
scholar does (as I may say) confer, or rather as it were reflect, a
marvellous kind of lustre on the fame of the master himself.

*Z.* There, Isaac! didst ever hear the like? he talks just as if it were all
out of a book; what wou'd you give to be able to utter such words?

*Isaac.* And what shou'd I do with them? them holiday terms wou'd
not pass in my shop; there's no buying and selling with them.

*Gruel.* Your observation is pithy and pertinent; different stations
different idioms demand, polished periods accord ill with the
mouths of mechanics; but as that tribe is permitted to circulate a
baser kind of coin, for the ease and convenience of inferior traffic,
so it is indulg'd with a vernacular or vicious vulgar phraseology, to
carry on their interlocutory commerce; but I doubt, Sir, I soar
above the region of your comprehension?

*I.* Why if you wou'd come down a step or two, I can't say but I shou'd
understand you the better.

*Z.* And I too.

*Gruel.* Then to the familiar I fall: if the gentleman has any ambition
to shine at a vestry, a common-hall, or even a convivial club, I can
supply him with ample materials.

*I.* No, I have no such desire.

*Gruel.* Not to lose time; your brother here, (for such I find the gentleman is) in other respects a common man like yourself—

*Z.* No better.

*Gruel.* Observe how alter'd by means of my art: are you prepar'd in
the speech on the great importance of trade?

*Z.* Pretty well, I believe.

*Gruel.* Let your gesticulations be chaste, and your muscular movements consistent.


*Z.* When I consider the vast importance of this day's debate; when I
revolve the various vicissitudes that this soil has sustain'd; when I
ponder what our painted progenitors were; and what we, their
civilized successors, are; when I reflect, that they fed on crab-
apples and chestnuts—

*Gruel.* Pignuts, good Sir, if you please.

*Z.* You are right; crab-apples and pignuts; and that we feast on green-
peas, and on custards: when I trace in the recording historical
page, that their floods gave them nothing but frogs, and now know
we have fish by land-carriage, I am lost in amazement at the prodigious power of commerce. Hail commerce! daughter of industry,

consort to credit, parent of opulence, full sister to liberty, and great grandmother to the art of navigation . . .

*I.* Why this gentlewoman has a pedigree as long as your wife's, brother Zac.[13]

However clumsy Zac may appear on stage, he is at least apprised of the elocutionary movement's standard lessons, "chaste gesticulation" and "consistent movements." He is also taught that the style of classical declamation depends on parallelism, antithesis, and figures of speech; an epideictic oration on trade would not be complete without an apostrophe ("Hail commerce!"), a personified lineage, and whatever other figures he might have employed if Isaac had not interrupted.

While the humor of this scene is broad, its ironies are incisive. First, there is the obvious irony that while Isaac, the plain-speaking tradesmen, usefully engages in commerce ("them holiday terms wou'd not pass in my shop; there's no buying and selling with them"), the "gentleman" merely apostrophizes Commerce, that is, addresses it in an elevated, noncommercial language. The second level of irony, however, is that the ornate declamatory style acquired by Zac is considered affected or puerile or simply vulgar by the polite standards of rhetorical restraint. Gruel is a quack, as his name indicates to all but Zac. If, as Robertson argues, politeness ultimately springs from commerce, then Zac doubly proves his imbecility by praising commerce in a gross imitation of a precommercial language, an otiose aristocratic idiom. Foote vindicates the blunt business sense and class modesty of Isaac in the denouement of his play, which exposes

---

13. On the personal satire of *The Commissary*, see Simon Trefman 146–48. Mr. Gruel was recognized by contemporary audiences as a caricature of the elocutionist Thomas Sheridan; Foote also satirized Sheridan in *The Orators* (1762), an earlier and less coherent play. Goldsmith, motivated by similarly antibourgeois politics, also numbers among Sheridan's detractors. In "The State of Literature" (1762), Goldsmith writes, "As Paracelsus attempted to cure all disorders with opium, so a celebrated Orator of the times proposed to effect all things by eloquence. . . . Cheesemongers were instructed to lay the proper emphasis on *Cheese*; and Taylors, taught by him, begged to take Measure in measured periods" (3:189). Cf. Goldsmith, "Of the Pride and Luxury of the Middling Class of People" 1:486–87; Charles Churchill, *The Rosciad* lines 633–48.

both Zac and those who would fleece him as "plunderers" and "frauds."[14]

The satire of *The Commissary* is leveled against the pretensions of the *novus homo*. Small tradesmen should not assume polite airs; certainly, their attempts at reputable speech are doomed to fail. The whole is fitting matter for a comedy, a genre whose effect Smith blandly explains with reference to our "[natural] inhumanity which disposes us to . . . trample under foot our inferiors" (124). An unprincipled upstart like Zac Fungus supplies an easy target for the social satire of any age; but for the socially mobilizing efforts of the elocutionary movement to be derided with such zest suggests a peculiar uneasiness among the polite. *The Commissary* intends to entertain and to reassure, in William C. Dowling's terms, "a newly ascendent bourgeoisie celebrating its own arrival at the ideological center of its society," but "it also reveals a middle-class acutely aware that it is insulated from a more demotic or openly bourgeois status" only by its "Augustan values" (*The Epistolary Moment* 141)—or, as I would say, by its polite speech.


## Hume's Generous Contradictions

It is tempting, and half-truthful, to portray the advocates of politeness as ruthlessly devising a self-serving history and politics of figurative eloquence, intended to protect themselves from oppositional discourse by discrediting it in advance.[15] They would invalidate the voices of the rabble and the grand seigneur, of Zac Fungus and the earl of Shaftesbury alike. The Enlightenment, as its Romantic detractors have been apt to note, does have its "totalitarian" air; it does attempt, at a certain ideological level, to

14. Just as Foote sides with Isaac against Zac's pretensions, so *The Weekly Magazine, or Edinburgh Amusement* (13 April 1769) asked its readers to sympathize with the plight of "Obadiah Olive," a plain-speaking tradesman whose wife and daughter have taken to reading "book[s] full of hard words." Olive complains: "According to my notion now, neither tradesmen, nor tradesmen's wives, nor any body belonging to them, have any business to talk like *skolards* [sic]. . . . For my part, I am sick of all books, but those belonging to my shop."
15. This is basically the position of Olivia Smith, *The Politics of Language, 1791–1819* chap. 1.

enforce philosophical and political uniformity on the plurifor-
mity of history and society.[16] Yet was the Enlightenment itself
ideologically consolidated? Was it as monolithic as we have sometimes conceived it?

Our contextual reading of Hume's "Of Eloquence" would suggest not. Hume's attitude toward eloquence certainly expresses
contradictions that a single ideology cannot quite manage. His
essay—especially but not only in its original incarnation—is profoundly ambivalent toward both classical eloquence and the republican form of government under which the orator flourished.
It exhibits a certain complacency in the politeness of modern
passion and administrative politics; yet it resonates with a stirring nostalgia, at once aesthetic and political, for the classical
orator's power to elicit moral sympathy and inflame a popular
assembly. Surely one cannot imagine Hume saying in 1742 what
Wilmington said of Carteret: "Had he studied parliament more
and Demosthenes less he would have been a more successful
minister" (quoted in Speck, 241).

Still, we cannot but concur—to some degree—with David
Womersley's judgment that "in the 1730s Hume's idea of human
nature was banal." However much his later historiography might
disabuse him of it, Hume's early "conviction [is] that the constitution of human nature is reasonable" (35): "reasonable" in the
sense of being tractable, predisposed to bathe undisturbedly in the
streams of custom. In reading Hume's early philosophical work
one often feels he is speaking of beings very unlike you and me,
beings of an animal or divine tranquility. Of course, Hume may in
part be engaged in a heuristic fiction: becalming advice offered as
an assumption of how calm we are. To postulate the banality of
human nature serves to reject a traditional Augustinian psychology of the kind we find in Johnson, with its temporal dissatisfac-
tions and unquenchable yearnings. Hume seems to have intuited
that a little throbbing is a dangerous thing; better to be, like
Burke's Britons, "thousands of great cattle, reposed beneath the

---

16. As I note in my review essay, "Hume's Practice," this charge has been
leveled by adherents and sympathizers of the Frankfurt School, from Horkheimer and Adorno's *Dialectic of Enlightenment* (chap. 1) up through Jerome
Christensen's critical biography of Hume.

shadow of the British oak." As Hume remarks with an air of regret, however, "'Tis almost impossible for the mind of man to rest, like those of beasts, in that narrow circle of objects, which are the subject of daily conversation and action" (*Treatise* 271). It is, at least, impossible for Hume's mind. And thus his halcyon image of human nature competes with flashes of admiration for the secular zeal of the political assembly, in which orator and his audience share a virtue rather sublime than prudent.

As Hume writes in his second *Enquiry*, "The ancients . . . have a grandeur and force of sentiment, which astonishes our narrow souls" (65–66): our "narrow souls" that lack precisely the *magnanimity* that Cicero recommends, and that Demosthenes both praises and embodies in his apostrophe to the dead at Marathon (see *De Officiis* 1.61). The sentiment that fills Demosthenes' soul is, as we have seen, his virtuous indignation at not only the self-regard of his fellow citizens but, a fortiori, their apostasy from the exalted selflessness of the past. His indignation, moreover, possesses or defines him: it purifies him of his lesser passions, it—in both senses of the phrase—"becomes him." Indignation to him is all in all. As Philip Fisher notes, "Anger and the vehement passions . . . are the highest evidence of self-identical, undivided being. . . . One meaning of vehemence is the capacity to be thoroughly, completely in a given state" (51). Indeed—so the myth goes—the sublime orator has an unsophisticated integrity of soul; in a phrase of Rousseau's that Lionel Trilling puts to good use, oratory alone of all the arts does not compromise "the unbroken sentiment of being" (68).

The orator, as an unshadowed political being under the hard Attic light, serves as a counterpoint to other images of the self more familiar to Hume and to his age: the Heraclitean fluidity of the closeted, self-reflective philosopher (*Treatise* 1.4.6); the uncertain ironies and uncentered dialogues of the urbane man of letters. These ironies tend to become dizzying: indeed, one may even ask, to what degree is Hume's ostensible ambivalence in "Of Eloquence" "really" just a self-conscious structural dialogism, a dispassionate or academic rehearsal of the pros and cons?[17] Certainly, Hume's self-divisions—be they purely cerebral or largely

17. On ironic endings and dialogic intent in Hume's essays (and in Johnson's *Rasselas*), see my essay "The Spirit of Ending in Johnson and Hume."

from the heart—are the effects of deliberation without pressure, meditation without vehemence. And it is precisely the reasonable person's desire to respond more fully to contingency and to nature that informs Hume's final praise of Demosthenes (added in 1753): Demosthenes' style "is *vehement reasoning*, without any appearance of art: It is disdain, anger, boldness, freedom, involved in a continued stream of argument: And of all human productions, the orations of Demosthenes present to us the models, which approach the nearest to perfection" (105–6, emphasis mine). Demosthenes is to Hume, as Donne is to T. S. Eliot, a paragon of undissociated sensibility, a being thoroughly vehement yet incessantly reasonable. Hume, not given to hyperbole, simply calls the eloquence of Demosthenes "perfection."

His admiration sometimes passes into emulation. In the essay "Of Public Credit" (1752) he inveighs with Demosthenic indignation against what he perceived as the encroaching evils of his age, stockjobbing and the national debt:

> In this unnatural state of society, the only persons, who possess any revenue beyond the immediate effects of their industry, are the stock-holders, who draw almost all the rent of the land and houses, besides the produce of all the customs and excises. These are men, who have no connexions with the state, who can enjoy their revenue in any part of the globe in which they chuse to reside, who will naturally bury themselves in the capital or in great cities, and who will sink into the lethargy of a stupid and pampered luxury, without spirit, ambition, or enjoyment. Adieu to all ideas of nobility, gentry, and family. (357–58)

Hume appeals to his fellow citizens in impassioned moral terms, blaming the national debt on the economic policies of Walpole and the stupifying spirit of "luxury" that they introduced. As a result of the debt, a rootless gang of stockholders threatens to undermine the "natural" civic virtues of the landed classes. Accordingly, the monstrous specter of credit calls forth Hume's most vehement reasoning:

> I must confess, that there is a strange supineness, from long custom, creeped into all ranks of men, with regard to public debts, not unlike

what divines so vehemently complain of with regard to their religious doctrines. We all own, that the most sanguine imagination
cannot hope, either that this or any future ministry will be possessed of such rigid and steady frugality, as to make a considerable
progress in the payment of our debts; or that the situation of foreign
affairs will, for any long time, allow them leisure and tranquillity
for such an undertaking. *What then is to become of us?* . . . It must,
indeed, be one of these two events; either the nation must destroy
public credit, or public credit will destroy the nation. (360–61)

Self-consciously or not, Hume re-creates "the inspired rapidity in
the play of question and answer" that Longinus so admires in
Demosthenes; as Longinus comments, "This method of asking
questions and providing your own answers gives the appearance
of being a natural outburst of feeling" (*On the Sublime* chap. 18).

But Hume seldom wrote with such ardor, real or apparent. He
was usually content to write with a sparkling blandness better
suited to the commerce of the new social sphere. The ideology of
commerce, indeed, supplies a key distinction between ancients
and moderns: whereas Xenophon doubted that commerce had
any advantages, and Plato was sure it had no benefits (*Essays* 88),
Hume and his contemporaries, though not untroubled by classical reservations, finally affirmed its power to civilize the passions.
It is through commerce that we are, in Zac Fungus's awkward but
ironically truthful phrase, the "civilized successors" of our
"painted progenitors." As Hume contends in "Of Luxury" (later
retitled "Of Refinement in the Arts"), the regulated exchanges of
urban life have occasioned an "encrease in humanity" (271)—a
genuinely hopeful phrase, it seems, that foretells even as it announces a time when politeness seems to pass from being (as
Smith advises) a restraint placed on our more boisterous passions
to being a true modification of our sentiments—in Sterne's
phrase, a true *politesse de coeur.* Perhaps, that is, the dictatorship
of guarded politeness will wither away and reveal the new utopia
of compassionate social equality—even if that equality pertains,
paradoxically, among only the polite.

Advocates of politeness cite Demosthenes' "democratic ease"
as a stylistic ideal—granted that it is shorn of its apostrophic
excesses. Apostrophe marks a style that unironically transgresses

boundaries not only between the living and the dead, and the transparent and the palpable, but also between the orator and "the lowest vulgar." This last transgression would seem particularly dangerous to persons whose own democratic sympathies are cautiously limited. The polite ideal, in effect, translates the communion of the classical assembly into the socially exclusive and philosophically tempered setting of the modern salon, club, coffeehouse, or grotto. Athens's sympathetic fire becomes the amiability of fireside conversation. Demosthenes' orations were adduced to support an ideal of discourse in which the intellectual speaks as an equal to other gentlemen—and also, according to the age's broadened sympathies, to refined women.

Indeed, the supreme fiction of polite society is the conversational voice: a voice that has regained some of its ancient simplicity, "free," in Adam Ferguson's formulation, "from the vulgar of [the mechanic], the pedantic of [the scholar], or the flippant [of the courtier]" (174). This conversational ideal supplies the norm for close encounters not only of the spoken but of the written kind, as when Madame du Deffand writes Horace Walpole: "I do not like to imagine an author is writing a book. I like to imagine he is talking to me. . . . Our writers of today have bodies of iron, not in their health, but in their style" (quoted in Lucas, 79). Wittingly or not, Deffand offers us a fable for the ways in which the simple and iron-hard language of Demosthenes bespeaks an ideal of community, even in a society in which Greek bodies have been supplanted by English letters.

# 3   Regretting Eloquence in Polite Letters: Pope, Gray, and Sterne

The tension we have seen in Hume between the old vehemence and a new civility, between regretting eloquence and extolling politeness, similarly animates the writings of other major authors of the period from 1742 to 1770—the years in which Hume wrote and revised "Of Eloquence." That Pope, Gray, and Sterne each stage the conflict between eloquence and polite style in terms that more or less resemble Hume's argues not only for the aptness of calling the mid–eighteenth century the age of Hume but, more fundamentally, for seeing this contest as *the* characteristic theme of the era.

## Pope: Heeding Bolingbroke in the Wake of Henley

In a letter dated 18 February 1724, Bolingbroke chided Pope for wasting his spirits on Homer. "Whilst you translate . . . you neglect to propagate the English tongue; and whilst you do so, you neglect to extend your own reputation, for depend upon it your writings will live as long and go as far as the language, longer or further they cannot." Should Pope observe his imperial duty to write original poems in his native tongue, English might be both spread and preserved. But if Bolingbroke could imagine Pope in the role of a British Virgil, he appears much less hopeful of finding a new Demosthenes to redeem English eloquence: "Eloquence . . . , God knows, [is] at the lowest ebb imaginable among us" (Pope, *Correspondence* 2:220).

What might be the proper way to cultivate eloquence in England? In addressing this question to a poet, Bolingbroke may have assumed that a simple sense of regret would prove most inspirational. As England is without eloquence, so Pope is left without an answer. Twelve years later, however, Bolingbroke suggests methods for reviving oratory in his *Letter on the Spirit of Patriotism*, written from France to the young Lord Cornbury in England. Bolingbroke advises Cornbury—and through him, the "Patriots" in general—"that opposition to an administration requires [neither] fewer preparatives, [nor] less constant application, than the conduct of it" (*Works* 3:29). He then expounds upon a familiar Ciceronian lesson. In book 1 of Cicero's *De Oratore*, the character Crassus argues at length that the orator must be a knowledgeable statesman and philosopher as well as an accomplished speaker (1.13, 3.16). In the same spirit, Bolingbroke urges the Opposition to prepare for speaking in public by first studying "every part of political knowledge," including history, philosophy, and, of course, rhetoric. The education of the modern orator must adhere to classical models. Only by knowing as much as Demosthenes and Cicero once knew will the orator possess the proper "fountain" from which eloquence can then "flow":

> Eloquence has charms to lead mankind, and gives a nobler superiority than power, that every dunce may use, or fraud, that every knave may employ. But eloquence must flow like a stream that is fed by an abundant spring, and not spout forth a little frothy water on some gaudy day, and remain dry the rest of the year. The famous orators of Greece and Rome were the statesmen and ministers of those commonwealths. The nature of their governments, and the humour of those ages, made elaborate orations necessary. . . . But as much pains as they took in learning how to conduct the stream of eloquence, they took more to enlarge the fountain from which it flowed. (3:24–25)

Bolingbroke's exhortation that learning precede eloquence became a standard piece of Opposition wisdom; among the Patriots and their fellow travelers it echoes at least as far as Fielding's *Tom Jones* (1749), in which William Pitt's eloquence is commended for following classical examples: "All the imagination, fire, and judgment of Pitt could [not] have produced those orations that have made the senate of England in these our times a rival in eloquence to Greece and Rome, if he had not been so well read in the writings of Demosthenes and Cicero, as to have transferred their whole spirit into his speeches, and with their spirit, their knowledge too" (2:739).

Pope, for his part, probably knew Bolingbroke's *Letter on the Spirit of Patriotism*, and surely he knew its lesson. He knew that "the full tide of Eloquence" (*Epistles of Horace* 2.2.171) must proceed from studiously acquired (if easily worn) political knowledge; he also knew that eloquence was indeed "at the lowest ebb imaginable" in Walpole's Britain. And these are precisely the assumptions, I would argue, that inform *The Dunciad* and give it, from first to last, its recognized affinity to Opposition concerns.[1] Pope shares with Hume an interest in the fate of ancient eloquence as well as the ironies that attend any modern handling of the theme. But while Hume offers measured prose meditations on the *absence* of sublime eloquence from modern Britain, Pope chooses the modern *debasement* of eloquence as the fit topic for his English song.[2]

---

1. Indeed, the dates of the poem's composition span the course of the Opposition to Walpole. The three-book *Dunciad* first appeared in May 1728, a year and a half after Bolingbroke launched *The Craftsman; The New Dunciad* came out in March 1742, the month after Walpole's resignation and two months after Hume's "Of Eloquence." Maynard Mack points out that a late note to book 1 of *The Dunciad* flagrantly identifies "the Hero of the Poem" as Walpole (162); Bertrand Goldgar calls the revised edition of the poem (October 1743) an "unforgiving indictment of [Walpole's] years of power" and an expression of the "anti-Hanoverian sentiment" prevalent in the wake of Walpole's fall (213–16). Frederick Keener argues that the poem, read through the lens of Le Bossu's epic theory, ultimately indicts not merely the minister but "the present monarch," George II (53–55).

2. Few will be surprised to hear that the theme of *The Dunciad* is, in a general way, "the decay of letters." Martin Price writes that the poem depicts the decay of poetry and rhetoric from means of communication to mere "excrement" (205–32); Ronald Paulson notes that "Pope projects a literature that is *about* literature—or, in the case of the dunces, about *non*-literature" (*Breaking and Remaking* 86). I would argue, however, that *The Dunciad* is more specifically

In the 1729 quarto *The Dunciad*, Pope illustrates oratory's lowest ebb in the figure of John "Orator" Henley (3.191–208).[3] The poem presents Henley as a supremely amphibious thing: preacher and huckster, City visionary and Walpole's creature, orator and opera singer, a duncical modern aspiring to be an ancient. The poem's portrait of Henley is supplemented by a long footnote cataloging his pretensions: these include "He preach'd on the Sundays Theological matters, and on the Wednesdays upon all other sciences"; he "compos'd three dissertations a week on all subjects; [and] undertook to teach in one year what Schools and Universities teach in five"; and he "styled himself the Restorer of ancient Eloquence."

Pope's source for most of this note is the biographical sketch of Henley prefixed to his *Oratory Transactions* no. 1 (1728), signed by a "Mr. Welstede" but generally believed to be written by Henley himself. In it, he advances his plan for "the Oratory," intended to be both a revival of the primitive church and "an academy of the sciences and languages." His schemes (like most academic proposals written today) combine a puffing assurance and a degree of charlatry. The latter fairly shines through his boast that he will "lay a foundation for the long desired English Academy; to give, by just degrees, a standard to the English tongue; to clear, regulate, ascertain and digest the English history; to revive an ancient Athenian and Roman school of philosophy, rhetorick, and elocution; which last is reckon'd among the Artes perditae: and to afford the best and readiest lights on all curious or occasional topicks" (iv, following 51). In the final turn from restoring the lost art of elocution to "affording lights on curious topics," we

---

about the decay of *eloquence*, particularly of the neo-Longinian strain long praised by Opposition poets and polemicists.

3. Graham Midgley's biography offers a balanced assessment of Henley's public life; the details of his "slanging match" with Pope are recounted on pp. 170–85 (see also the Twickenham *Dunciad*, ed. James Sutherland, 173–75, 444). Without ever fully abandoning his peculiar "Oratory" ambitions of the 1720s, Henley later achieved a more conventional eminence as a party writer for Walpole; his periodical *The Hyp-Doctor* (1730–41) ridiculed the arguments of *The Craftsman* and often engaged in ad hominem attacks on Pope. Pope's portrait of Henley is quoted from *The Dunciad Variorum* of 1729, as this was the version to which Henley responded.

may pinpoint the moment when an impossibly exalted ambition descends into what is unmistakably a huckster's pitch—though the two are never far apart. Despite Henley's later denial that he ever called himself "the Restorer of ancient Eloquence" (*How Now, Gossip Pope?* 7), this early pamphlet clearly shows that the epithet in no way misrepresents his ambitions.

Of course, the Henley that appears in Pope's poem, as distinct from his discursive note, is more or less abstracted into an emblem of debased eloquence. And just as Cicero and Bolingbroke argue that true eloquence must flow from reservoirs of history and philosophy, so Henley's entrance into the poem follows upon the emblematizing of these requisite arts. Dulness paints the scene:

> But, where each Science lifts its modern Type,
> Hist'ry her Pot, Divinity his Pipe,
> While proud Philosophy repines to show
> Dishonest sight! his breeches rent below;
> Imbrown'd with native Bronze, lo Henley stands,
> Tuning his voice, and balancing his hands.
> How fluent nonsense trickles from his tongue!
> How sweet the periods, neither said nor sung!
>
> (191–98)

Indeed, the historical Henley appointed himself the rather Herculean task of reuniting wisdom and eloquence; he would do so by teaching oratory as the culmination of all history, divinity, and philosophy. The feat smacks of heroic drama—or, in Pope's mock-heroic version, of tremendous simplicity: for modern historiography, like divinity, has relaxed into garrulousness or potvaliance, whereas philosophy, more ambitious, seems to illustrate Pope's later adage, "The higher you climb, the more you show your A——" (4.18n). The poet's "lo" directs us next to Henley, though it is difficult to visualize him "Imbrown'd with native Bronze," a descriptive phrase that may refer to the suntan of an open-air orator, the besmirchment that flows from Philosophy's rent breeches, or the "brazenness" the Opposition ever attributed to

Walpole and his creatures.[4] While each of these readings is appropriate, none receives any iconic privilege over the others. Pope authorizes us to imagine Henley "Imbrown'd" in a number of ways, none of which are enforced in the way that images enforce.

Pope thus avoids the type of visual simplification associated with Henley, who sought, according to "Welstede's" biography, to "introduce regular Action into the Pulpit." Henley, that is, would revive a transparent language of physical gesture, the "action" or "delivery" that the exemplary ancient orator possessed to a mythically perfect degree. Indeed, Henley identifies action as the defining excellence of ancient oratory: "Demosthenes has made the manner of delivery only to be the very essence of a public speaker. Quintilian has left us the most minute directions imaginable for each note and motion, and Tully was remarkable for this unweary'd application to the skill of it. . . . To see St. Paul preaching with a vehemence, an energy, like the blaze from heaven at his conversion, was a famous wish of one of the first doctors of the faith [Augustine?]" (*Appeal of the Oratory* 19). Reviving rhetorical action would indeed be an accomplishment, for if eloquence is all in all an ars perdita, action is its most lost aspect. Crassus of *De Oratore* laments that, already in his own day (91 B.C.), although "delivery has the sole and supreme power in oratory," to which Demosthenes famously assigned the first, second, and third places of importance, "the orators, who are the deliverers of truth itself, have neglected this whole department, and the players, who are only the imitators of truth, have taken possession of it" (3.56).

But if Henley would see himself restoring regular action to oratory, Pope depicts him as just another player in possession of oratory's lost prerogative. He describes Henley's speaking as a dumb show of gesture and sound, a tuned voice and balanced hands, devoid of truth or even sense. While Henley's preening recalls the ridiculously grandiose action of Swift's Lilliputian

4. *The Craftsman* no. 259 claims to translate an ancient Latin manuscript in which Verres (of Cicero's *Against Verres*) is described as "a whoreson round Man, of a brazen complexion"; the description is clearly meant to reflect Walpole. On Walpole's putative "brazenness," see also Maynard Mack 141–58.

Hurgo, his periods "neither said nor sung" look ahead to the inanity that *The Dunciad* book 4 attributes to opera's "quaint Recitativo" (4.52); indeed, for all his aspiration to be an orator, Henley appears rather to be the "zany" of an opera buffa:

> Oh great Restorer of the good old Stage,
> Preacher at once, and Zany of thy Age!
> Oh worthy thou of Ægypt's wise abodes,
> A decent Priest, where monkeys were the Gods!
>
> (201–4)

Henley may have styled himself the Restorer of ancient Eloquence, but Pope places him squarely in a lesser theatrical tradition. (Similarly, while Henley saw himself reviving the primitive Church, Pope associates him with a still more "primitive" ritual.) Indeed, Pope's attack on the would-be orator appears informed by Crassus's advice in *De Oratore*: "On all . . . emotions a proper gesture ought to attend; not the gesture of the stage, expressive of mere words, but one showing the whole force and meaning of a passage, not by gesticulation, but by emphatic delivery, by a strong and manly exertion of the lungs, not imitated from the theatre and the players, but rather from the camp and the palestra" (3.59).

Henley tended to defend his delivery, however, precisely by vindicating the gestures of the stage. His pamphlet *Milk for Babes* (1729) quotes and replies to each of the curiously Popean charges brought against him by the Grand-Jury of Westminster, where Henley had set up his Oratory in Newport-Market. Accused of using the "gestures of the theatre"—the charge implies, I assume, using them with the bad intention of roiling his audience— Henley replies, "There is not a man in the world, that does not use the same gestures as the theatre: for the theatre uses, or ought to use, the gestures of the world" (42). Henley may be too quick to collapse distinctions here; different types of gesture are indeed thought appropriate to the different contexts of theater, lectern, and "world." But then it is precisely Henley's refusal to acknowledge distinctions that so exasperated both Pope and the Westminster Jury.

The Grand-Jury objects to Henley's "holding unlawful assemblies, wherein riots and routs have been committed, and other unlawful practices"; moreover, his "rooms" purportedly contain maskers, and an unsavory air of carnival (26). Whatever the accuracy of these charges, they reveal a general perception that Henley is somehow a leveler; and however he may respond, it is a perception that he himself certainly encouraged in the first of his *Oratory Transactions*, which openly expresses the wish to reach *all* ranks of the London public. He vows "to supply the want of an university, or universal school in this capital, for the equal benefit of persons of all ranks, professions, circumstances, and capacities" (iii, following 51). To an ear attuned to degree, this must sound dangerously promiscuous. In response, Pope figures Henley's populist schemes—and his disquieting early success— in the seat-busting weight of his audience's buttocks: "Still break the benches, Henley! with thy strain, / While K**, B**, W**, preach in vain" (199–200). While the Twickenham edition cites Curl's *Key* in tentatively identifying "W**" as Dr. Robert Warren, whose sermons were published in 1723, at least some of Pope's contemporary readers would have thought rather of John Ward, the well-known lecturer on Ciceronian rhetoric at Gresham College. The contrast is certainly apt between Henley and Ward, two men who would establish such different views of oratory and do so at such different venues.

When Pope touched up his satire of Henley for *The Dunciad, in Four Books* (1743), K**, B**, and W** are replaced by "Sherlock, Hare, and Gibson" as updated types of preachers who do not break benches, but the ponderousness of Henley's audience remains the same. The irrational appeal of Henley's action will ever, it seems, attract crowds deaf to the blander suasion of an episcopal style. Again, Pope may have been minding Cicero's authority, for, as Crassus remarks, "in every thing appertaining to action there is a certain force bestowed by Nature herself; and it is by action accordingly that the illiterate, the vulgar, and even barbarians themselves, are principally moved" (3.xlix). Henley's power to attract a heterogenous crowd is what places him at the heart of *The Dunciad*, a poem, according to Pat Rogers, "about civil commotion" (99). In Rogers's provocative reading, the tu-

multuous crowd scenes of the poem allegorize the eighteenth-
century city riot, from the anti-Irish riots of 1736 through to a
proleptic vision of the Wilkite affrays of 1768 and the Gordon
Riots of 1780 (94–135). Pope, that is, represents "riots and
routs . . . and other unlawful practices" (in the words of the Westminster Jury) as a fairly cancerous threat to the nation. Indeed, to
employ a distinction made in *The Craftsman* no. 89, Pope envisions Henley not as an orator but as a haranguer: "The haranguer
is noisy in his accent, perplexed in his words, and disturbed in his
action. The orator is easy, clear and harmonious. The one is vol-
uble; the other eloquent. The one is wily, the other wise. . . . The
one sometimes receives a rude applause from a noisy audience. . . . Surely nothing is so formidable to a free people as an
indefatigable, imperious, artful disturber of the publick peace."
Mobs do indeed gravitate towards haranguers, and Henley is one
such cynosure in the London of *The Dunciad.*

But however many uproarious audiences Henley attracts, it is
the Goddess Dulness who supplies the ultimate gravitational
center of the poem. As she assumes her throne at the outset of
book 4, the captive Arts around her footstool include those initially degraded by Henley:

> There foam'd rebellious Logic, gagg'd and bound,
> There, stript, fair Rhet'ric languish'd on the ground;
> His blunted Arms by Sophistry are born,
> And shameless Billingsgate her Robes adorn.
>
> (23–26)

Pope had taken a great contemptuous delight in Henley's apt
residence at Butcher-Row, Haymarket ("But Fate with Butchers
plac'd thy priestly Stall," 3.205); here at Dulness's foot, rhetoric is
similarly debased by contact with fishwives and ruffians. Eloquence turns harangue when the taste of the vulgar forms that of
the orator.

Rhetoric not only declines into Billingsgate, however, but further decays in the course of Dulness's sessions into the conglom-
erating sound of "Fame's posterior Trumpet":

> And now had Fame's posterior Trumpet blown,
> And all the Nations summon'd to the Throne.
> The young, the old, who feel her inward sway,
> One instinct seizes, and transports away.
> None need a guide, by sure Attraction led
> And strong impulsive gravity of Head:
> None want a place, for all their Centre found,
> Hung to the Goddess, and coher'd around.
>
> (71–78)

Dulness's heralding trumpet may be read in a number of complementary contexts. It parodies the call to the Christian Last Judgment (as there is surely no judgment here); it also perverts the classical trumpet of fame that sounds to commemorate virtue and eloquence. As an example of the latter, consider Glover's ekphrastic description of Leonidas's shield:

> The form of Virtue dignified the scene.
> In her majestic sweetness was disclos'd
> The mind sublime and happy. From her lips
> Seem'd eloquence to flow. With looks serene . . .
> She wav'd her hand, where winding to the skies
> Her paths ascended. On the summit stood
> Fame, and protended her eternal trump,
> Incumbent on a trophy near to heav'n.
>
> (*Leonidas* 8.132–40)

In the larger narrative that graces the shield, the goddess Virtue contends with Pleasure for Hercules' allegiance; as we know, he chooses Virtue's arduous path to Fame over Pleasure's pneumatic allurements. Pope's modern dunces, on the contrary, levitate toward the sound of a different trumpet.

In *The Dunciad*, public sound becomes more attractive, in a purely mechanical way, the further it is divorced from sense, and particulary from any sense of duty or obligation. A certain type of assembly may be, as Longinus would say, "transported" by the civic pieties of the sublime orator, but a much larger and less discriminating throng will harken to a sound that brings bodies together while allowing spirits to remain separate or, in Dulness's words, "proud, selfish and dull" (582). And if in the City this sound issues from Butcher's Stalls and Billingsgate, in the fashionable world its locale is the opera. Fame's posterior Trumpet is, of course, merely an expulsion of air—and opera, in Opposition parlance, is itself nothing more.

Earlier, Addison indicted the rise of Italian opera in England as the triumph of sound over sense. According to *The Spectator* no. 18, the English audience, "to ease themselves entirely of the fatigue of thinking, have so ordered it at present that the whole Opera is performed in an unknown tongue. . . . It does not want any great measure of sense to see the ridicule of this monstrous practice; but what makes it the more astonishing, it is not the taste of the rabble, but of persons of the greatest politeness, which has established it." But Addison's objection to an imported opera, here as elsewhere, is stated purely as a matter of taste, ostensibly removed from political considerations.

Pope's ridicule of English operagoing, by contrast, draws upon Bolingbroke's overtly political reflections on Italian degeneracy. For example, "The Freeholder's Political Catechism" in *The Craftsman* no. 377 presents an ideal British citizen, well apprised that "Liberty, like the dew from heaven, fructifieth the barren mountains" and well prepared to answer questions about the deplorable condition of nations that are no longer free.

> *Q.* Why is enslaving mankind murdering human nature?
> *A.* Because mankind in a state of slavery and freedom is a different sort of creature. For proof of this I have read what the Greeks were of old, and what they are now in a state of slavery.
> *Q.* What is become of the heroes, philosophers, orators, and free citizens of Greece?
> *A.* They are now slaves to the great Turk.
> *Q.* What is become of the Scipio's and Cato's of Rome?
> *A.* They sing now on the English stage.

In Pope as in Bolingbroke, opera illustrates Italy's decline from her days of martial valor and austere Republican virtue. *The Craftsman* handles the contrast between "Scipio and Cato" and their Roman epigone bluffly, in a manner befitting a British freeholder, but Pope manages the same contrast in a more delicate shorthand when his satire on the Grand Tour leads

> To where the Seine, obsequious as she runs,
> Pours at great Bourbon's feet her silken sons;
> Or Tyber, now no longer Roman, rolls,
> Vain of Italian Arts, Italian Souls . . .
> To lands of singing, or of dancing slaves,
> Love-whisp'ring woods, and lute-resounding waves.
>
> (lines 297–306)

The Twickenham edition glosses these lines with the note that the Tiber, "no longer Roman . . . no longer contemplates with vanity Italian arts or Italian men." Equally appropriate is that the Tiber, corrupted with the rest of modern Italy, is vain of novel "Italian Arts" such as opera, and the "Italian souls" it may have recently received through the philosophical promptings of a man such as Count Radicati di Passerano, notorious in England for supporting the individual's right to suicide, and famously satirized in Pope's *Epilogue to the Satires*. "If Blount dispatch'd himself, he played the man / And so may'st Thou, illustrious Passeran!" (1.123–24).

Rome represents for the Opposition a city in which public forums have given place to inane musical spectacles and the shelter of "Love-whisp'ring woods," and dying *pro patria* has given way to merely indulgent and probably, as with poor Charles Blount, impulsively lovelorn self-murder. Thus, when Pope summarily refers to Italian opera singers as "eunuchs" in his *Imitations of Horace*, he intends their literal castration to ring with political significance. His animadversions upon the castrato's presence in Georgian England are intended to unsettle further a Country party audience little likely to assume the stability of either its own liberties or the English "tradition" of virile republicanism. Opera singers serve as not only an index of Italy's corruption but, in their importation, a symptom of England's own.

This is clearly a theme of *Epistle* 1.1 ("To Bolingbroke"), in which Pope responds to the Courtly counsel "Get Place and Wealth" with the pointed question "For what? to have a Box where Eunuchs sing, / And foremost in the Circle eye a King"

(105–6). He alludes, of course, to the fact that one might indeed see George II at the opera—he was a noted aficionado; but it is not altogether clear from Pope's description where the king is sitting. Is he in the circle seats of the theater, or in a circle of eunuchs on stage? Moreover, where would Pope be at the moment when he espies the king: would he be in his box, or would he rather find himself "foremost in the Circle," assuming a king's-eye view? The dizzying ambiguity of the lines suggests a double metamorphosis in which the poet becomes the king he eyes, while the king-as-spectator turns king-on-stage, or king-castrato. The danger of operagoing is that while thinking only to supplement one's self, one may find oneself supplanted. Though much of Rousseau's spartan attack on the theater in his *Letter to D'Alembert* would have seemed extreme to Pope, he would at least agree with Rousseau's premise: you are what you watch.

For Rousseau, the citizens of a republic should therefore attend only athletic entertainments and occasions for oratory—the latter because it is through regarding the virtuous orator that citizens may individually become their own best selves and collectively become the consolidated community that the orator beholds. As Lionel Trilling writes of Rousseau's communitarian vision, "The entertainments appropriate to a republic are those in which the citizen, participating in his own person, is reinforced in the sentiment of his own being and in his relation to his fellow beings" (65). Rousseau's ideal is, in essence, the classical republicanism we have seen in British letters throughout the 1730s and 1740s; it is the same ideal once approved by Voltaire, when he smiled on the Opposition's attraction to Demosthenic eloquence. Voltaire and Rousseau, however, would probably have had little sympathy for the Opposition's peculiarly John Bullish version of athletic entertainment, the beargarden.

Opposition writers tended to view the beargarden as England's indigenous equivalent to the Roman gladiatorial games, if not the Greek Olympics. Its praises are sung with particular ardor in Lyttelton's third *Letter from a Persian in England* (1735). Selim, the eponymous Persian observer, attends a Beargarden where a Frenchman complains of "the sanguinary disposition of the English, in delighting in such spectacles." Whereupon a rough English gentleman responds at length: "If more people came hither, and fewer loitered in the drawing room, it would not be worse for Old England. We are indeed a civilized state, as you are pleased to call it; but I could wish, upon certain occasions, we were not quite so civil. This gentleness and effeminacy in our manners will soften us by degrees into slaves. . . . You fine gentlemen are for the taste of Modern Rome, squeaking eunuchs and corruption: but I am for that of Ancient Rome, gladiators and liberty" (*Works* 1:138).

And opera, as Pope presents it, precisely negates that ancient republican ideal. The grand sessions of the Court of Dulness are opened by a "Phantom [that] represents the nature and genius of the Italian Opera" (Pope's note):

> When lo! a Harlot form soft sliding by,
> With mincing step, small voice, and languid eye;
> Foreign her air, her robe's discordant pride
> In patch-work flutt'ring, and her head aside:
> By singing Peers up-held on either hand,
> She tripp'd and laugh'd, too pretty much to stand;
> Cast on the prostrate Nine a scornful look,
> Then thus in quaint Recitativo spoke.
> "O *Cara! Cara!* silence all that train:
> Joy to great Chaos! let Division reign:
> Chromatic tortures soon shall drive them hence,
> Break all their nerves, and fritter all their sense:
> One Trill shall harmonize joy, grief, and rage,
> Wake the dull Church, and lull the ranting Stage;
> To the same notes thy sons shall hum, or snore,
> And all thy yawning daughters cry, *encore.*"
>
> (45–60)

Opera perverts the participatory scene of ancient eloquence: instead of the mutually rousing sympathies of the orator and the assembly, opera lulls the passive spectator into indifference and divides him from his fellows, even as it divides musical notes; instead of the orator's organic connection to the community he vivifies, the opera singer is an import, trilling in an alien tongue; instead of the orator's vigorous resistance to encroaching tyranny, the opera singer inspires, in the words of the Twickenham edition, "un-English affectations," and a generally supine attitude among the nobility who support it.

Moreover, as Pope's notes emphasize, the opera that absorbs the "fine Gentlemen of this age" is "languid and effeminate," full of "Chromatic tortures" that "the Spartans forbad the use of." As Bolingbroke had written in *The Craftsman* no. 29, "Musick has something so peculiar in it, that it exerts a willing tyranny over the mind, and forms the ductil soul into whatever shape the melody directs. . . . The soft Italian musick relaxes and unnerves the soul, and sinks it into weakness." The same essay quotes Herodotus on Croesus's method of subduing his subjects: "Order them to sing and play on the harp . . . and you'll soon see their spirits broken, and themselves changed from men into women." Pope's own vision presents this change as a fait accompli. English audiences will thus have no truck with Mr. Handel's introduction of martial elements into his orchestra: his alleged "Drums and Cannon" have proved "much too manly" for modern tastes. Significantly, it is Dulness's daughters who have the impetus to "cry, encore"—a fairly minimal impetus, to be sure, but nonetheless the only expression of will available to the opera audience.

In his useful study of Pope's friendship with Bolingbroke, Brean Hammond remarks that for the Opposition "the promotion of opera was part of the government's bread and circuses policy, a spectacular entertainment designed to keep the nation sweet while Walpole and his associates lined their pockets" (117). Since the Opposition blamed just about everything on Walpole's administration, Hammond's point, prima facie, would seem well taken; upon a closer inspection of at least Pope's writings, however, opera appears rather to be one force of national disintegration that transcends the administration's own intentions or designs. With regard to opera, the administration exercises as little will as anyone else. The growth of Italian opera in England is as threatening as it is incalculable, and the nature of that threat proves to be ontological as well as political. Much like the "Magus Cup" of lines 517–28, opera makes its devotees lose their virtue, their language, their very selves; but opera, more selectively, draws in the sons and daughters of peers—particularly, in *The Dunciad*, of new-made peers who have risen to prominence under the Whig administration:

> Others the Syren Sisters warble round,
> And empty heads console with empty sound.
> No more, alas! the voice of Fame they hear,
> The balm of Dulness trickling in their ear.
> Great C**, H**, P**, R**, K*,
> Why all your Toils? your Sons have learn'd to sing.
> How quick Ambition hastes to ridicule!
> The Sire is made a Peer, the Son a Fool.
>
> (541–48)

Frustrating the dynastic ambitions of the *novus homo*, opera participates in the same ironic moral economy that Pope sketched in the *Epistle to Bathurst* (161–218): after the father gathers, the son gives away. Except that here, the son's divestment—of ambition, learning, and any sense of affiliation—has no possible good effects for England as a whole.

Pope targets this dispersion of self in his satire on the Grand Tour, which climaxes with the young Tourist's absorption into the Italian opera. Because the "glorious Youth" has lost his language and his sense while abroad, his tale is told by his "attendant Orator" (281):

> Led by my hand, he saunter'd Europe round,
> And gather'd ev'ry Vice on Christian ground;
> Saw ev'ry Court, heard ev'ry King declare
> His royal Sense, of Op'ra's or the Fair . . .
> Dropt the dull lumber of the Latin store,
> Spoil'd his own language, and acquir'd no more;
> All Classic learning lost on Classic ground;
> And last turn'd *Air*, the Echo of a Sound!
>
> (311–22)

Pope notes that the young gentleman has become "less a Body than Echo itself; for Echo reflects Sense or Words at least, this Gentleman only Airs and Tunes." The youth turns into an operatic aria; and having thus abandoned all "matter," he quite literally vanishes into air. Delight in a bilingual pun seems to give rise to this metamorphosis, but the fate of the dissipated young tourist is not without a severer poetic justice, one that makes Pope's passage resemble an *Ovide moralisé.*

In this labile Ovidian universe where opera singers become parodies of orators and young peers reflections of opera singers, is true eloquence anywhere to be found? A handful of notes attest both to an underlying ideal of eloquence and to its seemingly irrevocable absence from Hanoverian Britain. Isaac Barrow and Dean Francis Atterbury, for example, were both "great Genius's and eloquent Preachers," but both are dead, Atterbury having died in Jacobite exile (245–46n). Eloquence, it seems, has passed away with the Good Old Cause (which would be briefly revived after Pope's death), or it is kept alive only in the ironic commentary of antiquarian footnotes. Thus, a note drily evokes Longinus's admiration for a sublime moment in the *Odyssey* when "the Ghost of Ajax turns sullenly from Ulysses"—a moment ironically similar to Aristarch's (or Bentley's) turning away at the approach of the Grand Tourist and his entourage, back from their own type of odyssey (271–74). The young gentleman having lost his mind to the "Syren Sisters" of opera, it devolves to his "attendant Orator" to narrate their journey; and in so doing he displays a hearty indifference to the values of experience. He relates with great gusto the progressive unencumbering of his "young Aeneas" (290), who scatters his learning, his language, and his sentiment of being amid the ancient ground where citizen orators—as opposed to attendant orators—once held sway.

The young peer on foreign soil, to quote Byron's self-dramatization, "stands a ruin amidst ruins," but his tutor, neither dramatizing nor moralizing this decline, offers only a tour guide's ethically neutral description. He speaks, in other words, as a "cicerone." Significantly, the *Oxford English Dictionary* attributes the first uses of the term to Addison (*Dialogues upon . . . Ancient Medals* [1726]) and to Pope, in a letter to Hugh Bethell dated 1 January 1742. But whereas Addison uses it as a term of approbation ("My cicerone [was] well acquainted with the bust and statues of . . . antiquity"), for Pope it already has a vaguely pejorative air. He writes, "One of my amusements has been writing a Poem [*The New Dunciad*], part of which is to abuse Travelling. . . . An Army of Virtuosi, Medalists, Ciceronis,

Royal Society Men . . . will encompass me with fury: It will be once more, *Concurrere Bellum atque Virum"* (*Correspondence* 3:377). As Pope's satire on the Grand Tour makes clear, the age of Cicero and Virgil has unhappily metamorphosed into an age of ciceroni and virtuosi.

In sum, the fourth book of *The Dunciad* depicts the ancient ideal of eloquence reduced in the City to Billingsgate, and at Court to "air." Given the republican topos that eloquence can flow only from humanely educated, disinterested citizens in a free commonwealth, Pope's world of "high priori" modern learning and the piecemeal restoration of "native Anarchy" is one in which words can merely "trickle," as nonsense merely trickles from Henley's tongue, and opera, "the balm of Dulness," trickles into the ears of young peers (544). Yet the poem draws toward a moment when even tricklings cease—when even the speaker's "Muse," who might have inspired a swan song to "hush the Nations," is peremptorily silenced by "Universal Darkness." Pope's dying strain recalls, with a great deal of elaboration, Bolingbroke's perception of the "universal quiet" that has prevailed and will prevail in Georgian politics in the absence of an eloquent Opposition (*Works* 1:274). Thus, Pope's final poem is an elegy not only to eloquence but to the Opposition that urged its revival—or, to personalize these terms, an elegy not only for a Ciceronian ideal but for the lost power of Bolingbroke, the man who brought that ideal home to Pope.

## Losing Sight of Eloquence

But as a lament, *The Dunciad* is much less wholehearted than is often recognized. Pope handles his most punitive set-pieces with a good deal of playfulness, a lightness that is reassuring because apparently so assured. Dunces turned orators and Grand Tourists turned to arias are more likely to delight us (or even the most dour Tory pessimist) with their wit than depress us with a Velleian vision of cyclical decline.[5] Even the much admired

---

5. Bolingbroke professed to believe in historical moments at which political decline becomes inevitable: he cautioned that patriots could not always return a

"apocalyptic" imagery of *The Dunciad*'s last lines, where the arts are extinguished one by one, must contend with a sprightly line that scans and bounces, and there is not a little humor in the spectacle of arts that "gaze, turn giddy, rave, and die" (648). Certainly, Pope laments the death of the arts—who would not?—but he does so with the peculiar complacency of wit that typically colors his relation to Opposition rhetoric.

Pope balances the moral enthusiasm he learned from Bolingbroke with a more savvy or "Horatian" sense of detachment, sometimes hard to distinguish from indifference. This tension in Pope's relation to Bolingbroke is curiously illustrated in his having printed fifteen hundred copies of *The Patriot King* and then leaving them, with no instructions for their future use, with his printer. Doubtless, it troubled Pope that a patriot king was not in the offing, but the pathos of Pope's complaint in *The Dunciad* is more properly, to borrow a term from *Peri Bathous*, "the Pathetic epigrammatical"; as Pope explains, "Nothing contributes so much to the *Cool*, as the Use of Wit in expressing Passion: The true Genius rarely fails of Points, Conceits, and proper Similes on such occasions" (chap. 9). Indeed, throughout *The Dunciad* Pope practices the bathos he earlier described in his mock-Longinian rhetoric. And his bathos aims, not altogether ironically, at the same mock-Longinian end, "the main End and principal Effect of the *Bathos* [being] to produce *Tranquillity of Mind*."

However, the tranquility Pope would achieve is not mere passivity or torpor but rather a coolness amid activity, a calm commensurate with exertion. The central paradox of *The Dunciad* is that it represents the end of the world as Pope knows it, and yet he feels fine—as we, who appreciate his poetic line, are also encouraged to feel. For his line enlivens the mind with tonic abstractions

government to its first principles, "but that when these principles are worn out in the minds of men, it is a vain enterprise to endeavour to renew them" (quoted by Howard Erskine-Hill, 351). According to Erskine-Hill, Pope shared Bolingbroke's belief in the inevitability of both destructive and creative periods in the pattern of history (350–53). Similarly, Walter Jackson Bate elegantly remarks Hume's influential revival of Velleius Paterculus, the first-century Roman historian who argued that the arts and sciences, having reached perfection in any nation, must subsequently decline (80–84).

and temporal surprises, while it correspondingly eschews the images, external or subjective, by which the mind is inflamed or engrossed, attracted or repulsed. In other words, Pope's style is politely iconoclastic—or, as I shall argue presently, polite precisely in being iconoclastic.

Pope is careful to set his style apart both from the pathetic visual displays of Henley and the opera and from the bathetic concreteness of Richard Blackmore's poetry, the butt of much of *Peri Bathous*:

> When Job says, in short, *He wash'd his Feet in Butter*, (a Circumstance some Poets would have soften'd, or past over) now hear how this Butter is spread out by the Great Genius.

> > With Teats distended with their milky Store,
> > Such num'rous lowing Herds, before my Door,
> > Their painful Burden to unload did meet,
> > That we with Butter might have wash'd our feet.
> >                                                   (chap. 8)

Blackmore's metonymic details appall Pope (however perversely appealing he may find them); as we know from his own practice, he is one of those Poets who would have politley softened rather than magnififed Job's homely locution. Certainly Pope's poetry has little of either the visual immediacy of Blackmore's line or its potential (if sorely miscalculated) emotional appeal. Pope's tableaux, if we may even call them that, are connotative and cerebral; their power derives not from what Pope refers to as the "minuteness" of "Dutch painters" (chap. 8) but from a Miltonic sublime of obscurity. Thus, in imbrowning Henley with native bronze and bidding Fame's posterior Trumpet blow, Pope borrows less from physical comedy or fabliau than, however ironically, from Milton's famous description of Death: "The other shape, / If shape it might be called that shape had none" (*Paradise Lost* 2.666–67).

Edmund Burke praised Milton's portrait of Death for its "judicious obscurity," its "significant and expressive uncertainty of strokes and colouring" (*Enquiry* 59). His praise may equally be applied to the various "portraits" of *The Dunciad*. Jean Hagstrum, in his seminal study of the sister arts, valiantly attempts to accommodate Burke's aesthetic and still salvage the later Pope for the pictorialist tradition.[6] But I would argue, on the contrary, that in *The Dunciad* Pope actively *parodies* his earlier *ut pictura poesis* assumptions. He explicitly announced those assumptions, of course, in his *Essay on Criticism*—a work that certainly illustrates if not a proper pictorialism then at least the extent to which visual theory, with its idiom of "design," idea," and "colours" (lines 484–93), could be used in describing the poet's craft. Even here, however, Pope's primary interest is with not spatial relations but rather an element of time that a picture could hardly capture: his moral is that "colour" proves "treach'rous," apt in time to fade just as Chaucer's diction has faded.

Taking off from this section of the *Essay*, Timothy Erwin persuasively reads *The Rape of the Lock* as an allegory of "the creative stages of invention, design, and coloring," arguing that the poem "affirms the morality of firm contour against the slippery appeal of color" (58). But in *The Dunciad* color is denied an appeal, and outline fares no better: imbrowning Henley "with native Bronze" subverts the very notion of both literary pictorial "design" and "coloring." For how are we to "see" the bronzed Henley: as a piece of Attic statuary, or a merely human figure tanned or spattered with excrement? And what are the visual possibilites offered by the main affective meaning of the passage, the sheerly abstract notion of "brass" or bold impudence? Surely the "Bronze"—the statue or visual image, its form as well as color—is what is shattered here. Pope in effect extends into the eighteenth century the iconoclastic strain that Ernest Gilman detects in much Renaissance literature, "at crucial moments when the visual resources of the poet are challenged by a concep-

6. Thus, while admitting that, to some extent, "Pope was suggestive and oblique, creating intellectual configurations rather than picturable details" (140), Hagstrum nonetheless maintains Pope's commitment to *enargeia*; he finally conflates these two aspects of Pope's art in speaking (somewhat obscurely) of a "richly suggestive pictorialism" that proves in *The Dunciad* not incompatible with Burke's values of "obscurity and darkness" (154). Later still in his discussion, Hagstrum reluctantly admits, "Pope learned from Dryden that a satirical character [is] not delineated chiefly by pictorial and visual detail" (235).

tion of language disinfected, in its blind and often violent purity, of any appeal to the eye" (11).

Pope effectively theorizes his iconoclasm in the *Elegy to the Memory of an Unfortunate Lady*. The narrator of the poem begins by seeing and addressing the "visionary" ghost of a lovelorn suicide (an apostrophic mode that "Ossian" would soon make famous); yet this apparition has, paradoxically, left behind her corporeal "Image," her "body's cage," "As into air the purer spirits flow, / And sep'rate from their kindred dregs below" (lines 1–26). As if in imitation of the unfortunate lady's tragic but ultimately triumphant fate, the rest of Pope's poem similarly concerns the renunciation of images, from praise of the lady's imageless grave—"What tho' no weeping Loves thy ashes grace, / Nor polished marble emulate thy face?" (59–60)—to the poet's anticipation of the lady's image finally parting "from his [own] closing eyes" (79), as darkness bittersweetly buries all.

Indeed, Pope's poem acquires its full force, it would seem, in unfolding across a blind man's eye: such, at least, is the moral of an anecdote told by David Hume. The story comes from Hume's description of his first meeting with the blind Scottish poet Thomas Blacklock: "I repeated to him Mr. Pope's Elegy to the Memory of an unfortunate Lady, which I happened to have by heart: And although I be a very bad reciter, I saw it affected him extremely. His eyes, indeed, the great index of the mind, could express no passion: but his whole body was thrown into agitation. That poem was equally qualified to touch the delicacy of his taste, and the tenderness of his feelings" (quoted in Mossner, *Life*, 379). Hume, the unmoved mover, observes the spiritual implosion of one whose passions cannot, like his own, be alleviated through voyeurism. Blacklock's physical agitation represents for Hume taste and feelings in excess of the body: it evinces, in Pope's phrase, a sign of a soul that melts (lines 46, 77). The circuit between Pope's poem and Blacklock's taste may be read as a fable for polite style itself—a style that aims to impress how much more the heart knows than the eye sees; a style that blurs the lineaments of the body in order to elicit the taste and feeling that putatively lie beyond the light of the senses. Thus, while the old eloquence is vitally (even when, as in Demosthenes, sparingly) metaphorical, able to give a face, as in marble or bronze, polite eloquence, by contrast, is only ironically metaphorical, a shuffling of masks.

## The Temporality of Pope's Rhetoric

Hagstrum contends that Pope attains the height of pictorialist virtuosity in *The Temple of Fame*, adverting in particular to his portrait of Cicero which "could, in fact, be a description of the statue of Augustus now in the Vatican" (266). We may well be prepared to see here something of "the monumental fixity of Roman art" (267); we might furthermore accept Erwin's contention that in Pope's visual imagination morality travels in firm outline. *The Dunciad*, however—perhaps as a temple of *impermanence*—presents us with decidedly anti-iconic portraits, descriptions that openly admit and exploit their construction in passing time. For it is not only through ambiguous imagery but through the very unfolding of his verse that Pope impedes or negates easy visualization.

Look again, for example, at Pope's passage on Logic and Rhetoric: "There foam'd rebellious Logic, gagg'd and bound, / There, stript, fair Rhet'ric languish'd on the ground" (4.23–24). Vincent Carretta uses these lines to illustrate "the emblematic side of *Dunciad* 4," arguing that to appreciate Pope's artistry here "we must *see* . . . the proper icon of [Rhetoric], as described in Ripa's *Iconologia*" (161–62). But while Carretta correctly notes that such an icon informs Pope's lines, what he does not notice is the way in which Pope deliberately transforms the visual image through the temporality of his poetic medium.[7] Because of the

7. My reading of Pope here is indebted to the method of Stanley Fish's *Surprised by Sin* (which is, in turn, indebted to Lessing's emphasis on the temporality of rhetoric). Like Milton, Pope "relies on the operation of three truths so obvious that many critics fail to take them into account: (1) the reading experience takes place in time, that is, we necessarily read one word after another; (2) the childish habit of moving the eyes along the page and back again is never really abandoned . . . therefore the line as a unit is a resting place even when rhyme is absent; (3) a mind asked to order a succession of rapidly given bits of detail (mental or

verb *foam'd* in the first line, one might well think *stript* an active verb, too, harkening back to the agency of Logic, until the final image of Rhetoric languishing on the ground forces the realization that it is she who *has been* stripped. This clever ambiguity between active verbs and adjectival past participles enforces a double take, an ongoing revisualization, leading the eye backward and the inner eye elsewhere with nearly every movement forward. Pope's temporal artistry thus arrests the reader's progress. Even the following couplet's fairly straightforward chiasmus—"His blunted Arms by Sophistry are born, / And shameless Billingsgate her Robes adorn"—requires an assimilative pause the first time we encounter it. Leslie Stephen found Pope's polished style "a mosaic rather than a continuous current of discourse" (68), and I find the description apt (though hardly, as in Stephen, a disparagement). Pope aimed at a discourse punctuated by discontinuities, one that would elicit the reflective pause rather than raise a huzzah and bring down the benches.

Thus, unlike Henley's "fluent nonsense" or Welsted's beery "o'erflowing" (3.172, 1743), Pope's lines do not principally flow. Indeed, according to Johnson, Pope's favorite couplet is one that embodies the theme of "hardly flowing":

> I have been told that the couplet by which he declared his own ear
> to be most gratified was this:
>
> > "Lo! where Maeotis sleeps, and hardly flows
> > The freezing Tanais thro' a waste of snows"
> > [*The Dunciad* 3.87]
>
> But the reason for this preference I cannot discover.
> > (*Lives of the Poets* 3:250)

In the couplet quoted by Johnson, Pope envisions the barbaric invaders of ancient Rome issuing from "The North," or the lands around the river Don ("Tanais") and the Sea of Azov ("Maeotis") into which it flows. In the following line, "The North by myriads

---

physical) seizes on the simplest scheme of organization which offers itself" (23). Syntactic "surprises" occur when that "simplest scheme" turns out, finally, not to be the correct one.

*pours* her mighty sons" (emphasis mine), in the way that Dulness, for Pope, always pours or flows forth. By contrast, Pope's own favorite lines hardly flow in describing a river similarly arrested. At the first line's end we think we see the sleeping Maeotis— however pleonastically—barely mobile, until the end of the couplet reveals that the scarce power of flowing belongs not to the lake but to the issuing river. The evolving sense of Pope's couplet makes us scan backward, even as its rhythm and rhyme propel us forward; in Geoffrey Tillotson's phrase, "the manner of proceeding" through Pope always involves time for reconsideration.

Tillotson's characterization of Pope's style may indeed serve to summarize much of what I have said: "In Pope a couplet will often suggest a figure in Euclid, its vowels and consonants, its sense-oppositions and sense-attractions, fitted together like arcs and lines. . . . A manner such as this keeps the reader's brain active, fetching and carrying. It is a metre for educated people. No meaning is possible for the 'mind' to review, or for the 'spirit' to kindle at, till the 'brain' has mastered the Euclidian relationships" (14–15). That "till" is key, as it recognizes the crucial element of time in reading Pope's poems. I find it surprising, then, that Tillotson chooses this couplet—"Lo! where Maeotis sleeps"—to illustrate his quite different contention that Pope's couplets resemble painting (130). Although "Lo!" by itself certainly serves as a visual index, Pope's use of it here (as elsewhere) seems largely ironic, since Lake Maeotis indeed possesses a "now you see it, now you don't" quality: now it flows, and now it does not. His introduction of Henley with a "Lo" is similarly ironic, as Henley's imbrownment remains not only visually uncertain but indeed a negation of the very principle of spectacle for which he stands. In the second edition of his popular *Cyclopaedia*, Ephraim Chambers notes that "Cicero calls [action] QUAEDAM CORPORIS ELOQUENTIA, a certain eloquence of the body"; Pope's line, by contrast, evinces an anticorporeal eloquence—the eloquence, precisely, of Enlightenment.

This antivisualism largely distinguishes Pope's pageant of London's stupefaction from the Dunce's genuinely stupefying productions, be they printed, spoken, or sung. His poem conjures a dun-

cical milieu "under erasure," so to speak: the dunces are there but
not there, arrant but invisible. This legerdemain confronts an
age whose visual imagination was, as I discuss in the next chapter, much readier than our own, especially in the realm of poetry.
Although Pope never renounced his Roman Catholicism in Prot-
estant England—and although Henley could thus resort to
the bigoted cant of calling *The Dunciad* "Catholic Invective"
(Midgley 177)—Pope's late poetry nonetheless wields a Prot-
estant poetics against the various idol-worshipers of the day. Dis-
mantling their own visual images, he reconstitutes them in a
manner almost sheerly verbal, turning them into monsters of
letters.

Iconoclasm can, of course, lead to leveling, and other writers
have perennially noted the promiscuity of Pope's transmogrifying
imagination: in "Verses Addressed to the Imitator of Horace,"
Lady Mary Wortley Montagu calls it "the gross Lust of Hate,
that still annoys, / Without distinction, as gross Love enjoys"
(ll. 30-31; Uphaus, ed., *The Other Eighteenth Century*). And her
"Epistle from Pope to Lord Bolingbroke," in an ironic reversal of
the charges Pope leveled against Henley, accuses Opposition eloquence of fomenting anarchy:

> And here, my Lord! let all mankind admire
> The bold efforts of unexhausted fire;
> You stand the champion of the people's cause,
> And bid the mob reform defective laws.
> Oh! was your pow'r, like your intention, good!
> Your native land wou'd stream with civic blood . . .
> Yet while you preach'd in prose, I scold in rhymes
> Against the injustice of flagitious times.
> You, learned Doctor of the public stage,
> Give gilded poison to corrupt the age;
> Your poor toad-eater I, around me scatter
> My scurril jests, and gaping crowds bespatter.
> 
> (37–42, 56–61)

Montagu is an early commentator on Pope's delight in disorder;
similarly, though more sympathetically, recent critics have noted

his only partly ironic affinities to the chaos he criticizes.[8] And indeed no reader of the late Pope can ignore his anarchic impulses, his apparent joy in bespattering excrement—or, more to the point, the "imbrownings" (and "sable streams," etc.) we may construe as excremental. It is important to note the difference between these circumlocutions and Montagu's much more direct remark that, having lined her commode with the works of Pope, Swift, and Bolingbroke, she had "the satisfaction of shitting on them every day" (quoted in Rumbold, 145).[9] For Pope's style obviously intends to transcend the corporeal; in it, we may witness the triumph of the Manichaean distrust of the body underwriting much of the Enlightenment. Because of its controlled distance from the bodies it mocks and the passions such mockery evokes, *The Dunciad* ranks not only as one of the most punitive poems in English literature but also among the most polite.

## Politeness and Violence

If *The Dunciad*'s dual nature seems paradoxical, this is only the paradox of politeness itself. Indeed, with due allowance made for the heightenings of poetry, *The Dunciad* shares crucial elements of the prose style that Hume recognized as polite. Pope's poem offers no crowd-catching glimpse of the violence it implies; it blocks any passionate identification with the scene of punishment it darkly enacts. And politeness largely refers to dispassionate representations of passion and halcyon representations of violence. It is a mode of fashioning both letters and lives in which style aims to transcend and perhaps to transmute substance. This

8. Thomas R. Edwards writes, "The sinking of the Dunces leads to repose and sleep, a kind of peace that Pope does not simply despise. . . . The satiric edge never withdraws, but there is also a tenderness in the tone and even a kind of yearning" (*Dark Estate*, 126–27). Edwards's sense of a Pope half in love with easeful disorder is elaborated by Dustin Griffin, 217–43.

9. Ironically, while eighteenth-century writers increasingly associated polite femininity with decorporealization—as Mary Poovey concludes, during the period "the ideal woman . . . cannot be seen at all" (22)—Montagu here plays the earthy huswife to Pope's feminized man. On the contemporary eighteenth-century perception of Pope's style as "feminized," see Claudia Thomas's article on Pope's "Appeal to the Ladies."

effort marks Pope's own mature style as clearly as it does the courtly politesse he depicts in *The Rape of the Lock*; we might say of both what Thomas R. Edwards says of the latter: even as Pope "expresses real admiration for the beauty and efficiency of manners," he nonetheless "shares our doubts about the wisdom of so wholly regularizing passion—which ceases to be itself when purged of its recognizably human disorder" (20). Sharing our doubt, the polite author is fascinated by the disruptive passion and force he would eschew, thus applying a fairly transparent veneer to the objects of his disapprobation.

This see-through covering seems to me the defining strategy of a "polite style," at least in Hume's influential understanding of that term. Thus, when Hume calls Swift's prose "the first polite prose we have" (*Essays* 91), there is no sense that Swift's matter jars with this style. For Hume—as for Adam Smith and the new rhetoricians after him—Swift's prose seems no less polite for its content of materialists, mad projectors, and cannibals. Rather, I would suggest it is this very tension between an easeful and familiar style and a startling substance that makes Swift a polite author. (Adam Smith's own polite gentleman is, we shall recall, never more himself than when at the beargarden.) Hume's own claim to a polite style, and indeed to belonging to a Swiftian tradition, derives from a similar tension in his own writing.[10] As David Womersley notes of Hume's *History of England*, "the cultivated blandness of Hume's style and his suave demeanour . . . are most palpable when [his] subject is atrocity"; only at such moments do we become fully aware of "an urbanity of finish quite foreign to the appalling event itself" (23).

Hume's celebrated polish consists not only in clear and measured prose and a voice that is all but never lifted but also in a reluctance to visualize events. Womersley adduces a well-known letter of 1739 in which Hume chooses to see himself as an anatomist rather than as a painter (*Letters* 1:32). And, as we have seen, Hume disapproved of Cicero's oratorical style precisely when it

10. Ernest C. Mossner notes, "Hume fancied himself as following in the tradition of Dean Swift. 'I have frequently had it in my Intentions,' he admitted to Gilbert Elliot in 1751, 'to write a Supplement to *Gulliver*, containing the Ridicule of Priests. Twas certainly a Pity that Swift was a Parson'" (234).

grew "too palpable," too visually "striking." It is better to deal
plainly in polite obfuscations. Indeed, just as Swift never offers
images of roasted babies, so Hume is similarly reticent about the
various savageries his histories recount. According to his *Natural
History of Religion*, in the benighted past people came to believe
in gods through fearing some natural "prodigy" or "monstrous
birth"—but Hume's readers will hardly respond similarly to such
generalized locutions. The motive of politeness, then, is to in-
demnify the self against modes of atavistic behavior: against not
only the cannibalism that ever, like Defoe's Friday, haunts modern competitive man but also large portions of the religious imagination, its own projection and ingestion of gods.

   Politeness typically involves an ironic discrepancy between an
abstract and convivial style and a thematic fascination with bodies and the unironic consciousness of barbarians. Norman N.
Knox notes that the term *irony* gained currency in English between 1720 and 1730, partly in connection with the publication
of Swift's major works (24). The concept of irony, however, not
only met a belletristic need but fueled the more basic drive of
modernity to distinguish itself from antecedent ages of innocence
and impulsiveness. Vico spoke for the Enlightenment when he
professed the profound consolation of irony. Historically, irony is
the ultimate trope, the badge of "the period of reflection," whereas "the first men of the gentile world had the simplicity of children, who are truthful by nature" (sec. 408). Irony thus distinguishes polite authors from both the unenlightened past and the
still unenlightened vulgar. As Madame du Deffand remarked,
"Our men of letters today have bodies of iron, not in their health,
but in their style"—but the iron of their disembodying style is,
precisely, irony. Or, as Pope puts it, "I have no way so good to
please [women], as by presenting 'em with any thing rather than
with my self" (quoted in Rumbold, 4).

   In other words, irony gives pleasure that the actual body takes
away. This polite antivisualism indeed informs any number of
social and even state practices by the mid–eighteenth century: for
example, Fielding was to argue against the theatricality of public
executions on the grounds that "the mind of man is so much
more capable of magnifying than his eye, that I question whether

every object is not lessened by being looked upon."[11] Fielding might have adduced *The Dunciad* to support (at least partially) his argument: for certainly no reader can claim to "look upon" Pope's exploded dunces, his Henleys and castrati. Unlike them, Pope would not absorb the gaze of others. Still, Pope and Fielding differ in their respective aims, for whereas the magistrate would inspire a restraining fear among the populace, the poet would but soothe and reassure an elite. Thus, however much a reader may mentally "magnify" Pope's pilloried dunces, they tend to become increasingly contemptible rather than threatening. Pope achieves the ease of a polite style that defuses any real threat represented by his subject matter and restrains any passionate response it might evoke. Even Lady Montagu, quick to hear in Bolingbroke's eloquence the potential for civic strife, is comparatively relaxed before Pope's "scurril jests," even those at her own expense. They appear to contain little that is truly intimidating. In part, of course, Montagu would insult Pope's impotence as a poet of the old "satyr-satirist" ilk.[12] But at the same time she willy-nilly acknowledges his politeness, a style that intends, with its dampened images and deferred passions, to ignite no fires.

Montagu's verses on Bolingbroke and Pope bear witness to the differences between the old eloquence and the new. Like Demosthenes' and Cicero's, Bolingbroke's eloquence is incendiary; and although, as Hume notes, Bolingbroke's force is attenuated through print, Montagu figures him, with the greater anxiety, as a viva voce orator, preaching upon the public stage, bidding the mob to be lawless. She grasps, in effect, that in Georgian England the republican idiom of manly and charismatic oratory, of drums, cannons, and patriotic death, represents a desire not so much for political stability as for illicit ecstasy. Illumined here is the dark

11. Quoted by John Bender, 239. Chap. 8 of Bender's *Imagining the Penitentiary* (231–52) has a general relevance to my discussion of Pope's aesthetic, as *The Dunciad* aetiolates the visual impact of punishment in a manner analogous to the withdrawal of real executions from the public gaze during the course of the eighteenth century.

12. As Ronald Paulson has noted, Renaissance etymology commonly linked "satire" to "satyr": "Since satire was thought of as uttered by a crude satyr, half man and half goat, it followed that the subject matter should be appropriate to him" (*Fictions of Satire* 89).

side of the republican eloquence memorialized not only in *The Craftsman* but in *The Dunciad.* The difference between Pope and Bolingbroke, however, is that Pope proves more binocular than his mentor; indeed, he evidently shares some of Montagu's distrust of the Opposition agenda. *The Dunciad*, as we have seen, is largely about the end of the ancient ideal of eloquence—an end ushered in not only by Billingsgate, Henley, and the opera but also, ironically, by Pope's own polite style. Pope commemorates an irretrievable eloquence in meters unmeet, acknowledging and perhaps even applauding the loss he nonetheless regrets. Thus, while Pope may finally cast his lot with well-mannered security, he keeps one eye on the civic sublimity left behind—for "even in its Ashes live its wonted Fires."

## Gray's *Elegy*: Between Civic Applause and the Cool Vale

The last sentence of the preceding section is of course adapted from the *Elegy Written in a Country Church-Yard*, a poem Gray began to write at about the time that Pope was dying. And in that poem Gray includes his own memorial stanzas to the passing of eloquence. The speaker surveys the "mould'ring heaps" of the country churchyard and reflects,

> Some village-Hampden, that with dauntless breast
> The little Tyrant of his fields withstood;
> Some mute inglorious Milton here may rest,
> Some Cromwell guiltless of his country's blood.
> Th'applause of list'ning senates to command,
> The threats of pain and ruin to despise,
> To scatter plenty o'er a smiling land,
> And read their hist'ry in a nation's eyes,
> Their lot forbad . . .
>
> (57–65 [stanzas 15–17])

Far from simply illustrating the thesis that peasants have unrealized potential, these stanzas evince a positive fascination with the Commonwealth period in its own right. Ironically, the heroes of the Commonwealth, in contrast to the peasants buried in the churchyard, have fulfilled not only their own but their nation's potential. The peasants underground did not become Hampdens and Miltons; but Hampden and Milton do, if only for a moment in Gray's lines, become Cato and Cicero. This reading is sanctioned, of course, by the fact that Hampden, Milton, and Cromwell assume the roles that Gray's Eton manuscript initially assigned to "some Village Cato," "some mute inglorious Tully," "some Caesar." Yet even without this fact of compositional history, the reader of the *Elegy* cannot but feel that the romance of Gray's Commonwealth men derives from their realization of classical republican prototypes: "th'applause of list'ning senates" and reading one's own "hist'ry in a nation's eyes" are clearly aspects of the ideal scene of ancient eloquence rather than some native English phenomenon. (Although it is not absolutely clear whether or not the lines on captivating the senate are in apposition to those on the Commonwealth, one certainly feels them to be.)

Hume's "Of Eloquence" had looked back to the Commonwealth as a time when a virtuous republican eloquence might have arisen; in the later *History of England*, by contrast, Hume treats the civil wars as an epoch in which eloquence may indeed have glimmered in England. Significantly, Hampden's speaking is singled out for praise: "Many were the virtues and talents of this eminent personage. . . . Affability in conversation; temper, art, and eloquence in debate; penetration and discernment in counsel" (5:407). Gray, too, grants eloquence to Hampden, as well as to Milton—the latter, presumably, in his role as Commonwealth apologist. Whether as a historical observation or as a self-consciously mythopoeic act, the *Elegy* suggests not only that ancient eloquence was indeed revived in England but that its revival was worth any subsequent, or even consequent, carnage. For "th'applause of list'ning senates" more or less drowns out any echo of the "country's blood" that carries over from the previous line; Gray clearly gives the final word to the glory of deliberative eloquence, and leaves us with an impression of republican heights.

That which kept the buried villagers from attaining such heights is not primarily their poverty but rather the more basic fact that by 1751 such heights had not existed in England for a

hundred years. The speaker of the *Elegy* surveys not only a country churchyard but an England in which the vivid assemblies of
the Commonwealth have passed away and the opportunities for
eloquence have all departed. If Gray's complaint had been, in
William Empson's well-known formulation, "that eighteenth-
century England had no scholarship system or *carrière ouverte
aux talents*" (4), then he would have shown the villager's inability
to rise to the status of plenipotentiary or prime minister. But his
point, rather, is that there is no public position now worth rising
to—or at least no position suitably exalted to be addressed in the
empyrean of poesy. There are at present no listening senates to
command with oratorical thunder, regardless of whether one is an
obscure rustic or, to recall Thomson's roughly coeval lines, the
earl of Chesterfield himself. Thomson's prophetic wish in "Winter" is only to "hail [Chesterfield] on some glorious day, / When
to the listening senate, ardent, crowd / Brittania's sons" (679–81).
But by the late 1740s, and to a poet of Gray's less than sanguine
disposition, it must have appeared evident that the day would
never come. The grand old line of eloquence was dead and gone—
it's with Hampden in the grave.

   It's no surprise that eloquence, as the very poetry of politics,
should win the retired man of letters' benignly idiotic admiration. Nor is it surprising that the poet's show of enthusiasm
should be met coolly in less susceptible quarters. John Young's
essay on the *Elegy*, published in 1783, takes issue with what he
perceives to be the "Whiggish prejudices" of Gray's fifteenth stanza: "Of liberty, the idea is so vague, and the dimension so little
settled, that the poet may make of it what he will. The fairy land
is all his own; and, however fantastic his combinations may be,
he will not want for fantastic hearers to listen to his tale" (40).
Young, however, goes on to qualify this assertion: the Poet might
have *once* been able to entice his readers with the fairyland of
liberty, but now Gray's "insertion . . . is *ill-timed.*"

   The zealots of rebellion are no longer heroes in Britain; and the
   appeal to the admiration of the Reader, is thrown back in the author's face. Other times have brought with them other principles.

*Tempora mutantur & nos*—. The subtle distinction, and inflammatory reasonings, that countenanced the shedding of sanctified blood,
are no longer allowed a hearing. . . . In the sixteenth stanza is con-
tained more, in the way of allusion to these heroes and their transactions; but allusion, at which criticism finds herself obliged to stop
short. Though the evil temper of the times *did* enable them to
"command the applause of listening senates," which is poetical
language, for being well heard in the House; yet, with what propriety, can any of them be said to have "scatter'd plenty o'er a smiling
land?" Of a land that has its ploughshare turned into a sword, the
plenty is not great; nor was England drest in smiles in the time of
the great rebellion. (41–43)

Young views Gray as an overtly republican incendiary whose
stanzas lament the demise of the Commonwealth and the commanding eloquence of its leaders.[13] His reading of Gray is, I would
contend, overstated but not unfounded. The *Elegy* is, in part, a
genuine political lament. The poet's readiness to write his own
epitaph is partly motivated by a desire to pass away with a passing
civic ideal, one "no longer allowed a hearing." The Elegist, that is,
would vanish along with England's vanished potential for sublime
eloquence. With the fairyland of liberty now curtained close from
future view, he casts his lot with death. In this gambit, he bears
some resemblance to Gray's other alter ego, the eponymous hero
of *The Bard*, who proudly announces his preparedness "to triumph, and to die" (142). The Bard's triumph comes, however,
with the prophetic accession of the patriot queen, Elizabeth—a
future that is already long past for the Elegist. His fate, by contrast, seems to be only to die, wishing without foretelling a restoration of liberty and eloquence.

But if Gray is thus torn between desiring liberty and desiring
death, Young, for his own part, would much rather be given death
with little ado. He complains that Gray has "suffered his mind to
be bewildered with politicks," while in "a work such as this, the

13. Young's indignation amply demonstrates that the political tone of Gray's
*Elegy* is more complex or ambivalent than a reader such as Richard Sha allows: for
Sha, the Elegist simply "aligns himself with those [like Soame Jenyns] who would
keep the poor ignorant in order to preserve the [post-Interregnum] social hegemo-
ny" (344).

sentiments ought to be such as every heart will return. . . . Death generalises the specifications of political tenets. The Grave takes in all parties" (43–44). The paradox of Young's critique, however, is that it makes Gray say what he should by borrowing the very sentiments his poem indeed expresses. Surely Gray recognized "th' inevitable hour," and taught that "the paths of glory lead but to the grave." Commanding the applause of senates is merely one such path and one that, viewed *sub specie aeternitatis*, is little worth admiring. Indeed, in a poem that never strays for long from the sight of "mould'ring heaps," it cannot but seem inevitable that the scene of eloquence should pass. And surely it is not only Empson who, in a Whiggish mood of his own, has been "irritated by the complacence in the massive calm of the poem" (5). Many of us, at times, have wished Gray less Stoic, less ready to let death level all political distinctions.

Thus, *pace* Young, Gray's note of sympathy for the Commonwealth hardly constitutes either a call for its revival or a protest against the present constitution of England. His contested stanzas read less like the rantings of an inveterate Whig than a student's reflections on sufficiently ancient history. And in the stanzas that follow, Gray, while not repudiating England's republican moment in the way that Young would have liked, expresses some relief at its being over. The grander civic virtues always run the risk of lapsing into equally grand crimes, such as wading "through slaughter to a throne" in the manner of a Caesar or Cromwell. And worshiping "Luxury and Pride / With incense kindled at the Muse's flame" (71–72) most likely refers, in context, to cultivating an eloquence vicious in style and intent. Gray admits that even the scene of eloquence can sour, and even senates be led where they ought not venture.

Rather than court such revolutions, Gray appears, finally, content with nothing happening at all. (This mode of bathos will be familiar to readers of Hume's "Of Eloquence.") He seems most satisfied with the unextraordinary lives of the hamlet's rude forefathers:

> Far from the madding crowd's ignoble strife,
> Their sober wishes never learn'd to stray;

> Along the cool sequester'd vale of life
> They kept the noiseless tenor of their way.
>
> (73–76 [stanza 19])

The noiseless tenor of the rustic represents a path to the grave that is considerably less circuitous than that of the statesman-orator, and perhaps Gray is far enough beyond the pleasure principle to appreciate such directness. But although the sequestered vale of life may finally imply an ache for death itself, in juxtaposition to four stanzas on civic tumult it most immediately signifies the desire to be among quiet things, far from the urban arenas of eloquence. The poem, that is, contrasts the "noiseless" tenor of the rustic's life with the *sound* of senates and madding crowds.

The relative silence of rural life is employed to rebuff the aspirations of oratory—especially its tendency to stir up commotion and, indeed, change of any sort. The topos is a common one; Pope, for example, writes from the vantage of his Twickenham retreat to prick the bubble of William Murray's parliamentary eloquence:

> The Greatest can but blaze, and pass away.
> Grac'd as thou art, with all the Pow'r of Words,
> So known, so honour'd, at the House of Lords;
> Conspicuous Scene! another yet is nigh,
> (More silent far) where Kings and Poets lye;
> Where MURRAY (long enough his Country's pride)
> Shall be no more than TULLY, or than HYDE!
>
> (*Epistles of Horace* 1.6.47–53)

Rural life serves the urban man of letters as, among other things, a memento mori. And just as the quiet of the grave and the inconspicuous scene of rustication may mutually figure one another, so may either serve as an antidote to the orator's stirrings.

Edmund Burke employs both; in the *Reflections*, the silence of bovine life and that of death equally serve as symbols of durability—indeed, of a sullen resistance to change that counters the "pert loquacity" of the French Revolution's sympathizers:

Because half a dozen grasshoppers under a fern make the field ring
with their importunate chink, whilst thousands of great cattle, reposed beneath the shadow of the British oak, chew the cud and are
silent, pray do not imagine, that those who make the noise are the
only inhabitants of the field. . . . We [English] know that *we* have
made no discoveries; and we think that no discoveries are to be
made, in morality; nor many in the great principles of government,
nor in the ideas of liberty, which were understood long before we
were born, altogether as well as they will be after the grave has
heaped its mould upon our presumption, and the silent tomb shall
have imposed its law on our pert loquacity. (*Reflections* 181–82)

Burke presents a world in which eloquence, where not deleterious, is at best unnecessary, because certain moral and political
prejudices have been universally shared time out of mind. They
have the inevitability of death itself; like death, they appear simply to be true. As strange as Burke's mute pastoral may seem to
us, it is finally not far removed in spirit from the *Elegy*'s nineteenth stanza. In both, voices inciting political change (for better
or for worse) fall upon fields without echoes. The speakers of both
passages would seem to concur with Shakespeare's Bassanio that
"paleness moves more than eloquence."

Of course, in Burke's case, the eloquence he deplores would
seem to run in his veins; "silence" may perhaps be a genuine
aspiration, but it is certainly a rhetorical effect, punctuating with
its very name Burke's torrential voice. Gray, by contrast, finds
silence truly congenial. He effectively buries a strident eloquence
not only in the substance but in the very style of his lines. From
his very first stanzas, he imitates the increasingly hushed quality
of a country twilight, from the tolling of the Curfew to the drowsy
tinklings of the beetle. And not only does the Elegist seem at
home amid rural silence but the still, sad tinklings of his voice
grace a setting that is well nigh invisible as well. Of course, a poet
does not look to a country churchyard at night to inspire a tale of
variegated sound and vision, but this fact should not mask exactly
how comfortable Gray feels with dimming the light of these
senses. Indeed, he possesses an antivisual streak that is, while
less conspicuous, probably more sincere than Pope's.

Thus, his representation of the civil wars, England's last great moment of sound and gesture and the poem's one moment of potential violence, turns out to be not quite a representation at all but rather a trick of presdigitation. The senates, threats, and triumphs that stanza 16 sketches are promptly withdrawn at the close of Gray's period, which reveals all this to be that which "Their lot forbad." The already generalized images of both stanzas 15 and 16 are finally images under erasure; as Henry Weinfield expresses it, "the subjunctive mood" of this section enables Gray to "convey presence and the 'presence of absence' simultaneously" (79). According to Weinfield, this "absence-presence dialectic" is epitomized in the oxymoronic "mute inglorious Milton," "a representation of what cannot literally be represented, a name for that which is nameless" (96).[14] Whereas Burke deals in parables and apostrophes, Gray's use of oxymoron allows for an aesthetic that is visually and emotionally etiolating—or, to use Hume's term, polite.

I believe that Gray looked upon the ages of a more rousing eloquence as dead and buried. While they may garner the passing tribute of a sigh, he hardly wishes wholeheartedly for their revival, despite Young's rather excited fears. As Gray's *Common Place Book* suggests, the progress from a rude to a polished age necessarily entails the loss of the old scene of eloquence: "The Province of Eloquence is to reign over minds of slow perception & little imagination, to set things in lights they never saw them in—to engage their attention by details & circumstances gradually unfolded, to adorn & heighten them with images & colours unknown to them to raise & engage their rude passions" (quoted in Jack, 139). But these rude and volatile passions have passed with the hamlet's "rude Forefathers"; other times have indeed, as Young observes, brought with them other types of men. And Gray's style is obviously suited to new polite tastes rather than to the province of eloquence.

14. I have found parts of Weinfield's dialectical reading of the poem illuminating, and I agree in part with his basic contention that the *Elegy* is "committed to the Enlightenment ideal of progress" (xviii). As I argue, Gray is at least content to see the disturbances of the past comfortably buried and duly elegized. My ear is not, however, sensitive to the millenarian overtones that Weinfield hears in the close of the poem (148–49).

F. R. Leavis wrote of mid-eighteenth-century poetry, generally, that "it keeps its monotonous tenour along the cool sequestered vale of Polite Letters" (105). Although the *Elegy* is excepted from this verdict—for having, as Leavis remarks, "social substance" (106)—Leavis's terms, ironically, would hardly have seemed obnoxious to Gray. He would have been particularly pleased with the stylistic connotations of "cool." And he knew that however much a cool style might be enjoyed in isolation, it needed to be cultivated in company.

## Mr. Yorick's Journey from Oratory to Conversation

Much of the comedy of Sterne's *A Sentimental Journey* turns precisely on confronting the ardor of the old eloquence with the coolness of polite manners. By 1768—the date of the novel's publication, and the era of Hume's late, "polite" revisions of "Of Eloquence"—the term *eloquence* was no longer an Opposition shibboleth; having lost much of its affective power as a high Ciceronian ideal, it was quickly becoming synonymous with mere public speaking, a practical concern of academies, elocutionists, and provincials who sought to rise in metropolitan London. In Sterne's world, however, thinking in terms of ancient oratory still occupies a variety of English gentlemen, all of whom the reader is invited to love if not admire. I refer chiefly, of course, to Walter Shandy, whose knack for impromptu oratory is well known; indeed, we may perhaps best understand Walter as an ironic vestige of the Country party's ideal of the retired Patriot, who is as well versed in the ancient orators as in the ancient constitution. But what is less commonly observed is that something of Walter's eloquence adheres to Mr. Yorick as he begins his sentimental journey.

A third of the way through the novel, however, Yorick's oratorical edge vanishes—rubbed off, in effect, by the more transactional universe of France. For midcentury Britons, France typifies a society in which commerce flourishes alongside civility; to some degree, it represents what Michael Ignatieff calls "a market society of strangers" (120), an international concourse where manners compensate for unfamiliarity. In Fielding's *Amelia*, Billy Booth maintains, "Being a stranger among [the French] entitles you to the better place, and to the greater degree of civility" (25); and even Rousseau, though best known as an advocate of classical polity, has his paragon Julie declare, "That which prepossesses all foreigners [is] the gracious hospitality of the French and the general manners of their society" (*Nouvelle Héloïse* 184).[15] Yorick himself initially apprehends that "the balance of sentimental commerce is always against the expatriated adventurer" (33), but he eventually finds himself, as a "poor stranger," admitted into conversation wherever he goes, from the shop to the theater (77–79). Yorick's good fortune may be attributed largely to a change in his own attitude toward the proper use of language and gesture; indeed, *A Sentimental Journey* may be read as Sterne's fable of the ways in which commerce, for better or for worse, supplants traditional forms of rhetoric with the new imperatives of polite style.

Yorick begins his adventures by playing the orator abroad, striking Demosthenic poses and expressing vehement passions. Inside the desobligeant in Calais, he eulogizes the cosmopolitan learning of England and apostrophizes the countrymen he has left behind: "It is an age so full of light, that there is scarce a country or a corner of Europe whose beams are not crossed and interchanged with others. . . . But there is no nation under heaven abounding with more variety of learning—where the sciences may be more fitly wooed, or more surely won than here—where art is encouraged, and will soon rise high . . . and, to close all, where there is more wit and variety of character to feed the mind with—Where then, my dear countrymen, are you going—" Yorick's speechify-

---

15. French manners were putatively introduced into England by Beau Nash: according to Goldsmith, "He first taught a familar intercourse among strangers at Bath and Tunbridge, which still subsists among them. That ease and open access first acquired there, our gentry brought back to the metropolis, and thus the whole kingdom by degrees became more refined by lessons originally derived from him" (3:288–89). For all the praise that manners might receive, however, they remained a bittersweet accomplishment in the eyes of many Britons—thus Charles Lamb wryly defines "good manners" as "an invention to take off the uneasy feeling which we derive from knowing ourselves to be less the object of love and esteem with a fellow creature than some other person is" (482).

ing recalls Zac Fungus's similarly stilted address to Commerce in *The Commissary,* a play produced three years earlier; in both, the comedy of the scene turns upon praising the fruits of commerce in a language that hardly shows the assimilative polish of commerce. Sterne, however, adds the fairly subtle touch of transplanting the *scene* of eloquence from the assemblies of men (even Zac, we will recall, commands a small audience) to a chaise that, as his note emphasizes, holds but one person. Eloquence, once the cement of civil society, has become an eccentricity, indeed a habit that is quite literally disobliging. (The disfavor of cigarette smoking in the 1990s provides a trivial but not altogether uninstructive analogy.)

On the other hand, Sterne broadens the comedy of the scene by appending the surprising reponse of Yorick's apostrophized countrymen: "—We are only looking at this chaise, said they—Your most obedient servant, said I, skipping out of it, and pulling off my hat" (36–37). It is an amusingly bathetic fall from the heights of apostrophe to the quotidian concerns of narrative, from the enthusiasm of eloquence to the mechanized routines of polite manners. Sterne knows before Yorick does that eloquence is out of place *sur la rue;* this (along with Yorick's steady tippling) goes far to explain the ironic discrepancy, especially at the novel's outset, between savvy author and naive narrator. We commonly speak of the "mock-heroic" mode of much eighteenth-century literature, but perhaps we need a more specialized term, the "mock-oratorical," to accomodate much of Sterne's comedy (and Foote's, et al.). For heroic oratory, no less than the other vitalities of the premodern hero, becomes suitable matter for amiable deflation in an age that would perfect a polite style.

Shortly after Yorick's embarrassment in the desobligeant, his oratorical reflexes are again made the occasion for Sterne's comedy of manners. Having determined to buy a different chaise from Monsieur Dessein, he suddenly becomes wary of the transaction, suspecting he will be swindled:

> I looked at Monsieur Dessein through and through—eyed him as he walked along in profile—then, *en face*—thought he looked like a Jew—then a Turk—disliked his wig—cursed him by my gods—wished him at the devil—

—And is all this to be lighted up in the heart for a beggarly account of three or four louis-d'ors, which is the most I can be over-reached in?—Base passion! said I, turning myself about, as a man naturally does upon a sudden reverse of sentiment—base, ungentle passion! thy hand is against every man, and every man's hand against thee—Heaven forbid! said she, raising her hand up to her forehead, for I had turned full in front upon the lady whom I had seen in conference with the monk—she had followed us unperceived—Heaven forbid indeed! said I, offering her my own— she had a black pair of gloves open only at the thumb and two fore-fingers, so accepted it without reserve—and I led her up to the door of the Remise. (39)

The scene neatly parodies not only apostrophe, but rhetorical action as well. Yorick raises his hand against an abstract entity his address has called into being, and frightens a gentlewoman who has in the meantime strolled over unnoticed. That Yorick subsequently takes her hand in his represents a transition from action to manners, from the old world of buskined address to the new world of easy social intercourse. In handing her to the Remise, he adapts himself to the mores of France. In abandoning rhetorical arts designed to seize the imaginations of large audiences, he also accommodates himself to the novelist's more intimate mode of representation. But whether Yorick's concession is to France or to the novel form—either of which may finally serve as a metonymy for the other—one point remains clear: his loose habit of sublime apostrophizing gives way to a code of manners predicated on the dispassionate containment of passion.

## The Logic of Double-Entendre

Of course, another source of Sterne's comedy is precisely his uncertain acceptance of polite pretensions. As *A Sentimental Journey* proceeds, it flaunts terms such as *commerce, conversation,* and the like, terms that, even as they figure in a panegyric on manners, acquire their own momentum of sexual connotation. Yorick, for his part, professes, "I have something within me which cannot bear the shock of the least indecent insinuation"

(108); his prudery (whether affected or not) serves to make the reader all the more sensitive to the sexual overtones enlivening his prose. Indeed, the language not only of commerce but of sensibility as well is practically inseparable from a pornographic idiom. Take, for example, the first "sentimental" exchange between Yorick and the Madame R***'s *fille de chambre*:

> —And what have you to do, my dear, said I, with *The Wanderings of the Heart*, who scarce know yet you have one? nor till love has first told you it, or some faithless shepherd has made it ache, can'st thou ever be sure it is so.—*Le Dieu m'en guard!* said the girl. . . . The young girl listened with a submissive attention, holding her sattin purse by its ribband in her hand all the time—'Tis a very small one, said I, taking hold of the bottom of it—she held it towards me—and there is very little in it, my dear, said I; but be but as good as thou art handsome, and heaven will fill it. (89–90)

The ribaldry in this scene—purses in need of filling, and so on—is of a fairly obvious sort. It becomes more interesting as it becomes more obscure:

> We stood still at the corner of the Rue de Nevers whilst this passed—We then stopped a moment whilst she disposed of her *Egarements de Coeur*, &c. more commodiously than carrying them in her hand—they were two volumes; so I held the second for her whilst she put the first into her pocket, and I put in the other after it.
> 'Tis sweet to feel by what fine-spun threads our affections are drawn together. (91)

These enigmatic "threads" may figure the bonds of sympathy, or even denote filaments in the "great SENSORIUM of the world! which vibrates, if a hair of our heads but falls upon the ground, in the remotest desert of thy creation" (141). Alternately, they may refer to the actual threads that bind the pages of *Les Egarements de Coeur*, or, indeed, any book at all, although the pun obviously works best with texts that cultivate the sensibility that draws us together. Finally, however, these "fine-spun threads" ask to be read on yet another level as pubic hairs, joining our affectionate organs—and so advancing the double-entendre of Yorick's earlier observations on the *fille de chambre*'s purse. This may seem a

fairly gratuitous joke, until one begins to work out its implications. For the double-entendres of *A Sentimental Journey* always
stress the quite serious point that sentimental commerce is a
polite restraint of the sexual passions that covertly fuel it. In
other words, sensibility *is* sexual sublimation.

Sex and sensibility thus operate both as opposites and as com-
plements in Yorick's narrative. They are not the same, even while
they are quite evidently just the same. Sterne finely polishes this
paradox of alterity and identitiy in the scene of "The Conquest,"
the final adventure (or nonadventure) between Yorick and the *fille
de chambre*. A series of mishaps has placed them both in more or
less recumbent positions on Yorick's bed:

> Yes—and then—Ye whose clay-cold heads and luke-warm hearts
> can argue down or mask your passions, tell me, what trespass is it
> that man should have them? or how his spirit stands answerable to
> the father of spirits, but for his conduct under them?
>
> If nature has so wove her web of kindness, that some threads of
> love and desire are entangled with the piece, must the whole web be
> rent in drawing them out?—Whip me such stoics, great governor of
> nature! said I to myself—Wherever thy providence shall place me
> for the trials of my virtue—whatever is my danger—whatever is my
> situation—let me feel the movements which rise out of it, and
> which belong to me as a man, and if I govern them as a good one, I
> will trust the issues to thy justice—for thou hast made us, and not
> we ourselves.
>
> As I finished my address, I raised the fair *fille de chambre* up by
> the hand, and led her out of the room—she stood by me till I locked
> the door and put the key in my pocket—*and then*—the victory
> being quite decisive—and not till then, I pressed my lips to her
> cheek, and, taking her by the hand again, led her safe to the gate of
> the hotel. (118)

The joke, of course, is that it is impossible to tell whether Yorick
is representing the conquest of his passions or of the *fille de
chambre*. Does he prove a feminized man of feeling or a womaniz-
ing Lothario?[16] Ambiguity prevails in the "threads of love," "the

16. The ambiguity of Yorick's conduct toward the *fille de chambre* may be read
as a reflection of the deeper quandary of the civilized male: as Carol Kay argues,

movements . . . which belong to me as a man," "the issues" of these movements, and so forth. Indeed, double-entendre supplies a full-blown counternarrative to Yorick's not implausible story of polite restraint.

In doing so, it effectively compromises the empirical realism of the novel, drawing it instead toward the ironic and antivisual modes of politeness we found in Swift, Pope, and Gray. For hearing double impedes one from seeing at all, at least in a steady or focused way; Max Byrd aptly compares Sterne's art of equivocation with "Wittgenstein's famous rabbit/duck drawing: the *coup d'oeil* sketch that flickers back and forth between two shapes so rapidly that the eye can never hold it to a single meaning" (105). Sterne's rigorously polite style blocks the reader's urge to identify (and identify with) simple images; it disenables him to simplify scenarios. If there is a lesson this style would convey, it may be to relegate single-mindedness beyond the pale of a modern social sphere. Simplicity of vision suits an ideal time when men were somehow integral and shadowless—like Demosthenes, standing erect under the hard Attic light. Impassioned gestures and bold apostrophes, fit for men like these, can only be out of place in the nuanced, bigendered world of the modern city. Here, polite persons must learn to sublimate, to maintain a double focus, to achieve a style that is distinct from the quickening of the pulse.

The section of *A Sentimental Journey* entitled "The Pulse" thematizes precisely this distinction. Yorick responds to the sustained "courtesy" of "the handsomest Grisset, I think, I ever saw":

Any one may do a casual act of good nature, but a continuation of them shews it is a part of the temperature; and certainly, added I, if it is the same blood which comes from the heart, which descends to the extremes (touching her wrist) I am sure you must have one of the best pulses of any woman in the world—Feel it, said she, holding out her arm. So laying down my hat, I took of her fingers in one hand, and applied the two fore-fingers of my other to the artery.—

though men competed with women for "the prestige of civilized sensitivity" (17), they also yearned for the prerogatives traditionally afforded them by a masculinist society—the rights of military and, I would add, sexual conquest (232–44).

—Would to heaven! my dear Eugenius, thou hadst passed by, and beheld me sitting in my black coat, and in my lack-a-day-sical manner, counting the throbs of it, one by one, with as much true devotion as if I had been watching the critical ebb or flow of her fever— How wouldst thou have laughed and moralized upon my new profession?—and thou shouldst have laughed and moralized on— Trust me, my dear Eugenius, I should have said, "there are worse occupations in this world *than feeling a woman's pulse."*— But a Grisset's! thou wouldst have said—and in an open shop! Yorick—
—So much the better: for when my views are direct, Eugenius, I care not if all the world saw me feel it. (75)

As Yorick feels the Grisset's pulse, that of his own prose subtly quickens; but still Yorick *acts* with suitable restraint, both in living and in recounting the moment. This tableau in the Paris shop is indeed so stylized that one may forget the eros that presumably motivates it; Yorick, for his part, pleads either its utter innocence or, more likely, its well-sanitized air in declaring, "I care not if all the world saw." To any passer-by—including, as it turns out, the Grisset's husband—the scene ought to represent a triumph of polished manners over the ruder throbbings of our nature. That a man must learn manners in situations such as this, amid the restraining presence of women, is the ostensible point of *A Sentimental Journey*, beginning with Yorick's encounter with the Lady in M. Dessein's coachyard. We have seen the same point made by Hume, whom Sterne met while in Paris and to whom he indeed tips his hat in *A Sentimental Journey*, calling him "a man of an excellent heart" (54).

## For and Against *Le Commerce des Femmes*

The "beautiful Grisset" not only fulfills a woman's duty in polishing men's hearts but instantiates as well the shaping influence of commerce upon polite culture. Steele's *The Spectator* no. 454, depicting a day's ramble through London, reserves particular praise for "the shops of agreeable females" in the Exchange; in the same vein, Yorick elaborates,

In Paris, there are scarce two orders of beings more different [than a shopkeeper and a shopkeeper's wife]: for the legislative and executive powers of the shop not resting in the husband, he seldom comes there—in some dark and dismal room behind, he sits commerceless in his thrum night-cap, the same rough son of Nature that Nature left him.

The genius of a people where nothing but the monarchy is *salique*, having ceded this department, with sundry others, totally to the women—by a continual higgling with customers of all ranks and sizes from morning to night, like so many rough pebbles shook long together in a bag, by amicable collisions, they have worn down their asperities and sharp angles, and not only become round and smooth, but will receive, some of them, a polish like a brilliant— Monsieur *le Mari* is little better than the stone under your feet— —Surely—surely man! it is not good for thee to sit alone—thou wast made for social intercourse and gentle greetings, and this improvement of our nature from it, I appeal to, as my evidence. (76)

Yorick offers a typically Whiggish tribute to the polishing effects of urban commerce. Indeed, he apparently associates politeness as much with *polir* as with polis; in this, he follows Shaftesbury's example: "All politeness is owing to liberty. We polish one another, and rub off our corners and rough sides by a sort of amicable collision" (1:46). For Yorick, these collisions may be of an economic or a purely social variety, but they are most effective when they occur between the sexes. (Tristram, indeed, praises the ennobling power of "that tender and delicious sentiment, which ever mixes in friendship, where there is a difference of sex" [*Tristram Shandy* 36].) Men have the most to gain from this commerce, tending as they do to remain "rough sons of Nature," while women appear—here as elsewhere in the novel (and the century's literature)—as habitués of social intercourse. Yet even *avant de commerce*, Yorick conceives of women as possessing a superior sensibility by nature. Thus, he declares to the somewhat salty Comte de B*** that he is interested not in the nakedness of women's bodies but in the "the *nakedness* of their hearts," apart from "the different disguises of customs, climates and religion": "I could wish . . . [to] find out what is good in them to fashion my own [heart] by" (108).

Finally, however, Yorick's ideal of woman marks but another discrepancy between narrator and author of *A Sentimental Journey*: for Sterne does not corroborate his alter-ego's notion of female exemplarity. No woman Yorick meets in France embodies his ideal *politesse de coeur* (114): the Grisset is not above charging him an extra livre on account of his sentimentality (78), and the *fille de chambre* who graciously receives his crown into her purse is not above suspicion in a text so laden with double-entendre. Yorick always seems satisfied with the women he meets, but the reader, though not perhaps any less indulgent toward human peccadillos, will nonetheless remark the difference between what Yorick professes to seek and what he is happy to find. And although Yorick takes pride in being "as weak [i.e., as lachrymose] as a woman" (45), we notice in the course of the novel that there is no woman so weak as Yorick—except, perhaps, for Maria of Moulines, whose derangement marks her as exceptional. In the normal course of things, effeminacy appears to be a male prerogative; Yorick at least affects it, and Captain Tobias Shandy unmistakably embodies it, in tandem with his "wound to the groin" (*Tristram Shandy* 48). French women are apt to have polished manners and amiable conversation, but they hardly attain to Sterne's nativist ideal of a sensibility that is authenticated by its very awkwardness, its patent dumbness.

In short, while *A Sentimental Journey* represents the commercial subversion of the old eloquence, it also suggests the shortcomings of the new commercial style.[17] Antique styles of eloquence seem antisocial, but the new social style courts insincerity. It also, to Sterne's greater dismay, risks homogenizing the characters of men. As Yorick explains to the Comte de B****:

17. Although Sterne partially conceives of true politeness as an internal quality in conflict with commerce and manners, this antagonism comes to fruition only in the sentimentality of the 1770s: it forms the basis of Charles Surface's opposition to Joseph in Sheridan's *School for Scandal* (1777) and of Harley's opposition to the world in Mackenzie's *Man of Feeling* (1771). Harley, like his aunt and like the "Ghost" writer who narrates the bulk of the novel, is positively alienated from the commercial world that his dwindling landed fortune will not allow him utterly to avoid. He is, moreover, devoid of *any* type of eloquence; his "remarkable silence" is a token of his "extreme sensibility" (10).

A polished nation, my dear Count, said I, makes every one its debt-
or; and besides, urbanity itself, like the fair sex, has so many
charms, it goes against the heart to say it can do ill: and yet, I
believe, there is but a certain line of perfection that man, take him
altogether, is impowered to arrive at—if he gets beyond, he rather
exchanges qualities, than gets them. I must not presume to say how
far this has affected the French in the subject we are speaking of—
but should it ever be the case of the English, in the progress of their
refinements, to arrive at the same polish which distinguishes the
French, if we did not lose the *politesse de coeur*, which inclines men
more to humane actions than courteous ones—we should at least
lose that distinct variety and originality of character, which distinguishes them, not only from each other, but from all the world
besides . . .
    The English, like ancient medals, kept more apart, and passing
but few peoples hands, preserve the first sharpnesses which the fine
hand of nature has given them—they are not so pleasant to feel—
but in return, the legend is so visible, that at the first look you see
whose image and superscription they bear. (114)

Preserved from the amicable collisions that France is famous for,
there are still "originals" among the English; their virtue lies in
being little capable of hypocrisy, as their rough surfaces tell all.
From a Menippean point of view, however, their attractiveness
lies precisely in their "distinct variety." While politeness (long
before television) threatened to homogenize even as it pacified the
world, the English comic mode came more and more to applaud
eccentricity. Oddballs proved the liberality of the overall British
system. The comedy of Sterne's properly English novel, *Tristram
Shandy*, concerns a whole family of originals who, aside from
exceptional moments of mute sympathy, preserve their first
sharpnesses by not really interacting at all.

## *Tristram Shandy*: The Comedic End of Oratorical Culture

While *A Sentimental Journey* represents Sterne's uneasy alliance with a rising cosmopolitan ideal of commerce, manners, and
women, *Tristram Shandy* contains his affectionate ridicule of an

older English ideal of the independent country gentleman. Up until the time of Pope's death, a chief desideratum of such gentlemen was (as we have seen) "eloquence": indeed, the very term was sent forth as a gadfly to sting the ministerial party. Sterne, who began his career as an apologist for the Court Whigs, takes his belated and tender revenge against the Opposition by rendering Walter's grand eloquence utterly harmless, even loveable in its impotence. Like Sir Roger de Coverley in *The Spectator* no. 2, Walter is all in all apt to be "rather beloved than esteemed"; by writing him into a comedy, Sterne effectively satirizes the past and lingering pretensions of the Country party. Thus, in party terms, whereas *A Sentimental Journey* serves, however qualifiedly, as a Whig panegyric to commercial progress, *Tristram Shandy* is a Whig satire in the tradition of Addison's de Coverley papers.

Wilbur L. Cross long ago noted Walter Shandy's resemblance to Philip Harland, the squire of Sterne's parish (Cross 65–66; cf. Cash 66–68, 90–91). Harland, a politically active Tory, was displeased that the vicarage should go to the nephew of Dr. Jaques Sterne, a prominent Whig politician; he was still more displeased when Laurence, on his uncle's behalf, wrote in support of Walpole's ministry party during the parliamentary elections of 1741– 42 (Cash 87–91). Sterne's own good-humored scorn for Harland, in turn, supplies a plausible motive for his portrait of Walter. Lewis Perry Curtis once meticulously distinguished between Sterne's early political career and his later novelistic achievement: "In 1741 Laurence Sterne . . . whose noblest study was mankind, was far removed from the interests by which he is known. . . . He was entangled in the mesh of artificial government, a man of society battling for society, a political theorist" (133–34). A considerable distance is indeed traversed between the *York Gazetteer* and *Tristram Shandy*, but, at the same time, the concerns of the political theorist are never *far* removed from those of the author, especially in the early chapters of volume 1.[18] And Curtis contradicts himself when he later explains that Samuel Johnson disliked Sterne's novels because, as he remarked to Bos-

18. As Cash notes, *Tristram Shandy*'s early chapters contain a more or less topical satire that loses prominence as the novel progresses, giving way to a more polite tone and a greater generality of reference (287–89).

well, he "hate[d] to see a Whig in a parson's gown" (136). Once a Whig, it would appear, always a Whig.

By the same token, Walter retains his ancient Tory mettle despite his former stint as a London merchant. He has, of course, been loath since before Tristram's birth to leave his ancestral estate of Shandy Hall. At the outset of the novel Walter is presented as a husband who adheres to strict domestic routines and as a political theorist wont to praise established rural ways. Indeed, he laments "the current of men and money towards the metropolis" and muses, "Was I an absolute prince . . . I would effectually provide, that the meadows and corn-fields, of my dominions, should laugh and sing;—that good cheer and hospitality flourish once more;—and that such weight and influence be put thereby into the hands of the Squirality of my kingdom, as should counterpoise what I perceive my Nobility are now taking from them" (33–34). He speaks on behalf of the squirearchy or, as he later calls it, the "country-interest"; he opposes the urban centralization of power seen in England since Elizabeth's reign and wickedly perfected in the France of Louis XIV. For although he is a Filmerian in regard to family governance, Walter is all for the gentry's "ancient liberties" in matters of state.

In outline, then, Walter is the very Country gentleman conjured by Bolingbroke's Opposition. The likeness is furthered by his attention to oratory, the putatively lost art whose revival the Patriots urged. But though they had advanced eloquence as a republican ideal, "there was not a subject in the world upon which [Walter] was so eloquent, as upon that of door-hinges"—notably, the squeaky hinges he will never find time to mend (147–48). For Walter, eloquence has become the purely domesticated means of (paradoxically) transcending the domestic. Thomson and Akenside invoke an eloquence that might assemble multitudes; oratory merely enables Walter to sequester himself in a decaying house. It guards him not only against the outside world but, as much as possible, against the descendental demands of both a manor house that is falling apart at the door hinges and window sashes, and a wife who minds the first Sunday of the month.

Walter is perhaps the midcentury's most notable orator, with his arguments *ad hominem* and *ad ignorantiam*, his epiphonema and erotesis, his adaptations of Socratic orations and his impromptu elegy to Bobby. "Persuasion hung upon his lips, and the elements of Logick and Rhetorick were so blended up in him . . . that NATURE might have stood up and said,—'This man is eloquent'" (37). And, as Tristram adds, Walter's eloquence is all the more impressive for owing nothing to the art of rhetoric: "He had never read *Cicero,* nor *Quintilian de Oratore,* nor *Isocrates,* nor *Aristotle,* nor *Longinus* amongst the ancients" (38). It is strange that a man so well versed in classical literature should have neglected all its authorities on rhetoric—unless we read the omission symbolically, as figuring Walter's dissociation from the classical political foundations of eloquence. "My father," writes Tristram, "was as proud of his eloquence, as MARCUS TULLIUS CICERO could be for his life, and for aught I am convinced of to the contrary at present, with as much reason" (246). But as Quintilian and nearly every neoclassical rhetorician contends, Tully took pride in his eloquence not (at least primarily) for its own sake but for the sake of the republic. Walter, quite to the contrary, represents oratory's retreat from a Ciceronian public sphere into an altogether private and eccentric milieu. In *Tristram Shandy,* "PATRIOT" is only the name of a horse that Walter has sold and subsequently forgotten the reason why (244).

As a comic character Walter's success derives from the loving detail with which Tristram reproduces and indeed *studies* his eloquence, deploying the Greco-Latin terms of rhetoric that his father presumably does not know. As Walter is an orator, so Tristram is a rhetorician: he names his father's figures, and observes the effects they have upon us. He takes explicit interest, for example, in the ways a figure such as aposiopesis acts and reacts upon the mind (70–72). Like his father, however, Tristram is also an orator, devoted to "the eloquence of the . . . fire-side" (87); finally, of course, his own copious oration is *Tristram Shandy* itself. Graham Petrie rightly suggests that, like Walter's, Tristram's style "is rhythmical and flowing, certainly, but it is not conversation; it is deliberate oratory" (487).[19] And behind Tristram's ora-

19. Petrie meticulously analyzes the arsenal of rhetorical figures employed by both Walter and Tristram, noting that "as with Walter, Apostrophe, Exclamation,

tory lies Sterne's, whose own genuine (if academic) *amor oratoris* shines through his creatures. As John Traugott argues, Sterne in *Tristram Shandy* "was a rhetorician and not a 'novelist.' . . . He argued to his readers, using their own responses as his illustrations" (xiii). Even the book's ostensible characters, according to Traugott, may best be understood as orator's prosopopoeias: "Walter, Toby, *et al.*, are his factors, are symbolic personifications. They make their entrances and exits according to the exigencies of the demonstration at hand" (48).[20]

As an extended oration, Tristram's book figures us as an audience, an assembly—though we remain a "community" merely of readers, reading sometimes to each other but more often alone, silent or quietly chuckling. Thus even while *Tristram Shandy* would effect a comedic inclusiveness, it recalls the loss of a truly political cohesion. It is no less ironic than perceptive, then, that Max Byrd relates the narrator's oratorical method to that of Demosthenes, as it is described by Longinus (chap. 22):

> He seems to invert the very order of his discourse, and, what is more, to utter every thing extempore; so that by means of his long Transpositions he drags his readers along, and conducts them through all the intricate mazes of his discourse; frequently arresting his thoughts in the midst of their career, he makes excursions into different subjects, and intermingles several seemingly unnecessary incidents: by this means he gives his audience a kind of anxiety, as if he has lost his subject, and forgotten what he was about; and so strongly engages their concern, that they tremble for, and bear their share in, the dangers of the speaker: at length, after a long ramble, he very pertinently, but unexpectedly, returns to his subject, and raises the surprise and admiration of all by these daring, but happy Transpositions. (Quoted in Byrd, 79)

---

Rhetorical Question, and Anthypophora [answering one's own question] are among the most frequent of the Narrator's rhetorical figures. But whereas Walter used them as a means of establishing his personality against the background of an audience, the Narrator uses them to build up a relationship *with* his audience, in order to involve them even more closely in the process of his narrative" (489–90).

20. Personally, I find it difficult to think of *Tristram Shandy* as anything but an oration after having seen it brilliantly staged as a one-man show by Stephen Oxley, at London's Finborough Theatre, 4 August 1990. Certainly no other eighteenth-century "novel" is so well suited to declamation.

Although Longinus affords a fitting description of Tristram's own formal methods, *Tristram Shandy* hardly possesses the pathos attributed to Demosthenes: few readers, I think, are apt to "tremble" for Tristram. Thus, while Tristram may be something of a Demosthenes *manqué,* a still more apt (if far less glorious) comparison is suggested by Richard Davies, who relates Tristram's "transpositional" as well as extravagantly metaphorical style to the "eccentric oratory" of John Henley (quoted in Reiman, 130). I would add, finally, that the narrator's affinities to Henley—or to Demosthenes—extend to a common appreciation of rhetorical action. One need only recall Tristram's well-known encomium to Trim's "dropping his hat upon the ground." Tristram concludes, "Ye who govern this mighty world and its mighty concerns with the *engines* of eloquence,—who heat it, and cool it, and melt it, and mollify it,—and then harden it again to *your purpose . . .* meditate, I beseech you, upon Trim's hat" (254).

Tristram urges the mighty to meditate on this instance of kitchen oratory because he knows—or at least knows the rhetorical topos—that the eloquence of the mighty is in sad disarray. He himself entertains Longinus's opinion that eloquence has woefully decayed since the collapse of popular government; indeed, it has declined so much that in the above passage the world's unacknowledged legislators appear to be huswives, whose "eloquence" is simply a power over penises. In this world in which the *oikos*—and, indeed, its most privy recesses—have replaced the polis as the stage of power, any other eloquence, including Tristram's own, will have little effect. He thus addresses the inefficacy of ancient eloquence in terms that are largely parodic but not a little rueful:

> It is a singular stroke of eloquence (at least it was so, when eloquence flourished at Athens and Rome, and would be so now, did orators wear mantlcs) not to mention the name of a thing, when you had the thing about you, *in petto,* ready to produce, pop, in the place you want it. A scar, an axe, a sword, a pink'd-doublet, a rusty helmet, a pound and a half of pot-ashes in an urn, or a three-halfpenny pickle pot,—but above all, a tender infant royally accoutred.—Tho' if it was too young, and the oration as long as Tully's second Philippick,—it must certainly have beshit the orator's mantle. . . .

> These feats however are not to be done, except in those states and
> times, I say, where orators wore mantles,—and pretty large ones too,
> my brethren, with some twenty or five and twenty yards of good
> purple, superfine, marketable cloth in them,—with large flowing
> folds and doubles, and in a great stile of design.—All which plainly
> shews, may it please your worships, that the decay of eloquence, and
> the little good service it does at present, both within, and without
> doors, is owing to nothing else in the world, but short coats, and the
> disuse of *trunk-hose.*—We can conceal nothing under ours, Madam,
> worth shewing. (135)

Tristram attributes the decay of eloquence not to the commonly
adduced political causes, but to the rather more mundane fact that
men no longer wear mantles, or even trunk-hose. The entire passage
culminates in a low-groan bawdy joke, but it is a joke that conceals a
serious reflection. In averring, "We can conceal nothing under our
[breeches], Madam, worth shewing," he demurely acknowledges
the loss of ancient eloquence's priapic energy. The ancient orators,
by contrast, had something to show, such as the "swelling . . . monstrous and gigantic" expressions that Hume remarked
in Cicero, and excused to his polite audience as "at least . . . giv[ing]
an idea of the stile of ancient eloquence" (*Essays* 101).

Like a caged fury, eloquence, no longer effective, becomes
merely diverting. Tristram aims simply to give us "somewhat to
make us merry with when the weather will not suffer us to go out
of doors" (46). His oratorical aspirations are wholly domesticated.
The English Demosthenes so ardently prophesied has arrived,
though not in a form that Bolingbroke or Pope or Gray would have
recognized. Rather than inspire civic virtue in men, the new orator is better suited, like Walter, to compose a "*chapter upon
sash-windows*, with a bitter *Phillipick* at the end of it, upon the
forgetfulness of chamber-maids" (269). For chambermaids, in ne-
glecting loose sash windows, allow them to fall upon the groins of
male children, rendering them domestic and more or less polite.
Inveighing against the loss of power will accomplish nothing, but
even pro forma display keeps the spirit alive. Thus Hume remarked in 1773, "The best Book, that has been writ by an Englishman these thirty years . . . is Tristram Shandy"—to which
he added, "bad as it is" (*Letters* 2:269).

# 4 Religious Eloquence: Hume on the Passions That Unite Us

James Boswell writes: "On Sunday forenoon the 7 of July 1776, being too late for church, I went to see Mr. David Hume, who was returned [to Edinburgh] from London and Bath, just a dying. I found him alone, in a reclining posture in his drawing room. He was lean, ghastly, and quite of an earthy appearance." In his last interview with Hume, Boswell attempts to make the "great Infidel" admit to a belief in a future state, or at least to some uneasiness concerning the prospect of annihilation. To Boswell's mortification, however, Hume "seemed to be placid and even cheerful" throughout their conversation. And in the place of any literature of Christian consolation, "He had before him Dr. Campbell's *Philosophy of Rhetorick*" (*Private Papers* 12:227–32).

Perusing a study of rhetoric may well seem a defiantly humanistic inquiry for one in extremis. Although Boswell does not comment on Hume's choice of deathbed reading, it does prompt him to introduce the subject of religion. Bringing to mind his "excellent Mother's pious instructions, [and] Dr. Johnson's noble lessons," he attempts to convince the philosopher to better mind his central self and eternal soul. But Hume remains "indecently and impolitely positive in his incredulity." We may suppose him eager to prove (in the words of his family shield) "true to the end" and thus happy to find in Boswell a foil for his own unflagging commitment to enlightenment. Boswell, ever a waverer, at last concedes, "I left him with impressions which disturbed me for some time." His afternoon endeavor to be *homo seriosus* had met with no success; but then what else could be expected from a visit occasioned by being "too late for church"?

The dying Hume, for his part, victoriously embodies what Richard Lanham calls "the rhetorical ideal of life." He may indeed be read as the type of Lanham's *homo rhetoricus*: pragmatic, shy of absolute convictions, and opposed to any type of zealousness (Lanham 1–8). Thus, to the degree that the values of rhetoric are Hume's own, Campbell's *Philosophy of Rhetoric* proves oddly analogous to the Bible that another dying man might hold to his breast. Of course, as we have seen in earlier chapters, Hume garnered from books of rhetoric not only an agile skepticism but also a rather more credulous tendency to believe in the scene of ancient eloquence: the orator's fabulous power to move and unite a political community in the grand manner of Demosthenes. However much Hume's enthusiasm for eloquence may have waned in the last two decades of his life, he still retained his verdict in "Of Eloquence" that "of all human productions, the orations of Demosthenes present to us the models, which approach the nearest to perfection."

In this chapter I hope to show that Hume not only regretted the power of Demosthenes but attempted in some way to salvage its purpose, its ability to bind people through a virtuous—and secular— appeal to their collective passions. The irony and perhaps the genius of Hume's endeavor is that it aims to preserve the coalescent power of eloquence in the very act of dissolving the bonds of religion. Hume would salvage the communal myths of rhetoric even as he rejects—indeed, in the very act of rejecting—those of historical religion. His own refutation of the "superstitious" belief in miracles and "a particular providence" is well known (*Enquiry concerning Human Understanding* secs. 10–11); I will argue, however, that he implicitly balances his critique of religious beliefs with an optimistic trust in the power of passional suasion.

Several of Hume's contemporaries do so overtly: Thomas Cooke's "Ode on the Powers of Eloquence" (1755), dedicated to William Murray, explicitly elevates the agency of eloquence over the exploded myth of divine intervention:

When Philip's gold with dire contagion ran
Thro all the states, and sap'd the heart of man . . .
Say, Murray, say, for thou can'st tell the pow'r
Which rous'd the nations in a perilous hour,
What dreams, what signs, what oracle, what god,
Mov'd the fierce Greeks to break the tyrant's rod?
No visionary forms by day or night,
No bleeding entrails, or propitious flight,
No answer from the groves, or delphic shrine,
No Pallas arm'd, but Eloquence like thine.

                                                    (lines 5–16)

And, with similar intent, John Quincy Adams interprets Aaron's role in the Book of Exodus as evidence of eloquence's superiority to wonder-working: "It was not sufficient . . . that the shepherd of his flock [Moses] should be invested with the power of performing signs and wonders to authenticate his mission, and command obedience to his words—the appropriate instrument, to appal the heart of the tyrant upon his throne, and to control the wayward dispositions of the people, was an eloquent speaker" (13).

Hume, however, knew that the needs of his age were different from those of the ancient polis or of the Israelites in the desert. The modern "orator" must establish consensus not primarily within the tribe but among a far more cosmopolitan community of men and women readers. In this new order, the old orator, Demosthenes or Aaron, would no longer do; the orator needs to be born again. The old myth must be given a new form. Thus, Hume's *The Natural History of Religion* strives to cement community by prompting a recognition of the passions that (like orators of the past) "actuate" us all—a recognition that is, ironically, a rejection of passion's untrammeled force. The polite community Hume would thus establish is, then, a tertium quid between Hellenic political community and the still more archaic— though, in Hume's own Britain, still more prevalent—nexus of religion.[1]

1. As David Womersley notes, midcentury Britain saw the arrival of a new spate of Christian apologists, "many fighting on the front of social utility, but others apparently motivated by an inner piety"; Hume in his letters comments on this development as a decline, remarking in 1765 that the English "are relapsing

## The *Ordo Cognoscendi* of Religion: Thinking in Figures

Warburton, disquieted by Hume's project, asked, "Would not the *Moral History of Meteors* be full as sensible as the *Natural History of Religion?*" (*Remarks* 15). Although he did not, presumably, expect an answer, we may nonetheless formulate one. Discounting revelation, Hume reasonably deduces religion's origins from two "natural" scenarios—man in nature, and nature in man. The former, as we shall see, is man dramatically situated in a precivilized setting, a rude and unpredictable "state of nature." The latter—nature inside of man—is the gale of passion.

As James Collins aptly notes, Hume's essay constitutes a "passional analysis of religion" (30). We need first recall that "passion" served as a more technical term in Hume's day than in our own. Lord Kames supplies a typical definition: "An internal motion or agitation of the mind, when it passeth away without desire, is denominated an *emotion*: when desire follows, the motion or agitation is denominated a *passion*" (*Elements* 1:41). A *sentiment*, in turn, is a "thought prompted by a passion" (1:451). As Kames's mechanistic terms suggest, the passions operate as forces of attraction and repulsion in an implicitly Newtonian system of human nature. Accordingly, passions are routinely invoked in contrarieties such as hope and fear, love and hate, sympathy and antipathy, liberality and avarice; for Hume as for his contemporaries, the self tends to be defined by, in Annette Baier's phrase, "the fiery circling of our successive passions," the alternation of opposed motions that cannot converge (145).

Of course, the analysis of the passions traditionally belongs to the domain of rhetoric. Book 2 of Aristotle's *Rhetoric* attempts to determine "the means . . . by which passions are excited in the breast, and are allayed" (2.11.7), in order to assist the aspiring orator in understanding the psychology of his audience. Aristotle's practical anatomy of the passions flourished once again in

---

fast into the deepest stupidity, Christianity & ignorance" (107–8). Paul Langford concurs that "there was a growing sense in the 1750s and 1760s that the tide of deism had been turned," and he dubs William Warburton "the literary lion of the day" (467–68).

numerous rhetorics of the eighteenth century. Campbell's *Philosophy of Rhetoric*, for example, contains a substantial section, Aristotelian in scope, on how to engage the passions (77–98). Still more comprehensively, Lord Kames characterizes his entire *Elements of Criticism* as a treatise on "the economy of the human passions," or the manner in which passions function in literature and the forms of rhetoric (1:193). Indeed, the only rhetoric of the period that precludes an analysis of the passions is Pope's *Peri Bathous*: as its narrator remarks, "It may be expected, that like other critics, I should next speak of the passions: but as the main end and principal effect of the bathos is to produce tranquillity of mind . . . we have little to say on this subject" (chap. 9).

The irony of Pope's demurral here is accentuated by the intense interest in the passions that he and his contemporaries express everywhere else: indeed, during the course of the century the analysis of the passions transcended its practical origins in classical rhetoric, exfoliating into the psychology of the ruling passion (Pope), the associationist analysis of complex passions (Hume, Hartley), the theodicy of the passions (Pope, Akenside), the passional foundation of morality (Shaftesbury, Hutcheson, Hume, Smith), poetic invocations of personified passions (the Wartons, Gray, Collins), and narrative enactment of passional agency (Richardson, Fielding). If, as Hume observed—and everyone else apparently believed—reason was to be the slave of the passions, it was important to know our passions reasonably well. All in all, this rather clinical attention served to sanitize the passions, allowing readers to view them as a mere technology, the motor of the human machine. And while the motor's basic efficiency merited praise, the strongly implied hope was that its freaks and sparks— its less reasonable firings—might be controlled or modified simply by recognizing them for what they are.

What was pursued, in other words, was a philosophical grammar of the passions—as well as of the rhetorical figures that serve as their reflections. The classically educated reader could hardly contemplate one without the other. For as Aristotle asserts, "The excitement of some passion" causes a person to depart from "ordinary" language (3.7.11); in an unbroken tradition, the Port Royalists claim, "The passions have a peculiar language, and are expressed only by what we call figures" (73). By consensus, the most conspicuous indexes of passion are apostrophe and prosopo-poeia—the twin pair that Quintilian classifies as "figures of thought" (9.2.38–39). Anthony Blackwall, for example, finds "an Excess of Passion, a Degree of Enthusiasm" in the "sublime fig-ure" of prosopopoeia (252). Similarly, Dumarsais holds that "there are, in truth, several figures which may only be used in the sub-lime style: such is the prosopopoeia" (6). Hume's essay "Of Elo-quence" does no more than register popular sentiment when it calls prosopopoeia and apostrophe the most "sublime" products of the imagination (*Essays* 100–101).

In Hume's *The Natural History of Religion*, the creation of the gods is neither more nor less sublime than the mental activity of apostrophe and prosopopoeia; these impetuous figures supply the purely formal principles of theogony. John Baillie credits *The Nat-ural History of Religion* with being the first work to put forward the principle that "theology should begin where faith itself begins and follow religion's own *ordo cognoscendi*" (103); I would argue, in turn, that for Hume the *ordo cognoscendi* of religion is specifi-cally an *ordo figurae*. Apostrophe and prosopopoeia elucidate reli-gion's cognitive origins, and vice versa. Indeed, Hume deems the figures of eloquence *homologous* to the concepts of religion, de-riving in common from an ancient and enduring moment of pas-sionate error.

Hume's primitive man—or "philosophically primitivized man," as James Collins puts it (36)—does not logically infer the existence of god from the regular design (or syntax) of nature, as seventeenth- and eighteenth-century natural theology contended. He is, rather, a prelogical creature, wholly governed by "wants and passions":

[A] barbarous, necessitous animal (such as man is on the first origin of society) . . . has no leisure to admire the regular face of nature, or make enquiries concerning the cause of those objects, to which from his infancy he has been gradually accustomed. On the con-trary, the more regular and uniform, that is, the more perfect nature appears, the more is he familiarized to it, and the less inclined to scrutinize and examine it. A monstrous birth excites his curiosity,

and is deemed a prodigy. It alarms him from its novelty; and immediately sets him a trembling, and sacrificing, and praying. But an
animal, compleat in all its limbs and organs, is to him an ordinary
spectacle, and produces no religious opinion or affection. (24–25)

Hume concurs with Burke's *Philosophical Enquiry into the Sublime and Beautiful* (a work that appeared in the same year as *The
Natural History of Religion* and that Hume commended as a
"very pretty treatise" [Mossner, *Life of David Hume* 394]) that the
"regular and uniform" aspects of nature—those appearances that
we are "familiarized to"—have a tranquilizing effect upon us. It
takes the obscurity and terror of "a monstrous birth" to rouse us
from our beautiful slumbers. We require the passion of fear or
self-preservation to open our eyes.

Accordingly, the concinnity of Hume's own prose here studiously mimes the shock of the sublime scene he envisions;
Hume, presumably, would have us share a portion of the primitive's fear, and an insight into the process by which deities are
born. Thus, while his description of the "regularity and uniformity" of nature is graced by a balanced period—"the more regular
and uniform, that is, the more perfect nature appears, the more
[the savage] is familiarized to it, and the less inclined to scrutinize
and examine it"—Hume shifts at the appearance of "a monstrous
birth" to an abrupt present-tense narration, in accord with Longinus's long-esteemed recipe for producing the rhetorical sublime
(chap. 25). Furthermore, the phrases "a monstrous birth" and "a
prodigy" are deliberately obscure, conjuring not only scenes of
malformed creatures but permitting thoughts of natural tumults,
the sudden and fearsome storms that Coleridge would call "a
mountain birth" in "Dejection: An Ode."

This combination of external monstrosity and the fear it in-
wardly inspires is what triggers the human propensities that give
rise to religious belief. Hume thus conceives of religious belief as
a secondary or complex passion, soluble into its component passions of fear and (to a lesser degree) hope, and dependent on external disturbance (27–31).[2] Yet while fear may be the ultimate

2. I am indebted to the work of Keith Yandell (see esp. 116–17) for sharpening
my understanding of Hume's analysis of religious belief. Yandell's rigorously ana-

cause of religion, its efficient cause is the speech act of apostrophe. Fear sets the savage "trembling, and sacrificing, and praying"; but only with the corollary act of "praying," or "asking," do the gods come into being. In Hume's primal scene of religion, the gods are given an ear before they are granted a face. Apostrophe gives birth to the gods who are supposed to have caused the "monstrous birth"; only after they are properly invoked do the gods then become the *personifications* of "unknown causes" (29).

Prosopopoeia is, for Hume, the inevitable result of our untutored propensity to "form some particular and distinct idea" of the various forces that act upon us:

> There is a universal tendency among mankind to conceive all beings like themselves, and to transfer to every object, those qualities, with which they are familiarly acquainted, and of which they are intimately conscious. We find human faces in the moon, armies in the clouds; and by a natural propensity, if not corrected by experience and reflection, ascribe malice or good-will to every thing, that hurts or pleases us. Hence the frequency and beauty of the *prosopopoeia* in poetry; where trees, mountains and streams are personified, and the inanimate parts of nature acquire sentiment and passion. And though these poetical figures and expressions gain not on the belief, they may serve, at least, to prove a certain tendency in the imagination, without which they could neither be beautiful nor natural. Nor is a river-god or hamadryad always taken for a mere poetical or imaginary personage; but may sometimes enter into the real creed of the ignorant vulgar; while each grove or field is represented as possessed of a particular *genius* or invisible power, which inhabits and protects it. Nay, philosophers cannot entirely exempt themselves from this natural frailty; but have oft ascribed to inanimate nature the horror of a *vacuum*, sympathies, antipathies, and other affections of human nature. (29–30)

Hume offers a thorough figural analysis of religion. He begins by noting our "universal tendency" to "transfer" qualities to objects that do not properly possess them. This act of transferrence

lytic work should, however, be complemented by Frank Manuel's historical survey of the neoclassical science of mythology, a study that well situates Hume's *Natural History of Religion* in the contexts of its time.

is precisely where, in all rhetorics, figuration begins. As Aristotle implied (and Lord Monboddo, for one, elaborated), all tropes are no more than a species of metaphor, a term that is variously Latinized—and hence Anglicized—as "translation," "transport," or, most commonly, "transference."[3] Hume accordingly establishes the general propensity to transfer qualities as the first principle of his analysis. Prosopopoeia is simply the more specific tendency to transfer to inanimate or abstract objects "human passions and infirmities" and "the limbs and figures of men" (30). And god-making, in turn, is only a specific instance of prosopopoeia.[4]

Hume's technical analysis of religion evidently serves a satiric purpose. He speaks as a connoisseur who finds personifications of "trees, mountains and streams" delectable in poetry but who is forced to note, with ironic understatement, that personification "may sometimes enter into the real creed of the ignorant vulgar." That is, while prosopopoeia may divert the enlightened mind, it provides the vulgar with a metaphysics. The same figures that the enlightened have cataloged for the purpose of rhetorical ornamentation enable the vulgar to posit reality. Put simply, the enlightened think *in terms of* figures, whereas the ignorant think *in* figures. As Gibbon would later remark, "Among a polished people, a taste for poetry is rather an amusement of the fancy than a passion of the soul" (1:249).

3. On metaphor as the genus of all tropes, see Aristotle, *Poetics* chap. 21; Monboddo 3:37–38. The earliest extant treatment of metaphor in Latin is found in the Pseudo-Ciceronian *Rhetorica ad Herennium* 4.34: "Metaphor [*translatio*] occurs when a word applying to one thing is transferred [*transferetur*] to another, because the similarity seems to justify this transferrence."

4. Eighteenth-century mythographers generally recognized prosopopoeia as the cornerstone of pagan or "poetical" religion. In "De L'Origine des Fables" (1724), Bernard Fontenelle anticipates Hume's view that the gods are the personified causes of nature's agitations: "To make sense of thunder and lightning, one represents a god with a human face [*un dieu de figure humaine*] hurling arrows of fire on us" (*Oeuvres* 2:388). Fontenelle's account of pagan myth corresponds in essentials to the considerably more elaborate "poetic theology" of Vico's *New Science* (1725; revised 1744). For Vico, the secular origins of god, conscience, and speech occur at the moment when a people see the thundering sky as a great, threatening body, which they name, in an onomatopoeic echo of the thunder, "Zeus" or "Jove" (secs. 447–48, 473–75). All distinctively human institutions are thus founded in a personifying speech act.

Midcentury theorists such as Kames and Priestley formally distinguished their culture's own taste for "rhetorical" personification from the "passionate," "serious," or otherwise credulous personifications of more primitive or vulgar minds (Kames, *Elements* 2:228–36; Priestley 254; cf. Jamieson 162–63). And Hume himself, in his review of William Wilkie's *Epigoniad* (his most extended piece of practical criticism), demonstrates a taste for woodenly self-conscious allegorical personifications. Wilkie's portrait of Jealousy—a goddess equipped with "arrows . . . of pointed steel / For sight too small, but terrible to feel," and so on—is praised by Hume as "a sublime beauty," "painted in the most splendid colours that poetry affords" (reprinted in French, 6:60–61). Perhaps the best we ourselves might say of Wilkie's allegorical art is that it shares the qualities that Hume in *The Natural History of Religion* attributes to "the god of poetry": it appears "elegant, polite, and amiable" (38). Presumably, what appeals to Hume is precisely Wilkie's control, the dispassionate eloquence with which he renders the passions.

Allegory itself, Hume knew, is as an orchestration of personification already a containment of its more primitive force; and thus he prefers the crafted stories of ancient polytheism (40) to the incandescent face of one God. For Hume, monotheism arises from nothing more than an aggravation of the passional impetus that accounts for all personification. While Hobbes as well as eighteenth-century deists held that monotheism, unlike the pagan religions, gloriously arises from man's rational speculation on the ultimate causes of the natural world (*Leviathan* 1.12), Hume, by contrast, maintains that monotheism merely issues from a "more urgent" fear, one that transfigures the original prosopopoeia of religion into something much more than human:

> It may readily happen, in an idolatrous nation, that though men admit the existence of several limited deities, yet is there some one God, whom, in a particular manner, they make the object of their worship and adoration. . . . Whether this god, therefore, be considered as their peculiar patron, or as the general sovereign of heaven, his votaries will endeavour, by every art, to insinuate themselves into his favour; and supposing him to be pleased, like themselves,

with praise and flattery, there is no eulogy or exaggeration, which will be spared in their addresses to him. In proportion as men's fears or distresses become more urgent, they still invent new strains of adulation; and even he who outdoes his predecessor in swelling up the titles of his divinity, is sure to be outdone by his successor in newer and more pompous epithets of praise. Thus they proceed; till at last they arrive at infinity itself, beyond which there is no farther progress. (42–43)

Hume presents monotheism, even of a sacred Hebrew variety (44), as the product of "eulogy or exaggeration"—that is, of hyperbole. The notion of an all-powerful god derives from imaginative exorbitance. Hume had suggested such a critique before; in his *Enquiry concerning Human Understanding* he argues that "the idea of God, as meaning an infinitely intelligent, wise, and good Being, arises from reflecting on the operations of our own mind and augmenting, without limit, those qualities of goodness and wisdom" (28). (Hume's source here is Locke's *Essay*, which describes the "complex Idea of God" as an "enlargement" of the mind's own ideas of reflection "with the idea of infinity" [2.23.33].) Elsewhere in the *Enquiry*, however, Hume more closely anticipates his later argument by attributing our conception of God's limitless power to "exaggeration and flattery" (146). *The Natural History of Religion* emphasizes—and politicizes—this point by comparing the infinite praise bestowed upon a supreme deity to the exaltation of "arbitrary princes" (43). Hume's analogy accords with the Renaissance commonplace that hyperbole is the courtier's trope (see Puttenham 202–3); through this analogy, Hume expresses his implicit distrust of the distortions practiced either by courtier or by celebrant. The politics of hyperbole evinces a dialectic of master and slave that Hume, in a spirt of polite equality, quietly deplores.

## Disfiguring the Deity

Apostrophe, prosopopoeia, allegory, hyperbole: these, then, are the philosopher's names for the formal principles of natural religion. The implied audience within Hume's text thinks in terms of figures, thus preserving an ironic distance from the modes of thought they deemed appropriate to less advanced stages of society. Hume's real audience, by the same token, would not necessarily be startled by his figural analysis of primitive superstition. But, as his contemporaries observed, the insinuation artfully couched in *The Natural History of Religion* is that all religion, Christianity not excepted, derives from the same scene of passionate error; that any and all figural conceptions of a deity evidence the narcissism of "barbarous, necessitous animals." William Rose noted in the *Monthly Review* (February 1757), "In his attacks upon the religion of his country, he acts not the part of an open and generous enemy, but endeavours to weaken its authority by oblique hints, and artful insinuations."

Still, even cautious readers were apt to find at least one unobjectionable sentiment in *The Natural History of Religion*: Hume's lament in his final chapter, "How is the deity disfigured in our representations of him! How much is he degraded even below the character, which we should naturally, in common life, ascribe to a man of sense and virtue!" (75). This complaint seems fairly designed to win the approval of moderate clergy, deist, and *philosophe* alike, and indeed it became a favorite extract from Hume's volume.[5] Many apparently shared Hume's distaste for the vulgar image of a vengeful and intractable deity. Just how "disfigured" the deity could be, when judged by polite standards, is evidenced by a pamphlet written against Hume in 1755.

*The Deist Stretched upon a Death-Bed, or a Lively Portraiture of a Dying Infidel* was published anonymously by Andrew Moir, a sympathizer of the Evangelical, or Highflying, party of the Church of Scotland.[6] In the pamphlet Moir "personates" the deathbed monologue of the "great infidel," David Hume. Realizing that he must die, the (implicitly converted) infidel trembles at the thought of God's exacting justice: "Must I then be arraigned before an injured angry judge, a powerful and incensed God?" He

5. Hume's sentence is cited approvingly by Caleb Fleming, "Three Questions Resoloved" 55; Pratt, *An Apology* 29. The sentiment Hume expresses hearkens back to Locke's *Essay* 1.4.16.

6. Mossner briefly notes Moir's pamphlet (343) in connection with the kirk's attempt to excommunicate the "three Humes" (David Hume; Henry Home, Lord Kames; and John Home, author of *Douglas*).

expects "a sentence insupportably severe, which inexorable Omnipotence, stimulated by just and infinite resentment, will put in execution, without the least abatement" (8–9). Amid such ruminations comes the truly gruesome period:

> Altho' all the devils, and fiery fiends of the infernal regions, were let loose upon me with redoubled fury; though their fury was exaggerated by their malice, and their malice belched out thundering cataracts of burning sulphur on me; tho' they lashed me with knotted whips of burning steel, then smeared my wounds with corroding fire, amidst the living steams of sulph'rous stench, and suffocating smoke, and that for myriad of ages, yet all this were nothing to the angry frowns of an irreconcileable God, consigning me over to eternal *vengeance*." (12–13)

One can hardly imagine a deity with a more malevolent face. Yet Moir was not alone in his wild imaginings: indeed, one may compare his style to the similarly vivid eloquence of Orator Henley's sermons, *The Pangs of Expiring Penitents*, and *The Atheist Tormented by Sure Prognosticks of* HELL FIRE (quoted in Midgley, 100–102).

But although the polite certainly viewed the God of hellfire as a disfigured deity, Hume's deeper implication is that the very act of figuration paradoxically "disfigures" the deity. (As Hume remarks of style in general, "too much ornament" proves a "disfigurement" [*Essays* 192].) Prosopopoeia—"giving a face"—is a disfigurement because there is no reason to assume that the supreme intelligence of the world (if there is one) possesses human form or intellect. *The Natural History of Religion* begins with Hume's (at least tactical) profession of rational belief in "an intelligent author" of nature (21);[7] what he proceeds to adumbrate, however, is a deity who is radically different from us: rarefied, inaccessible, and, by an implicit consequence, irrelevant.

7. James Noxon shrewdly attributes Hume's opening claim that his work concerns only the "foundation [of religion] in human nature," not the "foundation [of religion] in reason," to a "strategy of limited offensives": although *The Natural History of Religion* traces popular religion to its source in our "least estimable passions," it is the subsequent task of the *Dialogues concerning Natural Religion* to undermine a rational confidence in natural religion (174).

Yet there is still another level of irony in the sentence "How is the deity disfigured in our representations of him!" for "figure" may read not only as face but also as trope. The pun is inescapable in the romance languages: Dumarsais, for one, feels compelled to rationalize it, arguing for a logical relation between the term's two senses (1:7–8). Hume himself uses the term both ways. In the course of a paragraph he describes prosopopoeia both as an entertaining "poetical figure" and as the attribution of "limbs and figures" to the deities (29–30). To "figure" a diety, then, could mean either to bestow an appearance on an invisible power or, conversely, to render that apparent power fabulous.

By the same logic, "disfigured" may refer either to a marred appearance or to the loss of a fable's figural potency; this latter sense is clearly intended in Thomas Blackwell's observation that "[ancient mythology's] power is retrenched since its figures were effaced." An effaced figure is, for Blackwell, an allegory that has lost its power of "striking the fancy, and winning the Heart" (80–82). And what the mythic figures are, Hume would have the deity become. Hence the "disfigurement" of the deity may refer to nothing less than the demystifying exhibition of the deity's figural construction. And whereas in the Renaissance rhetoricians often conceive of figures as descending from heaven—Thomas Wilson calls the eloquent man "halfe a God" (11), and Donne ascribes the genius of figures to the Lord of the Testaments, "a figurative, a metaphorical God" (99)—Hume by contrast argues that figures merely ascend from the mouths of ignorant men. His analysis of the deity into figures of speech may thus be compared to Newton's reduction of the rainbow to prismatic colors; Keats, for one, could never view the rainbow with the same eyes again.

## Hume's Catachrestic Logic

In sum, Hume would "efface" the figures upon which religion depends, implicitly offering in their place a perfect lucidity of thought and expression. Viewed in this light, *The Natural History of Religion* evidently serves as an Enlightenment text, a contribution to the demythologizing of the world; for what do we mean by *enlightenment* if not, in the words of a sympathetic critic, a call for "a disenchanted universe, and an end to myth" (Crocker 340)? Indeed, even unsympathetic critics concur: "The program of the Enlightenment was the disenchantment of the world; the dissolution of myths and the substitution of knowledge for fancy" (Horkheimer and Adorno 3).

But are there no new figures within enlightened discourse? Was the Enlightenment truly free from myths of its own? To use a phrase that even "philosophers cannot entirely exempt themselves from" (*The Natural History of Religion* 30), what "fills the vacuum" left by the absented gods? A familiar modern answer is that in eighteenth-century literature, "abstract personifications . . . feebly replaced the gods" (Engell 252). As Bertrand Bronson notes, "Although the age might derive excitement and pleasure from the new revelations of science, men were temperamentally no more 'scientific' then than at other times: they needed to humanize their abstractions and generalizations" (147). The "humanized abstractions" of the eighteenth century are most obviously the incarnations of human passions that populate its odes and moral poems, and indeed its prose narratives—to these I shall turn shortly. First, however, I would like to glance at a subtler mode of personification that inhabits Hume's writing.

*The Natural History of Religion* replaces the disfigured deity with "the regular face of nature," the face that "a barbarous, necessitous animal . . . has no leisure to admire" (24). It is a face that Hume, by contrast, consistently admires. Monstrous births may make an impression on the minds of the vulgar, but Hume presents himself as ultimately capable of admiring the beautiful regularity of nature. In his role as rational theist, he contends that the god of the enlightened is a purely intellectual inference from the orderly design of nature. How purely intellectual, however, can a "face" ever be? A certain sensuality clings to "the face of nature"; the phrase feels too palpable to be reduced to sheer argument. In rhetorical terms, we may label that "face" a catachresis verging on personification.

But though "the face of nature" is an accepted poetic locution from Homer to Thomson, it is not a face that one often sees. Poets typically represent the face of nature as veiled or obfuscated, hid-

den beneath storms, or clouds, or night. The tradition begins with
Homer:

> As when in the sky Zeus strings for mortals the shimmering
> rainbow, to be a portent and a sign of war, or of wintry
> storm, when heat perishes, such storm as stops mortals'
> work upon *the face of the earth*, and afflicts their cattle,
> So Athene shrouded in the shimmering cloud about her
> merged among the swarming Achaians, and wakened each man.
>
> (*Iliad* 17.547–52; emphasis mine)[8]

Pope's translation of these lines is too loose to be telling, but
elsewhere he conjures the face of the waters covered by "a gen'ral
Darkness": "The Waves scarce heave, the Face of Ocean sleeps"
(*Iliad* 7.71–73).

Throughout the eighteenth century poets liberally invoke "the
face of nature" or, somewhat more characteristically, "the face of
things." In *The Seasons* (1746), Thomson describes a winter night
in which "in sable cincture, shadows vast, / Deep-ting'd and
damp, and congregated clouds, / And all the vapoury turbulence
of heaven / Involve the face of things" ("Winter" 54–57). Of a
snowfall at sunset, he writes, "Earth's universal face, deep-hid,
and chill, / Is one wild dazzling waste, that buries wide / The
works of man" (238–40). And in summer, "sober evening" sends
shadows "to close the face of things" ("Summer" 1647–54). Similarly, Thomas Warton's "Pleasures of Melancholy" (1747) presents nature's face well-hid:

> Yet not ungrateful is the morn's approach,
> When dropping wet she comes, and clad in clouds,
> While thro' the damp air scowls the louring south,
> Blackening the landscape's face, that grove and hill
> In formless vapours undistinguish'd swim . . .
> Fix'd in th'unfinished furrow rests the plough:
> Rings not the high word with enliven'd shouts
> Of early hunter: all is silence drear;
> And deepest sadness wraps the face of things.
>
> (135–52)

8. "The face of the earth" is a stock translation of Homer's *cthon*; the phrase is
retained in both the Loeb and the Lattimore translations of the *Iliad*.

The conventional image of nature's cloud-wrapped face even enters into Hume's little-known lines on the countenance of a beloved "Clarinda":

> Tell me, Clarinda, why this scorn,
> Why hatred give for love?
> Why for a gentler purpose born,
> Wouldst thou a tyrant prove?
> Why draw a cloud upon that face,
> Made to enslave mankind?
> Why through your lip does thunder pass,
> Those lips for love designed.[9]

Indeed, so prevalent did the veiled face of nature become that Hurd, in his "On the Idea of Universal Poetry" (1766), interprets it as a metaphor for the act of poetry itself: "For [poetry's] purpose is, not to delineate truth simply, but to represent it in the most taking forms; not to reflect the real face of things, but to illustrate and adorn it" (*Works* 2:8). Hume, however—unlike the poet, the lover, or the barbarian—professes in *The Natural History of Religion* to see "the regular face of nature," unadorned by clouds or catastrophes. Unveiling the face of nature, he offers a lucid or "enlightened" personification of natural order.

## Pathopoeia in Enlightened Prose

Though he gives external nature a face, Hume is still more concerned to animate aspects of man's inner nature. Indeed, our irresistible passions come to life in his prose, albeit as shadowy beings:

[The] first ideas of religion arose not from a contemplation of the works of nature, but from a concern with regard to the events of life, and from the incessant hopes and fears, which actuate the human mind. . . . It must necessarily, indeed, be allowed, that, in order to

9. Three manuscript poems attributed to Hume are reproduced in John Hill Burton 1:228–31. J. V. Price maintains that the poems "are undoubtedly Hume's" (164).

carry men's intention beyond the present course of things, or lead
them into any inference concerning invisible intelligent power, they
must be actuated by some passion, which prompts their thought
and reflection; some motive, which urges their first enquiry. . . . No
passions . . . can be supposed to work upon such barbarians, but the
ordinary affections of human life; the anxious concern for happi-
ness, the dread of future misery, the terror of death, the thirst of
revenge, the appetite for food and other necessaries. Agitated by
hopes and fears of this nature, especially the latter, men scrutinize,
with a trembling curiosity, the course of future causes, and examine
the various and contrary events of human life. And in this disordered scene, with an eye still more disordered and astonished, they
see the first obscure traces of divinity. (27–28)

As Hume here describes it, human nature is a congeries of passions that incessantly "actuate," "prompt," "urge," "work
upon," and "agitate" us. To borrow a term recalled by Henry
Weinfield, Hume employs "what the sixteenth-century rhetorician Richard Sherry called *pathopoeia*: 'whereby the passions of
the mind . . . are personified.'" Weinfield proceeds to argue that
passion "is treated as an external agency for the perfectly legitimate reason that it exerts a real impact on human beings: the
individual who succumbs to it becomes caught up in forces beyond his control" (64).

The question that remains, however, is to what *degree* Hume's
passions take on an external agency. Certainly we are not likely to
envision them rising up from his page in full iconic regalia; Hume
is careful to distinguish his quasi-personifications from the full-
blown visualizations of vulgar religion. Still, eighteenth-century
readers possessed, in Chester Chapin's phrase, "a 'ready' allegorical imagination" and were apt to turn to shape the abstractions
they encountered on the written page (59). Hume could count on
an audience whose rage for personification would take fire with
relatively little detail. According to Bertrand Bronson, the verbs
that actively qualify Hume's train of passions might of themselves indicate the presence of personification (126): thus for the
eighteenth-century reader even grammar, that ideal mirror of logic, betrays a propensity toward prosopopoeia.

Accordingly, *The Natural History of Religion* brings before us,

"as in a great theatre," a polite pageant of personified passions
(28); hope, fear, diffidence, terror, and melancholy are all part of
Hume's passion play. He personifies not only these causative passions but causation itself (that relation which famously eludes
reason in book 1 of the *Treatise*) is figured as procreation in his
closing proverb: "Ignorance is the mother of Devotion" (75). Yet it
is with still more zest that Hume's *History of England* (1754–62)
presents a panoply of "actuating" passions and estates—among
them zeal, ambition, composure, society, solitude. Witness
Hume's description of Cromwell's anxious last days: "Of assas-
sination likewise he was apprehensive, from the zealous spirit,
which actuated the soldiers. . . . Fleetwood, his son-in-law, actuated by the wildest zeal, began to estrange himself from him. . . .
[Cromwell's] fatal ambition had betrayed him. . . . All composure
of mind was now for ever fled from the protector. . . . Society
terrified him. . . . Solitude astonished him" (6:104–5).

The relentless determinism of Hume's style is set in relief by
the contrasting sensibility of Cowley's *Discourses*, the one source
on Cromwell's character quoted at length in the *History*. Cowley's rhythms are panegyrical:

> What can be more extraordinary than that a person, of private birth
> and education . . . should have the courage to attempt and the abili-
> ties to execute so great a design as the subverting one of the most
> ancient and best established monarchies in the world? That he
> should have the power and boldness to put his prince and master to
> an open and infamous death? . . . Cover all these temerities under a
> seeming obedience to a parliament. . . . Trample too upon that par-
> liament, in their turn. . . . Erect in their place the dominion of the
> saints. (6:107–8)

As Cowley continues to recount Cromwell's achievements, he
piles on a daunting list of active verbs: Cromwell has the "power
and boldness" to "give reality . . . suppress . . . set himself
up . . . overcome . . . serve . . . command . . . overrun . . . sub-
due," and so on. Cromwell heroically acts and acts again, in full
possession of his own passions and virtues. The disparity between
Cowley's sense of heroic agency and the *History*'s overwhelming
determinism must have proved amusing to Hume, who notes

dryly that Cowley's picture of Cromwell smacks of "the marvellous" (6:108).

Thus, in both Hume's natural and political histories passion is
the demiurge that impels or "actuates" us. But by something
more than coincidence, the term *actuate* also appears in the period as a predicate of the orator. Condillac writes of the power of
classical eloquence to "agir si puissamment sur l'âme des audi-
teurs"; in Thomas Nugent's translation, the ancient orators
"powerfully actuated the minds of their hearers" (208). That eloquence and passion should be equally capable of actuating us is
not surprising, because eloquence was theorized as being primarily an appeal to the passions. In a sense, eloquence *is* passion, once
removed: it works on us indirectly, by inciting our passions to
impel us immediately. Of course it was lamented that eloquence
no longer fulfilled this task; but the loss of eloquence was rather
bittersweet than bitter to an age that was never certain whether it
wished to be ancient or modern. One of its most profound attempts to reconcile an ideal past with an uncertain future—to
glance both forward and backward—lies precisely in its psychology of passion. Passion, as it was theorized by the moderns, takes
on the work anciently assigned to eloquence.

Quite simply, personified passions act as the guiding orators of
a modern ideal of community. The nature of that community
being broadly social rather than narrowly political, the passions
provide the perfect cosmopolitan substitute for the necessarily
parochial appeal of the orator. Our passions actuate us in common, as equals, across boundaries both regional and national.
This is the lesson not only of Hume but of the early novelists as
well. Fielding in particular luxuriates in imagining the individual
as a puppet of the passions shared by all. George Eliot famously
remarks that Fielding "seems to bring his arm-chair to the pro-
scenium" and address his reader, as it were, face to face (*Mid-
dlemarch* 2.15); but Fielding himself lets us know that, far from
being the true orator here, he is only the handmaiden to passions
that "are the managers and directors of this theatre" of common
life (*Tom Jones* 1:328).

Fielding indeed insists on the agency of the passions to the
exclusion of other personified abstractions: thus, while Martin

Battestin notes that *Tom Jones*'s mock-Homeric churchyard brawl draws upon the first battle scene of the Greek and Trojan armies in the *Iliad* (4.490–511, Pope trans.), I would add that Fielding significantly transforms the presiding personifications of Homer's passage, "flight" and "discord," into a confederacy of passions—"fear," "envy," and the bathetic "love of fun" (1:178–79). Throughout his novels, love advocates, and honor endeavors to vindicate and pity to mitigate, while pride and revenge often speak just as loudly: it is not merely Lady Booby who is subject to the psychomachia of "opposite Passions distracting and tearing her mind [in] different ways" (*Joseph Andrews* 36; cf. 68, 218). A still more dramatic denial of individual agency occurs in *Amelia*, in which the fatalistic Billy Booth uses the pronoun *I* and the names of passions interchangeably as the subjects of his sentences (70–71), thereby emptying his own individuality, quite graphically, into a common reservoir of passion. As Sterne's Yorick says, his good deeds accrue to "the passion—not myself" (57); as passion blesses him with anonymity, so it follows that "there is not a more perplexing affair in life to me, than to set about telling anyone who I am" (109). For we are all together.

Of course, eighteenth-century authors always assume that membership has its price. Clifford Siskin, in the course of arguing, much as I do, that personifying the passions at once assumes and instates an ideally unified community, does well to note that Augustan texts in fact address the personified qualities shared by a very limited number of people—that is, the elite that reads Augustan texts (379). As Alan McKenzie states with admirable directness, "The passions had always been most effectively articulated by and for a narrow band of the social structure" (18). This elite community corresponds to what I would call the polite: those who are actuated in common not so much by raw passion as by the civilized recognition and refined echo of the less circumspect feelings of others. Polite society seeks to unite itself through shared passions it would outwardly restrain. Ideologically, this myth of secret sharing may be prompted by the loneliness of market society; it may respond to the sorrows of private readers, each in his or her own home; it may, too, respond to the threat of a London mob actuated not by a classical vocabulary of

passions but, in Alexander Wedderburn's indignant phrase, "actuated solely by the word Wilkes" (quoted in Rudé, 173).

   Politics and political economy do not, however, entirely explain
the comfort that polite writers derive from a common domain of
actuating passions. Surely part of that comfort comes from the
relief it brought to a universe in which at least some people were
publicly losing their religion—though few so publicly as Hume.
Lukacs may exaggerate in quipping, "The novel is the epic of a
world that has been abandoned by God" (88), but it is no over-
statement to call *The Natural History of Religion* the rhetoric of a
world abandoned not only by God but by the orator—or rather,
abandoned by a God who formerly had extirpated the orator. For
Hume, in *philosophe* manner, accuses Christianity of disrupting
an ancient oratorical tradition founded on the union of religious
and political virtue. According to Hume, it is one thing for Demosthenes to swear "by the *manes* of those heroes" who died at
Marathon and Plataea (*Essays* 100); it is quite another to believe
in the "supreme government and administration" of a despotic
God (*The Natural History of Religion* 33). Whereas Judeo-
Christian scripture is apt "to sink the human mind into the lowest submission and abasement," the hallowed spirits and traditional deities of ancient polytheism tend to encourage "activity,
spirit, courage, magnanimity, love of liberty, and all the virtues
which aggrandize a people" (52). The rise of Christianity signaled
the end of civic virtue as the ancients, and the Enlightenment,
understood it. Even in the *Poems of Ossian*, Macpherson in his
role as "editor" contends that the Fingalian era of virtuous pagan
heroism ended with the ascendance of Christianity in the fourth
century (40–44).

   The common agency of the passions thus serves, if only for
those versed in polite letters, as an escape from the Christian
millennium and a ghostly evocation of the secular bond of the
ancient polis. Indeed, the polis, and not the city of God, represents, in Carl Becker's phrase, "the heavenly city of the
eighteenth-century philosophers." The type of unified community associated with the ancients may have been irretrievably lost
to politics, but the psychology of the passions attempts its re-
trieval at the level of theory, while enlightened prose attempts its

re-creation among a sphere of readers—for, as an essay on eloquence in the *Edinburgh Magazine* (March 1785) puts it, "what
was formerly done by the tongue, is now performed by the press"
(228). Thus the signal service of both the passions and writing
about the passions is to bind persons together, and to do so in the
manner not of Paul but of the more ancient orators—in the manner, finally, of Demosthenes.

## Campbell Reads Hume's
## Philosophical Rhetoric

Having touched upon the role of pathopoeia within a broad
economy of eighteenth-century thought, let us once again return
to focus on the exemplary writings of David Hume. The question
I would ask is this: did eighteenth-century readers appreciate
Hume's debt to the ideals of ancient oratory? How aware were
Hume's contemporaries of the Demosthenic nostalgia that lie
behind the cultivation of polite community? In response I would
maintain that by 1776 George Campbell, for one, had recognized
the scene of ancient eloquence underlying so much of Hume's
thought. As Lloyd Bitzer demonstrates, Campbell indeed bases
his own psychological analysis of effective speaking on terms and
concepts derived from Hume's theory of belief. He is able to do so,
I shall argue, precisely because in Hume's *Treatise* the general act
of "perception"—like the more specific force of passion in *The
Natural History of Religion*—is personified as the action of an
orator upon a community of minds. That is, Hume, in describing
the impact of perceptions (some but not all of them passions)
upon the mind, implies an analogy with the orator's impact upon
an audience: in particular, with Demosthenes' impact upon the
Greek polloi. Drawing upon the descriptions of Demosthenic eloquence in classical rhetoric, Hume grants perceptions the "force"
and "vivacity" necessary to "persuade" the assembled capacities
of the mind.

Hume's theory of belief is properly a psychology of belief, although Hume does not use the term. (It was introduced into English by David Hartley). According to Hume, all belief is essen-

tially irrational: it derives simply from the "vivacity" with which
a given perception strikes the mind. Hume writes, "Thus it appears, that the *belief* or *assent*, which always attends the memory
and senses, is nothing but the vivacity of those perceptions they
present; and that this alone distinguishes them from the imagination. To believe is in this case to feel an immediate impression of
the senses, or a repetition of that impression in the memory"
(*Treatise* 86). We believe in our impressions, as we feel or remember them, because of their "superior force and vivacity" to the
"mere fictions of the imagination" (85).

Yet though we always believe in our impressions, we only
sometimes believe in our "ideas." As Hume defines them, ideas
originate as the fainter representations of our original perceptions. Ideas can, however, be compounded and arranged by the
"feigning" imagination, as they routinely are in works of art and
"vulgar" superstition. Thus we can have an idea of a fire-
breathing dragon, or an ill-visaged deity, without actually having
seen or felt one. We are not bound, however, to believe in such
ideas; nor is it indeed likely that we will believe in a fire-
breathing dragon in the same way we believe that fire burns. According to Hume, "Impressions always actuate the soul, and that
in the highest degree; but 'tis not every idea which has the same
effect" (118).

An idea is vivified, or made to approximate the force of an
impression, either by a trick of nature or by a device of art. Chief
among naturally induced beliefs is our inclination to associate
causes and effects; chief among the artificial means of procuring
belief are the methods of oratory. Having stated that "belief must
please the imagination by means of the force and vivacity which
attends it," Hume conversely argues "that belief not only gives
vigour to the imagination, but that a vigorous and strong imagination is of all talents the most proper to procure belief and
authority. 'Tis difficult for us to withhold our assent from what is
painted out to us in all the colours of eloquence; and the vivacity
produc'd by the fancy is in many cases greater than that which
arises from custom and experience" (122–23). Hume proceeds to
assert that a speaker's "fire and genius," or simply "a blaze of

poetical figures and images," will suffice to allow "any shadow of argument" to procure our "full conviction" (123).

The distinction I have drawn between naturally induced and artificially imposed belief is, however, often blurred by Hume's rhetorical practice. He tends, for example, to describe our naturally determined beliefs as "persuasion": thus he concludes his discussion of belief with the contention (or solace) that despite any "sceptical doubt" the reader may have acquired from perusing the *Treatise*'s first book, "an hour hence he will be persuaded there is both an external and internal world" (218). Although Hume may be right, he begs the question of agency: who is doing the persuading here? What force proves more encompassing than both the "external and internal world"? Logically, it can only be perception itself that persuades us to believe in the veracity of our impressions, in real existences, in cause and effect. That we believe in anything at all is the effect of the sheer persuasiveness of our perceptions. Perception serves as the *non plus ultra* orator. Plato criticizes oratory for producing only belief (*pistin*), not true knowledge (*episteme*) (*Gorgias* 454e); but for Hume, our knowlege of matters of fact is always and only belief, and belief is simply an effect of persuasion.

John Richetti has indeed commented upon the manner in which Hume rhetoricizes belief: "Impressions persuade or irresistably enforce belief by their vividness. Hume's terms are strikingly aesthetic. . . . The epistemological process takes place within a naturalistic psychology that resembles a rhetorical situation: our ideas are 'representations' of impressions, copies that are more or less vivid; we are persuaded to belief not by argument but by image and forceful sequence" (*Philosophical Writing* 208–9). Richetti's assertions would, however, be still more forceful—that is, believable—were he to elaborate on the intellectual-historical context of Hume's terms. For Hume borrows his distinctive phrases—"force," "vivacity," "liveliness," "strike"—from classical rhetorical descriptions of the scene of eloquence. Longinus praises the characteristic "force" (*bia*) of Demosthenes's oratory (chaps. 12 and 34) and notes the orator's ability to "strike" (*hubrizo*) as when an opponent "strikes you with his fists, when he strikes you like a slave" (chap. 20).

These terms—filtered through Quintilian's and Cicero's insistence on the *vis* of sublime eloquence (*Institutio Oratoria.* 2.15.22; *De Oratore* 2.44.187)—flourished in French neoclassical rhetorical theory. Dumarsais, for one, speaks of "la vivacité . . . la force" of figurative eloquence (1.11); Condillac speaks of "la force" and "le vif langage" of ancient eloquence, and its corresponding ability to actuate an audience (*Oeuvres* 1:235–36, 260). For Rousseau, speech itself anciently possessed a "force" and "vivacité" that served as the prop and product of liberty (*Essai* 197). Hume knowingly echoes this rhetorical vocabulary in maintaining that "Lord Bolingbroke's productions . . . contain a force and energy which our orators scarcely aim at" (*Essays* 108).

Thus, the reason that Campbell could easily adopt the main concepts of Hume's epistemology into his *Philosophy of Rhetoric* is that, as he was well aware, those concepts originate in the discourse of rhetoric. And by (re-) applying Hume's terms to the powers of persuasive speech, Campbell effectively uncovers the theory of oratory that informs Hume's science of mind. Lloyd Bitzer notes that the notion of "vivacity" in particular "establishes the historical link between Hume and Campbell": "Vivacity, or the liveliness of ideas—according to Hume the essential quality of belief—became in Campbell's theory the essential quality in effective rhetorical discourse: the success of nearly every instance of discourse hinges upon the creation of 'lively and glowing ideas'" (4–5). Campbell follows Hume in holding that sense, memory, and imagination possess decreasing amounts of vivacity; accordingly, the orator's task is to find ways to enliven the ideas raised in the imagination to such a degree that they resemble the perceptions of the senses and the transcripts of the memory. As Campbell phrases it, the orator must "make the ideas he summons up in the imaginations of his hearers, resemble, in lustre and steadiness, those of sensation and remembrance" (81).

Particularly conducive to vivacity are the tropes of synecdoche, metaphor, metonymy, and personification—the last of which, Campbell remarks, makes such a strong impression on the mind that it "hath [itself] come to be termed vivacity, or liveliness of style" (299–310). With this comment Campbell returns us to the familiar theme of sublime prosopopoeia, recalling the terms in which rhetoricians—and Hume in "Of Eloquence"—praise the stylistic flourishes of *On the Crown* and *Against Verres*. As Vincent Bevilacqua points out, Campbell's concept of vivacity is not entirely indebted to Hume but "rests also on principles in the tradition of Longinus that by the mid–eighteenth century were commonplace in English aesthetic theory" (11). I would add, quite simply, that neither is Hume's concept of vivacity entirely or even chiefly his own but rests squarely within that same rhetorical tradition.

In short, for Hume forceful and vivacious perceptions strike the mind in a manner analogous to strong oratory's operation upon an assembly. It follows, associatively, that Hume's theory of perception imitates rhetorical accounts of Demosthenes' impact upon an audience. When Hume figures perception as oratory, he thus figures it—however loosely or suggestively—as Demosthenes. And by the same figurative logic, the percipient mind is analogous to a democratic assembly, susceptible to forceful persuasion. Indeed, Hume's preferred analogue for the mind is "a republic or commonwealth," for in both mind and republic "the several members" are assembled according to constitutive principles of association (*Treatise* 261). Like the republican assembly, the mind is at once a location and a collection of perceptions.[10] And at any given moment, the mind is struck by a particular perception that dominates the assembled perceptions of the mind; this striking perception issues from an assembly to which it belongs and to which it will soon return. We may "see" behind Hume's metaphysics the ghostly outlines of the orator who speaks before the republic, a citizen among citizens, privileged only for the moment of his speech—for a moment, *primus inter pares*. In Hume, no less than Plato, statecraft proves the mirror of soulcraft.

10. As Robert Anderson observes, Hume tends to equivocate between an image of the mind as a mere collection of perceptions, and one as a substantial container or location for perceptions (1–35). Hume's metaphor of the mind-as-republic serves to resolve this inconsistency, as the republican assembly is at once a place *and* a collection of individuals.

## Hume's Deathbed Revisited

Received opinion holds that the *Treatise* aims at "a total negation of myth," or the revelation of a world in which "meaning
does not transcend the boundaries of perceptual actuality" (Kolakowski 64–65). Yet as we have seen, Hume styles his philosophy of mind as an allegory of eloquence. Despite its positivist air,
the *Treatise* in fact establishes that our understanding can be
understood only in terms of vivifying analogies drawn from classical politics. As Thomas Blackwell notes in his *Letters concerning Mythology*, "There be no science unadorned by allegory"
(285): Hume's science of mind is evidently no exception—nor is
his science of religion. Indeed, while *The Natural History of Religion* criticizes the old gods for being no more than the personifications of "unknown causes" (30), the essay in turn personifies
the passions in order to explain the motivating causes of human
action. Thus, although Hume may explode the content of religion, he remains within the realm of figural representation identified as the provenance of religion.

With this paradox in mind, Hume's choice of deathbed reading
appears still more apposite than it did at first. Surely his mortal
serenity, which so disturbed Boswell, belies the lurid predictions
of Andrew Moir's "Deist Stretched Upon a Deathbed." Hume
indeed dies contentedly without a Bible on his breast. But in a
less obvious and perhaps less heroic sense, Campbell's *Philosophy of Rhetoric* serves, for Hume, as a surrogate Bible insofar
as the figures of rhetoric represent the limit of his own understanding. Hume sought as a critic of religion to satirize the passionate, credulous figures of the unenlightened mind; it is thus
ironic that his own scientific analyses of motivation and credibil-
ity resort to a rhetoric of personification. At first glance, Hume
seems to smile condescendingly at the figures he discovers in
both the religious imagination and the "striking and palpable"
protrusions of classical eloquence ("Of Eloquence"); he would
ostensibly rid polite culture of both the error and the class vulgarity of residual figurative thinking. Yet in throwing superstitious figures out the front door, he admits a subtler set of
animating figures at the rear. His own prosopopoeia mirrors, how-

ever darkly, religion's prosopopoeia, as passion replaces the God he would extirpate.

Of course, Hume's mirroring act differs significantly from the spontaneous figures of his rude theists. Unlike these "necessitous animals," Hume appears to *recognize* the necessity of metaphor; he knows what he is doing, even if he does not have perfect liberty to do otherwise. Hume indeed reflects upon the very process of necessity, and minimally personifies that process in terms of the "passions." As an act of figuration that doubles back on its own birth, his manipulation of the passions tends to undermine any naively literal understanding of that which passion has wrought. Hume inherits this reflective strategy, I believe, from Lucretius's *De Rerum Natura*, the other book he pondered upon his deathbed.

As Boswell recounts in his final interview with Hume: "I asked him if the thought of annihilation never gave him any uneasiness. He said not the least; no more than the thought that he had not been, as Lucretius observes." Hume alludes here to a couple of passages in the third book of Lucretius: "Rest assured, therefore, that we have nothing to fear in death. One who no longer is cannot suffer, or differ in any way from one who has never been born. . . . Look back at the eternity, that passed before we were born, and mark how utterly it counts to us as nothing. This is a mirror that Nature holds up to us, in which we may see the time that shall be after we are dead" (122–25). Hume's Lucretian allusion represents a certain liberation from the syntax of passions— the pathology, so to speak—established in *The Natural History of Religion*. Moreover, it implies a source for Hume's ethos of imperturbability in the Lucretian mirror that deflects our primal passions. Lucretius suspends fear, a forward-looking passion, by showing it a mirror—that is, by showing it the past. Thus the prospective is balanced against the retrospective, fear against the unmemorable, projection against nothing that is not there and the nothing that is.

Lucretius would short-circuit passion's proper course, taming its charge on behalf of our tranquil interests. In a related move, Hume employs Lucretius's mirror to explain the moment at which a society of passions becomes one of interests: in book 3 of the *Treatise*, the savage within us beholds himself in a mirror, and "the least reflection" transforms his avidity, "by an alteration of its direction," into a regard for private property. Hume holds that "this alteration must necessarily take place . . . since 'tis evident, that the passion is much better satisfied by its restraint, than by its liberty, and that by preserving society, we make much greater advances in the acquiring [of] possessions, than by running into the solitary and forlorn condition, which must follow upon violence and a universal license" (492). The savage best serves his self-interest by seeing it for what it is; as in all polite scenarios (as well as Freud's ego mechanisms), reflection ultimately abets the passion it restrains. And for Hume, serving a passion that reflects back upon itself makes better sense than bowing to the pathetic fallacy that calls itself God.

Thus Hume's necessary fictions—the face of nature, the rostrum of passions, the voice of perception—recoup the form but not the innocence of earlier poetic thought. In a type of the Romantic "circuitous journey home," Hume returns to where we began, in order to recognize the place for the first time.[11] Concerning our rude beginnings, we might say with Nietzsche: "All rhetorical figures (i.e., the essence of language) are logically erroneous reasonings. It is with them that reasoning begins!" (*Das Philosophenbuch* 132). And, albeit ironically, it is with them that enlightened reasoning ends.

11. M. H. Abrams elaborates on the "circuitous journey" or "Romantic spiral" in *Natural Supernaturalism*, drawing upon Hugo von Hoffmannsthal's description of the idea: "Every development moves in a spiral line, leaves nothing behind, reverts to the same point on a higher turning" (184).

# 5 Eloquence and Manners in Macpherson's *Poems of Ossian*

Hume and his contemporaries admired the ancient ideal of eloquence, but they did so, finally, with a certain charitable irony. Despite their neo-Longinian praise of captivating speech, they nonetheless considered the republican orators—and, a fortiori, the spokesmen of religion—to be outside the pale of an evolving ideal of perspicuity and polite restraint. Hume's essays on eloquence—"Of Eloquence" and *The Natural History of Religion*—variously manage to accommodate both praise and blame, emulation and rejection of the figurative imagination. Demonstrating what Madame de Boufflers calls his "divine impartiality," Hume delicately balances admiration and contempt for the sublime strokes of ancient speech.[1] Indeed, faced with an inheritance perceived as no less vain than glorious, all a modern could honestly do was differ from himself. Hume's countryman James Macpherson managed to transcend irony, however, by denying his modernity. In becoming an ancient, he revealed the dilemma of eloquence and manners to be inessential. He offered a world in which passionate eloquence proves compatible with the

1. The Comtesse de Boufflers's appreciation of Hume's "divine impartiality" is recounted in Mossner, *Life of Hume* 425–26; compare Rousseau's judgment: "[Hume] has seen from all points of view what passion has let me see only from one" (*Life* 507).

most refined sentiment, a world in which polished behavior and civic sublimity are one.[2]

## Questions of Authenticity and Popularity

Macpherson's earliest defenders, most notably Blair and Lord Kames, viewed the Ossian poems as the unadulterated remnants of a heroic Celtic past, having at once an established provenance

2. In the early 1760s, Macpherson published three volumes of poetry alleged to be translations from antique Gaelic manuscripts that preserved the still more ancient oral poetry of the third-century Highland bard, Ossian. The first volume, *Fragments of Ancient Poetry Collected in the Highlands of Scotland and Translated from the Gaelic and Erse Languages*, appeared in 1760; the second, *Fingal, an Ancient Epic in Six Books*, in 1762. In addition to the title work the second volume includes sixteen Ossianic prose-poems that narrate related events in the military and amorous careers of Fingal, the king of Morven in northern Scotland, and his sons Ossian, Ryno, and Fillan; Ossian's own son, Oscar; and their several Irish clients and Scandinavian antagonists. The *Fingal* volume also contains a preface and Macpherson's sixteen-page "Dissertation Concerning the Antiquity, etc., of the Poems of Ossian the Son of Fingal." The third and final Ossianic volume, published the following year, comprises *Temora, an Ancient Epic in Eight Books* and six other poems, as well as a dedication to Lord Bute, and a new thirty-four-page "Dissertation." Finally, Macpherson revised the sequence of the Ossi- anic repetoire for the 1773 edition of the *Poems of Ossian*; the 1839 Philadelphia edition, which I cite, preserves this order and prefaces the poems with a daunting critical apparatus that includes Macpherson's "Dissertations," Hugh Blair's "A Critical Dissertation on the Poems of Ossian" (1763), and several anonymous nineteenth-century essays. A more detailed bibliographic history of the *Poems* is much needed; the valiant first steps toward such an undertaking may be found in Fiona Stafford's selective list of the "major editions" of Ossian (185–87). As How- ard Gaskill notes in his introduction to *Ossian Revisited*, there is at present no single satisfactory volume of the poems (4), though Gaskill's contributor's note announces that he and Stafford are at work on a new edition.

Among Macpherson's supporters in the 1760s were John Home, Hugh Blair, Adam Ferguson, Lord Kames, William Wilkie, Anna Seward, Thomas Gray, Thomas Warton, Thomas Sheridan, and, for a longer time than has often been thought, David Hume (see David Raynor, "Ossian and Hume," *Ossian Revisited* 147–63). Ossian's popularity among the Scottish literati is discussed by Richard Sher (242–61); Ian Gordon Brown (in Craig, *History of Scottish Literature* 2.33–49) addresses the relevant context of mid–eighteenth-century Scottish antiquaria- nism. A number of recent critics have suggested aesthetic or broadly cultural explanations for Ossian's *succès d'estime*: see Robert Folkenflik's essay, as well as the relevant sections of Fredric Bogel (97–101, 123–35) and Ian Haywood (73–100). Stafford's excellent monograph on Macpherson, published after this book was substantially written, foreshadows elements of my own argument.

and a universal appeal. However, the major stumbling block for those who would establish Ossian's authenticity proved to be the surprising representation of "manners" in the poems. In September 1763, Hume wrote to Blair:

> I must own, for my part, that though I have had many particular reasons to believe these poems genuine, more than it is possible for any Englishmen of letters to have, yet I am not entirely without my scruples on that head. You think that the internal proofs in favor of the poems are very convincing: so they are; but there are also internal reasons against them, *particularly from the manners*, notwithstanding all the art with which you [in the "Critical Dissertation"] have endeavored to throw a vernish [*sic*] on that circumstance . . . (Cited in *Poems of Ossian*, 16; emphasis mine)

Blair notes in his *Dissertation* that the Fingalian heroes possessed an ostensibly modern "delicacy of sentiment," but he explains this circumstance, in an awkwardly circular fashion, with reference to the civilizing effect of bardic song. Manners flourished, he maintains, because bards praised them in panegyrics. (Bishop Hurd similarly argues that the savage Irish, like the ancient Greeks, held "their Rhymers in principal estimation" [*Letters* 102–3].) The bards, in turn, derived their wisdom from an ancient order of philosophical Druids (who, according to Macpherson's own "Dissertations," had vanished by Fingal's time). Macpherson, in perfect agreement with Blair, writes that the Gaelic bards had their minds "opened" by Druidical learning (*Poems* 42, 74–77). Alternatively, Lord Kames sets aside the whole question of historical evidence and adopts a purely philosophical argument for the authenticity of the Ossian poems. Sophistically, he transforms the problem of anachronistic manners into proof of Ossian's antiquity. Precisely because the "system of manners" in Ossian is "so opposite to any notion [the modern writer] could frame of savage manners," the Ossian poems, he contends, must be authentic (*Sketches* 1:283–84).

Such arguments did not satisfy any great number of readers. Johnson famously demanded that Macpherson present his manuscript sources (and Macpherson just as famously refused to do so); and in 1775, Hume, long a supporter of the Ossian poems, wrote an essay debunking their authenticity as well as dismissing their aesthetic merit. He never published this essay; David Raynor speculates that his reticence proceeded less from deference to his friend Blair than from a deeper ambivalence about the art of the poems ("Ossian and Hume," *Ossian Revisited* 159–61). While Ossian's cadences continued to please, the publication of Malcolm Laing's heavily annotated edition of *The Poems of Ossian* in 1805 dealt a decisive blow to the plausibilty of Ossianic manners. Laing reveals the poems' modern sources by pointing out allusions to almost a hundred authors from the King James Bible and Pope's Homer through to Thomson and Gray, noting along the way that "the modern Ossian" possesses the exaggerated delicacy of "a French critic" (43) and that Ossian's tender descriptions of women in particular possess "the sentimental extravagance of a modern romance" (50) or "a mere modern prettiness of thought" (144). Yet while Laing's edition helped to shatter the myth that Macpherson had delivered intact the words of a third-century Gaelic bard, it hardly put a dent in the popularity of the Ossian poems. As George Chalmers observed in the same year as Laing's edition appeared, "Except the Bible and Shakespeare, there is not any book that sells better than Ossian" (quoted in Stafford, 171).

What made the poems of Ossian so well liked? Unquestionably, their popularity derived in part from their representation of archaic modes of thought and uncorrupted civic practices. But primitivism cannot entirely explain their appeal. Rather, their particular attraction lies precisely in the fact that, unlike the ballads collected by Percy or the genuine Ossianic fragments known to Irish scholars, they are impressed with distinctly modern concerns. Macpherson's Ossian poetry is, to borrow a phrase from *Fingal* (240), a "half-enlightened" work, which meditates on *éclaircissement* even as it conjures a darkly noble past. As I argue in Chapter 4, the eighteenth-century psychology of passion attempts to re-create the communal bonds of the past within a modern situation; conversely, the Ossian poems would reconcile the modern condition with an idealized past. Macpherson himself suggests the appeal of such a synthesis in his remark to Boswell: "Let me have something in perfection: either the noble rudeness of barbarous manners or the highest relish of polished society.

There is no medium" (*London Journal* 73–74). Macpherson may have had to make exclusive choices in the real world—either Highland primitivism or London polish—but the heterocosm of his poetry renders all sacrifice unnecessary. In the poems of Ossian extremes are united and preserved, without sterile compromise.

## Ancient Virtue Meets Modern Manners

On the surface, the Ossian poems treat the reader to a splendid vision of civic primitivism, "the noble rudeness of barbarous manners" in perfection. One can hardly imagine a more remote setting. Macpherson's "translation" presents the heroic age of Fingal to eighteenth-century commercial society, in which heroes are notoriously hard to find. In Fingalian culture, property and law (not to mention modern litigiousness) are as yet unknown. The collectivity of the clan is all in all. According to one strain of eighteenth-century political thought, which Macpherson did much to advance, only the "savage" could be a true citizen; the veritable republicans of history thus become Native Americans and Scottish clansmen.[3] Although Fingal is nominally "king," he

3. Adam Ferguson technically defines a "savage" state of society as one in which private property does not yet exist; by contrast, "barbarians" have property but no settled law (181–82). Although this distinction is useful, it is not consistently upheld by eighteenth-century writers. On the midcentury tendency to equate savages and true citizens, see Pocock, *The Machiavellian Moment* 501–5. A vivid example of this equation may be found in Richard Polewhele's *English Orator* (1786), which, after exhorting the student of eloquence to read Demosthenes and Cicero, adds that "the scenes of barb'rous life" afford still better instruction:

> Survey the uncultur'd breast
> How simple in its energies! How pure
> From artificial tincture! See yon chief
> Beneath his plantain-canopy of shade,
> The hoary father of his Indian tribe,
> In attitude to speak! And hark—his voice,
> Rude orator! awards in solemn tones
> The fearful sentence; or announces, urg'd
> By social spirit, the decrees of law . . .
> Meantime the untutor'd hearers, with rude signs

conducts himself as *primus inter pares* among the hunters and warriors whom he leads. This state of affairs accords with what Hume, for one, would have expected of third-century Scotland: as he writes in his essay "Of the Original Contract," "If we trace government to its first origin in the woods and deserts, [the people] are the source of all power and jurisdiction. . . . The chieftain, who had probably acquired his influence during the continuance of war, ruled more by persuasion than command" (*Essays* 468). Macpherson says much the same in a lengthy footnote to *Temora*, book 6: "The first ages of society are not the times of arbitrary power. As the wants of mankind are few, they retain their independence. It is an advanced state of civilization that moulds the mind to that submission to government, of which ambitious magistrates take advantage and raise themselves into absolute power" (375).

Throughout the poems, the Fingalian heroes jealously cling to their independence and self-sufficiency; they remain defiantly noncommercial. When the defeated and forgiven Scandinavian king Swaran offers Fingal Viking ships (the symbols of trade and conquest), Fingal replies austerely, "The desert is enough for me, with its deer and woods" (276). Yet Macpherson's representation of primitive virtue is complicated by his apparent sympathy for the eighteenth-century ideology of manners. He is no less concerned than Hume or Adam Smith with the polite reserve and condescension that mark the perfect gentleman; his "gentlemen," however, are Celtic warriors. Modern politeness and ancient virtue were, as we have seen, often viewed as antithetical; polished manners ideally served to compensate for virtue lost through commercial progress. Macpherson, however, envisions an ancient Highland utopia where republican solidarity proves compatible with the most civilized manners. Indeed, his utopia resolves the troubling ethical dialectic of progress and "corruption." William C. Dowling's comment on eighteenth-century

Not inexpressive of the moral sense
Stamp'd on each heart . . . the veteran chieftain hail
Their judge, their legislator, father, friend.

(219–25, 231–36)

ancient constitutionalism applies equally well to the Ossian poems: they tell "a story about the national past that . . . attempts to resolve in imaginary or symbolic terms a contradiction at the level of the real" ("Ideology" 138). This cultural wish-fulfillment may account for the popularity of the poems among a wide readership; few aesthetic formulas are more likely to please than the representation of a past that relieves the strains we are likely to feel in the present.

It is important to note that the polished manners of the Fingalian heroes are not simply chivalric. Modern critics sometimes attribute Ossian's popularity to the midcentury taste for the Gothic; Macpherson, according to this view, exploited the "Gothic revival" evident in the writings of Gray, Horace Walpole, Thomas Warton, and Bishop Hurd. There are two problems with this interpretation. First, Gothicism was rarefied, and hardly extended across the Tweed. In Scotland, "the Grecian Taste" held sway: Hume's early preference for Demosthenes over Cicero represents a moment in a growing Hellenic enthusiasm that would later engage Kames, Monboddo, Wilkie, James "Athenian" Stuart, and indeed Macpherson, who translated the *Iliad* in 1773. Second, and most important, Macpherson carefully notes in his prefatory dissertations that the Ossianic era predates the Middle Ages. He equates the medieval stage of history with "barbarity" and tyranny. Ossian belongs to the first stage of history, which Macpherson labels "consanguinity," and which we might call "patriarchy." According to Macpherson, Scotland passed from this idyllic state into the second, "barbaric" stage of history in the early fifth century, a full hundred years after the death of Ossian (*Poems* 51). Macpherson is at pains to emphasize, even at the risk of anachronism, the absolute simplicity of Fingalian manners and accoutrements. The Gothic period was known for its goldsmiths, and no image of a medieval hall is complete without chalices; the Fingalian heroes, by contrast, drink out of seashells.

Nonetheless, as Edward Davies noted in 1825, certain Ossianic manners do accord better with Gothic practices than with those attributed to ancient Caledonians by "the Romans and Southern Britons"—for example, their "disdain to engage the enemy by night, or to bring superior forces into the field, concluding that glory was to be acquired only in the equal combat" (Davies 6–7). Davies concludes, however, that "the manners and sentiments which present themselves in the poems of Ossian, were not fully appropriate, either to the Celts, or the Goths. . . . Indeed, under the circumstances in which his heroes are placed, such mental refinement could not have been appropriate to mortals. Scarcely has it graced the contemplative philosopher of the most enlightened age, and under the most favorable circumstances" (35).

Blair, by contrast, is ever more sanguine in attributing a philosophic temperament to the ancient Celts. He, too, notes the similarities between chivalric and Ossianic manners—but he emphasizes the differences. Ossian's heroes "have all the gallantry and generosity of those fabulous knights, without their extravagance; and his love-scenes have native tenderness, without any mixture of those forced and unnatural conceits which abound in the old romances." In Ossian "we find tenderness, and even delicacy of sentiment"; the Fingalian heroes are actuated by "magnanimity, generosity, and true heroism." Ossian, reflecting in his blind old age on "the heroes among whom he had flourished," attains, "more perhaps than . . . any other writer," to "the Poetry of the Heart" (Poems 74, 76, 81, 100). In short, the Fingalian heroes possess the politesse de coeur to which modern men and women of feeling aspire. Macpherson's own prefatory dissertation adds that the virtue of our present "jurisprudential" stage of history is that it affords us the freedom and leisure to cultivate "primeval dignity of sentiment" (Poems 51).

While the critical dissertations of Blair and Macpherson provide a point of entry into Ossian's moral universe, the manners on display in the poems still come as something of a surprise. Macpherson's headnote to the first poem in the collection, Cath-Loda (named after Loda, the ruthless genius loci of the Scandinavians), sets forth the "Argument" of the first part of the poem: "Fingal, when very young, making a voyage to the Orkney islands, was driven, by stress of weather, into a bay of Scandinavia, near the residence of Starno, king of Lochlin. Starno invites Fingal to a feast. Fingal, doubting the faith of the king, and mindful of a former breach of hospitality, refuses to go. Starno gathers his tribes; Fingal resolves to defend himself" (125). We move from the

"Argument" to Ossian's bardic prologue (which begins, "A tale of the times of old!") and then to the abrupt introduction of Fingal, who embodies, amid "the times of old," conspicuous delicacy of sentiment:

> Starno sent a dweller of Loda [i.e., a Scandinavian] to bid Fingal to the feast; but the king remembered the past, and all his rage arose. "Nor Gormal's mossy towers, nor Starno, shall Fingal behold. Deaths wander like shadows over his fiery soul! Do I forget that beam of light, the white-handed daughter of kings? [*Macpherson's note*: "Agandecca, the daughter of Starno, whom her father killed, on account of her discovering to Fingal a plot laid against his life . . ."] Go, son of Loda! his words are wind to Fingal: wind that, to and fro, drives the thistle in autumn's dusky vale!"

This is the "rage" of the elegiac poet, not the warrior-king. Despite the emphatic punctuation of the passage, Fingal maintains an equal tenor of melancholic introspection. Here, as elsewhere, his thoughts are with the dead; accordingly, he draws his elevating tropes from the "shadows" and "winds" of a symbolically autumnal setting.

Fingal's meditative tone and delicate manners vary little through *Cath-Loda*. The poet displays a similar decorum. Fingal's so-called rage leads to a battle scene, which is rendered with great obscurity and tact:

> Starno came murmuring on. Fingal arose in arms. "Who art thou, son of night!" Silent, he threw the spear. They mixed their gloomy strife. The shield of Starno fell, cleft in twain. He is bound to an oak. The early beam arose. It was then Fingal beheld the king. He rolled awhile his silent eyes. He thought of other days, when white-bosomed Agandecca moved like the music of songs. He loosed the thong from his hands. Son of Annir, he said, retire. Retire to Gormal of shells [Starno's royal seat]; a beam that was set returns. I remember thy white-bosomed daughter; dreadful king, away! Go to thy troubled dwelling, cloudy foe of the lovely! Let the stranger shun thee, thou gloomy in the hall. A tale of the times of old! (140)

The poet merely implies the combat between Fingal and Starno. Details of the fighting are abstracted in "They mixed their gloomy strife"; the outcome is condensed into the hushed metonymy "The shield of Starno fell, cleft in twain."

In their characteristic reticence about violence, the Ossian poems are stunted at precisely the point where primary epics are most expansive. Ruthlessness in war, as a recognized hallmark of ancient culture, did not fail to garner the praise, however qualified, of Adam Ferguson:

> The amiable plea of humanity was little regarded by [the ancients] in operations of war. Cities were razed, or inslaved; the captive sold, mutilated, or condemned to die. . . . And yet they have, in other respects, merited and obtained our praise. . . . If their animosities were great, their affections were proportionate: they, perhaps, loved, where we only pity; and were stern and inexorable, where we are not merciful, but only irresolute. (199)

For Ferguson, the capacity for violence is the capacity for love; and both, lamentably, are lost in the modern age.

Indeed, in Macpherson's Ossian forgeries, even the ability to depict animosity is lost. It appears that Macpherson makes the aged Ossian a blind poet precisely in order to hide the violence of the past. Primeval force is advertised, but concealed; paraded, but veiled behind a polite aesthetic. Blood, noise, and death feature in many of Ossian's martial descriptions, such as the following battle scene between Irish and Scandinavian armies in Fingal: "Helmets are cleft on high. Blood bursts and smokes around. Strings murmur on the polished yews. Darts rush along the sky. Spears fall like the circles of light which gild the face of the night" (233). Yet Ossian's language purposefully distracts us from the brutality it implies: the metonymic catalog of martial accoutrements ("Helmets . . . Strings . . . Darts . . . Spears") is oddly depersonalized, and "blood" appears to "burst" out of no one and nowhere in particular; the passive mood and smoothly balanced lines have a soothing effect; and the intellectual difficulty of visualizing the final, farfetched simile ("Spears fall like the circles of light") tends to efface any impression of warfare we may have had.

Laing notes that Macpherson adapts a number of his battle descriptions from Pope's Homer; and as an essay in the Edinburgh Magazine (September 1785) complains, the ferocity of

Pope's Homeric heroes "is often soothed and tamed away so effectually, that, instead of the smartness and acrimony of the original, we find nothing but the milkiness of the best good manners" (167).[4] But Macpherson, even more than Pope, glosses over his glimpses of martial culture. Pope, though equally fond of bloodless metonymies such as "To Armour Armour, Lance to Lance oppos'd," sometimes intrudes upon our ease with the relative impetus and active voice of a summation such as this: "With streaming Blood the slipp'ry Fields are dy'd, / While slaughter'd Heroes swell the dreadful Tide" (*Iliad* 4.509–15). Ossian, by contrast, never approaches this degree of *enargeia*.

Moreover, as the *Poems* proceed, Ossian's martial descriptions become increasingly abstracted and obscure. In the last major contest in the *Poems*, the fight between Fingal and the Irish rebel Cathmor in the eighth and last book of *Temora*, Ossian compares the mist-covered combat to "the contending of spirits in a nightly cloud, when they strive for the wintry wings of winds, and the rolling of the foam-covered waves" (394). The phrase "the wintry wings of winds" seems composed mechanically for sheer alliteration: not only is the notion of combat eluded, but reference itself is bracketed. In an explanatory "antiquarian" footnote to this scene Macpherson defends Ossian's technique of evoking battle: "A column of mist is thrown over the whole, and the combat is left to the imagination of the reader. . . . Our imagination stretches beyond, and consequently despises, [attempts at minute] description." As Macpherson implies, combat assumes its proper proportions only in a blind bard's eye; the literal and figurative mystification of violence derives its aesthetic power from Burke's sublime of obscurity, according to which "a clear idea is . . . another name for a little idea" (*Philosophical Enquiry* 63).

Ultimately, however, Macpherson's technique subordinates aesthetic considerations to a more comprehensive ethos of polite-

---

4. In his study of Pope's *Iliad*, Steven Shankman dubs the era of Pope's writing "the Age of Passion" (xv–xvii)—a phrase that seems to me to demand some qualification. However much Pope may have admired Homer's "unequal'd Fire and Rapture," it is a fire that Pope's own poetic line would decorously contain, and indeed Shankman suggests as much in his observation that "it was Pope's intention to make Homer appear as elevated, as fiery an author *as good English would allow*" (131; emphasis mine).

ness. Indeed, disguising violence in "columns of mist" may be said to define the ideology of manners itself. The key to manners is the restraint of the passions, a feat that the vulgar putatively cannot accomplish; placidity of manners is, accordingly, a more or less aggressive response to the real or perceived encroachments of an underclass. Adam Smith writes that "polite persons" are "no-ways ruffled by passion," even at a beargarden (198): how much more admirably difficult to maintain a polite reserve on the bat-tlefield. "The epithets *civilized* or . . . *polished*," according to Ferguson, are bestowed on modern nations "principally" on ac-count of "the laws of war and . . . the lenitives which have been devised to soften its rigours" (199–200). In Ossian, one such leni-tive is the mist of verbiage used to conceal rather than imitate violence.

Another lenitive is the spirit with which the victor spares or forgives the vanquished. Thus, in the final paragraph of *Cath-Loda* Fingal allows Starno to depart peaceably—after rebuking him for his unseemly manners. Ferguson notes that "in the mod-ern nations of Europe . . . we have mingled politeness with the use of the sword"; accordingly, "glory is more successfully ob-tained by saving and protecting, than by destroying the van-quished" (199–200). Ferguson commends, rather than admires, this peculiarly modern lenity. Blair, however, is wholly pleased to observe that lenity is the very "moral" of the ancient Fingalian epics: "*Fingal* obviously furnishes [a general moral], not inferior to that of any other poet, viz: That wisdom and bravery will always triumph over brutal force; or another, nobler still: That the most complete victory over an enemy is obtained by that modesty and generosity which convert him into a friend" (84). It would seem that pre-Christian Celts already have an intimation of a fully moral sense of good and evil.

However, since the Ossianic voice is indeed an eighteenth-century fantasy, the manners of the Fingalian heroes do not mark an intuitive approach toward Christian morality; rather, they are securely *beyond* good and evil. For Fingal's actions are determined not by the dictates of morality but by the impulses of reminis-cence. Fingal's motivation in pardoning Starno at the end of *Cath-Loda* is neither modesty nor humility but the softening remembrance of Starno's "white-bosomed daughter," Agandecca. Symmetrically, the same nostalgic image of Agandecca animates Fingal at the outset of the poem, where she appears as "that beam of light, the white-handed daughter of kings." When Fingal allows Starno to "retire to Gormal of shells," his appositive statement— "a beam that was set returns"—refers ambiguously to the rising sun; the recollected glimmer of Agandecca, "that beam of light"; and to Starno himself, who has been vanquished and, because of Agandecca, restored. It is hardly an exaggeration to assert that the ghostly, overseeing image of Agandecca is the main agency in the poem.

The resolution of *Cath-Loda*, moreover, accords with that of the other Ossianic poems: *Fingal* ends in an almost identical manner, as the hero spares his Scandinavian antagonist Swaran (Starno's son and successor) with the words "Raise, tomorrow, raise thy white sails to the wind, thou brother of Agandecca! Bright as the beam of noon, she comes on my mournful soul" (276). While Fingal's lenity toward his foes may have an underlying affinity with the Enlightenment ethic of sympathy, its more immediate source is always recollected "loveliness." Beauty itself, especially the bright image of a dead woman, anchors the thought and softens the rage of the ancient warrior.

The poems of Ossian are littered with the corpses of women who have died from their love of warriors and who are, like Agandecca, posthumously revived in the minds of the men they loved. King Starno is particularly adept at supplying young warriors with food for future thought. As Macpherson notes at the beginning of *Cath-Loda* (and elaborates in book 3 of *Fingal*), Starno murdered Agandecca for alerting her beloved Fingal to the plot set against him. Moreover, as we are informed later in *Cath-Loda* (138–39), Starno also murdered his sister, Foina-bragal, for falling in love with a foreign warrior. Finally, immediately prior to the time of the poem, Starno murdered a king of Sweden, abducted the king's daughter, Conban-carglas, and confined her to a cave; during the course of the poem, she "dies of grief."

Starno's brutal treatment of women serves as a foil for the politeness of the Fingalian heroes. Macpherson's footnotes to *Cath-Loda* repeatedly advert to Ossian's civilized compassion for women and even to the "feminized" qualities of the Fingalian heroes themselves. (It is worth noting that there are no fewer female corpses in ancient Caledonia than in Scandinavia, but Celtic maidens tend to die by elegiac "grief" rather than by murder). Commenting on Ossian's description of Foina-bragal as she "bursts into tears" at the news of her father's death, Macpherson writes: "Ossian is very partial to the fair sex. Even [Foina-bragal], the sister of the revengeful and bloody Starno, partakes not of the disagreeable characters so peculiar to her family. She is altogether tender and delicate" (139). Nor are tenderness and delicacy exclusive to the fair sex. Fingal displays *tendresse* in addressing the enslaved Conban-carglas: "The maids are not shut in our caves of streams. They toss not their white arms alone. They bend fair within their locks, above the harps of Selma. Their voice is not in the desert wild. We melt along the pleasing sound!" (129). Listening to the "pleasing sound" of women's voices in the royal hall of Selma, Fingal and his heroes "melt" with love, sympathy, or ruth. Although "melting" is presumably a figure of sensation common to many ages, in eighteenth-century sentimental argot it is the prerogative of the man or woman of feeling to "melt into a flood of tears" (as Richard Steele phrases it in *The Tatler* 104).[5] Fingal's profession of melting tears thus attests most eloquently to the modern cast of his manners. Appropriately, it was Henry Mackenzie, the creator of the deliquescent *Man of Feeling*, who, as head of a special Highland Society Committee, first authoritatively declared the Ossian poems a modern imposture.

To Fingal's sentimental avowal Macpherson appends the footnote "From this contrast which Fingal draws between his own nation and the inhabitants of Scandinavia, we may learn, that the former were much less barbarous than the latter. The distinction is so much observed throughout the poems of Ossian, that there can be no doubt that he followed the real manners of both nations

5. Hume writes to Blair of a particularly sentimental episode in which Rousseau "threw his hands about my neck, and bedewing all my face with tears, exclaim'd . . . *I love you, I esteem you.* . . . I was . . . melted on this occasion: I assure you I kissd him and embrac'd him twenty times, with a plentiful effusion of tears" (*Letters* 2:30). Utter and Needham offer an excellent survey and analysis of sentimental tears in *Pamela's Daughters* chap. 4, "Liquid Sorrow," 96–137.

in his own time." Does consistently maintaining a distinction make it a "real" distinction? The strained logic of this footnote may alert us to the precariousness of the Ossianic attempt to fuse ancient passions with modern manners. But Macpherson's early readers were more willing than we are to suspend their disbelief, especially at moments when Ossian "proved" the opposition between rigor and softness, *virtù* and *politesse*, to be without historical foundation. Many, apparently, wanted to believe that the Celtic citizen-warrior, the incarnation of a civic ideal of stern "masculinity," also possessed typically "feminine" qualities such as delicacy of sentiment and a naturally polite judgment. (Historically, Macpherson's sentimental depiction of Celtic women did much to naturalize his age's ideal of femininity, and it did so against the grain of the fierce, "masculine" images of Celtic women established by Roman reporters like Ammianus Marcellinus and Dio Cassius.)[6] Applying a reverse spin to Pope's well-known lines from "To a Lady"—"Heav'n, when it strives to polish all it can / Its last best work, but forms a softer Man"— Macpherson realizes his own ideal of a "softer man" by feminizing male heroes.

The attraction of Ossian's tender heroes becomes clearer when we place them in the context of a concurrent debate on gender roles and civic character. In later eighteenth- century Britain, manners came to be associated less with France and more with home: as Henry Mackenzie remarks, "In a cultivated society this *sentiment of Home* cherishes the useful virtues of domestic life" (quoted in Dwyer, "Imperative of Sociability," 175). Politeness came increasingly to be seen as an offspring of the "feminine"

6. Nora Chadwick (50) conveniently quotes Ammianus and Dio on the martial fierceness of Celtic women. It should be noted, however, that in his *Essay on the Authenticity of the Poems of Ossian* (1807), Patrick Graham argues that Dio's representation of Celtic women is not incompatible, on the whole, with that of Ossian. Furthermore, Graham adduces Tacitus to discover "the high consideration, in which the female character was held among the Celts." Tactius observed "that the Britons were wont to make war under the conduct of females; and that they placed their wives near the field of battle, that they might witness the successes of their husbands." Quite fantastically, Graham gathers from this quotation that the ancient Celts were more susceptible to "the refined charms of female character and manners" than the Greeks and Romans—who were thus, "according to every feeling of modern times, themselves barbarians!" (Graham 21).

sphere; domesticity and delicacy of affections became linked in the popular imagination. Thus Fingal, a reluctant warrior, responds to the hostile customs and terrain of Scandinavia by conjuring homely images of his royal hall and the melting feelings he has had listening to the songs of his countrywomen. And, as the Ossian poems repeatedly demonstrate, Celtic maidens sing jealously private love songs, and elegies for loved ones who are dead. Their songs hearken back to Akenside's evocation of "Sappho's melting airs" ("On Lyric Poetry" 31) or to the Song of Solomon, a poem from which Macpherson indeed borrows liberally; in thus integrating the love lyric within the epic of male adventure, Macpherson synthesizes the two poles of ancient experience: feminine and masculine, private and public, *heimlich* and *unheimlich*.

It hardly needs saying that neither all cultural periods nor all currents of eighteenth-century British opinion were so eager to cross gender and genre boundaries. Macpherson complains in a note to *Cath-Loda* that "Homer, of all ancient poets, uses [women] with least ceremony. His cold contempt is even worse than the downright abuse of the moderns, for to draw abuse implies the possession of some merit" (139). "The downright abuse of the moderns" to which Macpherson alludes was, in effect, the obverse of the respect newly paid to "the fair sex." Antifeminist polemics flourished in midcentury Britain. With a sense of urgency unknown to Lyttelton and Pope, writers such as Ferguson, John Brown, and Rousseau denounced the "feminine" ethos that threatened to eclipse their Spartan ideal of political society.

Misogyny figured prominently in an agenda that, no longer satisfied with the culture of Rome or Athens, applauded the still purer or more "masculine" virtue of Sparta, the Scottish Highlands, and Native America. (Herder may have been the first to remark, but doubtless was not the first to notice, that the manners of the Fingalians resemble those of the North American savages [Smart 7].) Deploring the lack of generous civic passion in polite society, Ferguson and Brown accused their contemporaries of "effeminacy," a blanket term that connotes self-interest, luxury, and an undue emphasis on privacy and domesticity at the expense of a public life. Ferguson's *Essay on the History of Civil*

*Society* (1767) matter-of-factly refers to the "weakness and effeminacy of polished nations" (228), while John Brown's more inflammatory (and tremendously popular) *Estimate of the Manners and Principles of the Times* (1757) is a sustained invective against the "vain, luxurious, and selfish EFFEMINACY" of modern manners (19).[7]

The *Estimate* is a full-scale attack on "manners" in the Humean sense; indeed, Brown satirizes Hume's *Essays* for falling "within the Compass of a Breakfast-reading" and thus catering to the fashionable amateurism of pampered men and women (33). The very fact that Hume intended his *Essays* to break down the barriers between the "learned" (men) and the "conversible" (women) must have proved sufficiently intolerable to Brown's rigidly sexist temperament. Brown persistently decries the loss of classical gender distinctions, remarking (to his presumedly male audience), "The ruling manners of our women [have become] essentially the same as those of the men, and are therefore included in this Estimate. The sexes have now little other apparent distinction, beyond that of person and dress: Their peculiar and characteristic manners, are confounded and lost: The one sex having advanced into boldness, as the other have sunk into effeminacy" (30).

Brown attributes disastrous consequences to the effeminacy of modern manners; like many late Augustan satires, his *Estimate* concludes with an image of apocalyptic inundation, which he here gives a historical name: a British defeat at the hands of the French in the colonial and commercial war declared in 1756 (known retrospectively as the Seven Years' War). He writes, "In

7. Blaming a debilitating "luxury" on the extravagance of women is a topos that extends back, in the Latin tradition, to Livy's representations of the orations of Cato: see John Sekora, *Luxury* 37–38. Though the "effeminate luxury" of the times was a familiar theme of Bolingbroke's *The Craftsman*, Sekora suggests, as I do, that "the controversy over luxury probably reached its highest pitch in British history in the years 1756–63" (66). As Edmund Burke writes in his first *Letter on a Regicide Peace*, "I remember, in the beginning of what has lately been called the Seven Years' War, that an eloquent writer and ingenious speculator, Dr. Brown, published an elaborate philosophical discourse to prove that the distinguishing features of the people of England had been totally changed, and that a frivolous effeminacy was become the national character. Nothing could be more popular than that work" (*On Revolution* 253).

the present effeminate tho' factious times, we have no danger [of civil war] to fear. For as our manners are degenerated into those of women, so are our weapons of offence. But as this home-security arises only from the common impotence; it is probable, that other nations may soon know of what materials we are made; and therefore our danger is likely to arise from without" (65). In the figurative logic of Brown's text, the threat of foreign invasion proceeds from castration anxiety at home: "our weapons" are "degenerated into those of women." It is "the common impotence."[8] (Ironically, Brown gives lurid coloring to a palpably civic and military—that is, "masculine"—danger by borrowing the terms of a private or domestic crisis).

The *Poems of Ossian* may be understood as a response to this type of Brownian chauvinism. The ethos of the Fingalian hero gives the lie to Brown's ideal of ancient and uncorrupted masculinity. Fingal himself can enjoy not only security but even melting sensations at home, and still ward off invaders from without (his eponymous epic concerns the repulsion of Scandinavians who have attacked neighboring Ireland). He is an ideal reconciliation of eighteenth-century oppositions: in him, the passionate fierceness of the citizen-warrior blends with the delicate affections fostered by domesticity; precommercial civic virtue joins with modern manners; the traditional attributes of masculinity combine with those of femininity. Macpherson's cultural poetics do not treat the primitive and the modern as mutually exclusive categories. Rather, his impersonation of an ancient Caledonian voice makes the Scots' savage ancestors forebears to the Scottish Enlightenment's most cherished ideals of polity and manners.

Of course, Macpherson consigns Fingal to a past within a past, lamented even by the aged poet Ossian as he reviews the heroes of his youth. For elegy enhances as it preserves the integrity of ideals—especially ideals that have died too soon, or people that have passed prematurely. Thus, before Macpherson, Hume populated the Scotland of his *History* with what Donald Siebert aptly calls "heroes of feeling": Mary, Queen of Scots, Charles I, and

8. For a brilliant examination of the ways in which political crisis may be figured as the fear of castration, see Neil Hertz, "Medusa's Head: Male Hysteria under Political Pressure," *The End of the Line* 161–216.

above all the Marquess of Montrose, whose untimely deaths evince even as they seal in amber their estimable combinations of classical magnanimity and modern benevolence (*Moral Animus* 25–61). Hume applauds Scots who maintain a union of ancient and modern virtues in parting with their heads; similarly, Macpherson's Ossian praises the virtuous dead for allowing their lives to end before their ideals wane. However, in a distinctive twist, Ossian focuses not on the men but on the *women* who have gone before us.

Of the dozens of heroines introduced in the Ossian poems, hardly one remains unscathed. In the heat of the controversy over Ossian's authenticity, Edward Davies remarked that the poems do not display the "*Varios casus*, the *Tot discrimina rerum*, which are generally found in real life and authentic history"; rather, "the same object perpetually returns, in a different point of view." Davies evidences "the sentimental deaths of Ossian's heroines," painstakingly (though not exhaustively) cataloging nineteen examples (40–46). Scandinavian heroines have little choice but to love and be undone. Though some Celtic heroines take more positive action—in the poem "Oithona," the heroine valiantly disguises herself as a soldier to enter and die in battle—most mourn and "die of grief"; as Ossianic legend explains it, they are summoned by "the voices of the dead" (*Poems* 360, 381). This curious means of death raises a number of important questions. First, what did enlightened readers imagine these voices of the dead to be? And second, why do such voices plague women in particular? That is, why does Macpherson's union of virtue and manners require the sacrifice of so many ancient maidens? Why should feminizing an ancient ideal of civic and martial valor coincide with the death of women?

## Conversing with the Dead

In this section I shall address my first question: how did Macpherson's early readers, and how should we, understand the voices of the dead? I would argue that this question invariably leads us, in Paul de Man's dramatic phrase, to "the complex and philosophically challenging epistemology of the tropes" (*Allegories* 130). Hearing the voices of the dead, or of inanimate nature more generally, belongs to the turn of mind the rhetoricians classify as prosopopoeia. The *Rhetorica ad Herennium* teaches that the figure "represents an absent person as present, or makes a mute or shapeless thing articulate" (4.53). In the Ossianic era, however, prosopopoeia is not yet a self-conscious rhetorical practice but a more immediate way of knowing the world. Like Hume's exemplary primitives in *The Natural History of Religion*, Macpherson's ancient Celts think *in* figures; they intuitively confer faces upon natural events and the viewless dead. As Hugh Blair notes, Ossian's poetry abounds in apostrophes, and "inanimate objects, such as winds, trees, flowers, he sometimes personifies with great beauty" (*Poems* 80, 115).

However, the Ossian poems also suggest a *new* sense of prosopopoeia, one which (mutatis mutandis) accords with de Man's analysis of the figure. In its classical sense, prosopopoeia confers the power of speech on an absent, dead, or otherwise voiceless entity. For de Man, however, attributing a voice to the dead serves to demonstrate the illusory nature of our own possession of voice. He evokes prosopopoeia to describe an assymetry between meaning and intention that inheres in language use itself: in giving a voice to the dead, we recognize ourselves as (figuratively speaking) "mute," or alienated from the meaning of our own utterances. De Man thus describes prosopopoeia as essentially a "linguistic predicament" (*Rhetoric of Romanticism* 78–81). Yet we may translate the terms of de Man's conceptual rhetoric into a more familiar experiential vocabulary by defining prosopopoeia as the chiasmic figure that turns the dead into the living, and the living into the dead. Psychologically, it becomes the condition in which the imagery of the mind—especially the speaking images of those who are dead or absent from us—become more real to us than a corporeal reality we no longer trust.

Prosopopoeia, as the expression of a peculiarly modern (or Romantic) subjectivism, suffuses the poems of Ossian. Yet though the preoccupation with nostalgic or phantasmagoric images properly belongs not to third-century Scotland but to eighteenth-century Europe, Macpherson's Ossian myth provides a smooth segue between the two epochs; thus, just as the manners of the Fingalians possess a surprising continuity with those of the moderns, so the primitive anthropomorphism of the Celts shades into a distinctly modern version of haunted consciousness.[9]

Along with savage manners, anthropomorphism enjoyed a mid-century vogue, and Macpherson's "translation" of Ossian provided its compendious sourcebook. Ossian's poetry teems with what Kames calls "passionate personifications," or figures that evince the speaker's impetuous belief in the sympathy of external nature. (The poets of a polished age, by contrast, recognize the purely fictive quality of their personifications, be they simply decorative or elaborately "descriptive"; indeed, while the savage poet appears to literalize his personifications, the modern allegorical poet runs the alternate risk, as Steven Knapp argues, of personfiying his literalizations [58–61].) Kames ranks Ossian alongside Homer and the Old Testament prophets as a poet of sublime projection. According to Kames,

> [When] a passion becomes excessive, it cannot be gratified but by sympathy from others; and if denied that consolation in a natural way, it will convert even things inanimate into sympathetic beings. . . . That such personification is derived from nature, will not admit the least remaining doubt, after finding it in poems of the darkest ages and remotest countries. No figure is more common in Ossian's works; for example,
>> The battle is over, said the King, and I behold the blood of my friends. Sad is the heath of Lena, and mournful the oaks of Cromla.
> Again:
>> The sword of Gaul trembles at his side, and longs to glitter in his hand.
> Terror produceth the same effect: it is communicated in thought to every thing around, even to things inanimate:
>> Go, view the settling sea. The stormy wind is laid; but the billows

---

9. Neil Tolchin demonstrates the similar haunting of nineteenth-century consciousness with this quotation from Orville Dewey: "The world is filled with the voices of the dead. They speak . . . from the private history of our own experiences. . . . Though they are invisible, yet life is filled with their presence. . . . Go where we will, the dead are with us" (8).

still tremble on the deep, and seem to fear the blast. *Fingal.* (*Elements* 2:230–33)

Heaths, oaks, seas, and swords not only are endowed with human passions but may also acquire human speech. Fingal is better able to imagine his own effacement than the silence of nature: "Soon shall my voice be heard no more, and my footsteps cease to be seen. The bards will tell of Fingal's name. The stones will talk of me" (*Poems* 268). In the Port-Royalist *Art of Speaking*, prosopopoeia is the figure that "makes the Stones speak": Ossian evinces the ancient belief upon which the rhetorician bases his figure.

Ossian draws no very firm distinction between the human and the nonhuman but freely bestows the attributes of human passion and activity upon all aspects of his grim northern world. He animates the face of nature with the same grievances, terrors, and longings felt by the Fingalian heroes and heroines; their actions and passions, in turn, are described in terms of the elemental nature that surrounds them, particularly the volatile elements of wind and sea. As Priestley notes, "Ossian . . . always illustrates human actions by the appearances of inanimate nature" (178). Thus, *Fingal* describes advancing armies as the "roar of streams," or "as waves white-bubbling over the deep," while a woman's white arms are "as the foam of waves." A hero describes his mourning, "I sighed as the wind in the cleft of a rock" (245, 248, 260). Somewhat more abstractly, Fingal's troubled thoughts are figured in *Temora* as "waves on a secret mountain top, each with its back of foam" (374). This metaphor may be glossed by Warburton's observation that "the first ages, uncultivated, and immersed in sense, could express their rude conceptions of abstract ideas, and the reflex operations of the mind, only by material images; which, so applied, became *metaphors*" (*Divine Legation* 2:59–60). Finally, throughout the Ossian poems heroes in motion are "pillars of fire," an image that would seem to be copied from Exodus, not nature, if Ossian's ignorance of revealed religion and all canonical Western texts had not been insisted upon by Macpherson and his followers.

According to Macpherson, any similarities between Ossian and previously canonized authors may be accounted for by the limitations of nature itself. He first offers this explanation in the preface to *Temora*: "If . . . in the form of his poems, and in several passages of his diction, [Ossian] resembles Homer, the similarity must proceed from Nature, the original from which both drew their ideas." A later commentator (1806) pens the aphorism "The book of nature is open to all, and in her pages there are no new readings" (*Poems* 24).[10] This "naturalizing" of nature imagery, or obstruction of allusion, was crucial to Ossian's early reception. Aestheticians agreed that ancient poetry derived its bold force from the direct experience and passionate transformation of nature. Whereas mankind's progressive alienation from poetic modes of thought began with literacy, Macpherson claims that the Ossian poems he partially translated from Gaelic manuscripts belong primarily to an ancient *oral* tradition preserved in the Highlands. From literacy came learning; learned poets introduced allusion (or what Edward Young would call "imitative" rather than "original" composition), and the attendant sense of a literary canon. Through his Ossianic impersonation, Macpherson would transform emulation and allusion into unmediated creation; his attempt, however transparent it seems to us now, struck a responsive chord in contemporaries who wished without hope they could do the same.[11]

10. Hurd writes that similarities in "original" poets as diverse as Homer and Shakespeare may be accounted for by the "fact [that] quick, perceptive, intelligent minds . . . will hardly fail of seeing nature in the same light, and of noting the same distinct features and proportions" (*Works* 2.159). Hurd, like Macpherson, believes that not only distinctive modes of eloquence but even specific mimetic observations are available to all peoples at corresponding stages in their cultural and psychological development. The Enlightenment in general opposed the still prevalent theory of cultural "diffusionism" that was advanced, for example, in James Adair's *History of the American Indians* (1775), a work that argues, on the grounds of cultural and particularly oratorical similarities, that Native Americans must be *descended from* the ancient tribes of Israel (12). Adair assumes that all eloquence ultimately derives from one oriental font; by contrast, Ossian's defenders would account for the similarities among North American, ancient Hebrew, and Ossianic eloquence by reference not to one genealogical source but rather to one process of parallel development.

11. Walter Jackson Bate and Harold Bloom variously attest that history became a particularly vivid nightmare for the modern poet; and Robert Folkenflik notes that it was a nightmare from which Macpherson, no less than his admirer Blake,

In re-creating a rude state of language and manners, Macpherson wrote primarily as what we would now call a "cultural historian" or even a "historian of consciousness." Yet the distinctively modern quality of his rhetorical achievement should not be overlooked. William Duff, in his *Critical Observations on the Writing of the Most Celebrated Original Geniuses in Poetry* (1770), locates the "force" of Ossian's genius in his "assigning an existence and offices, [and] appropriating speech and action to ghosts and spirits." In this, "Ossian is without a superior" (125). The ability to conjure such unseen presences is an aspect of prosopopoeia similar but not identical to the anthropomorphism noted by Kames. The ghosts and spirits of the Ossian poems are related, in part, to primitive "daemonism"—the belief that particular locations or activities are inhabited or guided by animating spirits; but Ossian's ghosts are not primarily *genii loci*, spirits tied to natural sites. Rather, they are specters of the private imagination, inhabiting a decidedly modern, individualistic world. Indeed, J. S. Smart notes that the ghosts of Ossian have no foundation in actual Celtic legend but are wholly Macpherson's interpolation (24).

Still, Macpherson masterfully blurs the distinction between daemonism and more privatized forms of haunted consciousness. Witness the opening lines of *Cath-Loda*:

> A tale of the times of old!
> Why, thou wanderer unseen! thou bender of the thistle of Lora; why, thou breeze of the valley, hast thou left mine ear? I hear no distant roar of streams! No sound of the harp from the rock! Come, thou huntress of Lutha, Malvina, call back his soul to the bard. I look forward to Lochlin of lakes, to the dark billowy bay of U-thorno, where Fingal descends from ocean, from the roar of winds. Few are the heroes of Morven in a land unknown!

The pace of this opening paragraph is dizzying. Blair's *Dissertation* warns the unsuspecting reader that Ossian's style "is so con-

---

tried to awake. Folkenflik elegantly summarizes Macpherson's ambition: "By becoming an ancient, Macpherson places [the] Herculean burden of the past on other shoulders" (381).

cise; and so much crowded with imagery; the mind is kept at such a stretch in accompanying the author, that an ordinary reader is at first apt to be dazzled and fatigued, rather than pleased" (*Poems* 82). The reader may eventually puzzle out the initially opaque references to "Lora" (a stream-filled district of Fingal's kingdom of Morven), "Malvina" (the betrothed of Ossian's dead son, Oscar, who attends Ossian in his old age), and "Lochlin" (the Scandinavian kingdom of Starno). This barrage of proper names simply belongs to the "primitive" style, which was thought to be highly "particularized";[12] once the reader has learned the peculiar geography of the Ossian poems these names no longer pose a difficulty.

But Ossian's concision, coupled with his primitive sensuousness, make the opening apostrophe to the "wanderer unseen" *fundamentally* difficult to read. Who or what is "the wanderer unseen"? Is it literally the thistle-bending "breeze of the valley" of the following line, invoked by Ossian as a symbol of his own renewed inspiration? This reading would seem to be supported by Fingal's subsequent speech, in which the wind of autumn is said to wander "to and fro." Alternately, however, might not the "wanderer unseen" be the ghost of Fingal, envisioned by Ossian in his blind old age? (The shapes of the past are not to Ossian as a landscape to a blind man's eye: rather, in the words of Fingal's companion Duth-maruno, "The deeds of old . . . are like paths to our eyes" [132–33].) Might not the "wanderer" be the specter of Fingal, gliding like a breeze over the valleys he once inhabited? Clearly, by the time that Ossian invokes Malvina's aid in "call[ing] back *his* soul," his reference is to Fingal; and later in the poem King Starno indeed calls Fingal the "wanderer." But how much of this ongoing information is simply irrelevant to the forceful unreadability of the poem's opening image? We are ultimately left with an unanswerable question: is the breeze the tenor or the vehicle of the metaphor that draws us into the poem? Does Ossian sense a daemon in the viewless winds, or is he apostrophizing his dead father? Are we witnessing a confident

12. Blair writes, "The ideas of men, at first, were all particular" (*Poems* 80); cf. Priestley 161–62, and Adam Smith's account of the progress of language from names of particular objects to general terms (203–5).

animism, or the modern suspicion that our fathers are every-where?

The answer is probably that we are witnessing both. However, I would like now to consider the modern aspect of Ossian's consciousness. As the bardic narrator of his people's former glories, Ossian is obsessed with images of the dead; he conceives of them as more real, more substantial, than the "little men" who surround him in the present. Ossian feels himself to be an epigone, blind and forlorn among "the sons of the feeble" (255, 278). Of course, this is largely the nostalgia of the Iliadic Homer, who persistently observes how much better the heroes at Troy were "than men are now" (Pope's translation indicts "such men as live in these degen'rate Days"). But Ossian senses with a greater profundity than Homer the insubstantiality of the present moment and the emptiness of all that surrounds him. As William Hazlitt puts it, Ossian "converses only with the spirit of the departed. . . . The feeling of cheerless desolation, of the loss of the pith and sap of existence, of the annihilation of the substance, and the clinging to the shadow of all things as in a mock-embrace, is here perfect" (quoted in Stafford, 149). This aspect of Ossian attracted such melancholic readers as Werther, Napoleon, and Byron. It also situates Macpherson squarely within the existential crisis that a number of modern critics have identified in eighteenth-century literary culture: in Fredric Bogel's words, "What the poems and prose works of the later eighteenth century disclose is . . . a common attitude towards human experience: specifically, a pervasive awareness of its insubstantiality" (24).

Paradoxically, in the experience of both the aged Ossian and his mournful heroes and heroines, the living are reduced to ghostly presences less affectively real than the specters that haunt private memory. The dead acquire a substantiality denied to the living. Terry Castle argues that the later eighteenth century ushers in "an obsessional concentration on nolstalgic images of the dead," in which the perceptions of memory may seem more palpable than those of sense (246). (This ability to mistake memory for present experience is entirely consonant with the popular epistemology of later eighteenth-century Britain, which followed Hume in treating the impressions of sense and memory as fundamentally equivalent, and distinguished only by the ordinarily superior "vivacity" of sense perception.) Castle's thesis on Anne Radcliffe applies, a fortiori, to the poems of Ossian: "What was once real (the supernatural) has become unreal; what was once unreal (the imagery of the mind) has become real. . . . Ghosts and specters retain their ambiguous grip on the human imagination; they simply migrate into the space of the mind" (248).

Thus, the several incursions of the supernatural in Ossian's poems—shrieking ghosts, second sight, and the descent of Odin—are summarily demystified in Macpherson's "antiquarian" footnotes. For example, book 4 of *Temora* ends with the heroine Sul-malla's apostrophe to her dead father, Conmor, as she anticipates the death of her beloved Cathmor:

> Spirit of departed Conmor! are thy steps on the bosom of winds? Comest thou, at times, to other lands, father of sad Sul-malla? Thou dost come! I have heard thy voice at night; while yet I rose on the wave to Erin of the streams. . . . The ghosts of fathers, they say, call away the souls of their race, while they behold them lonely in the midst of wo. Call me, my father, away! When Cathmor is low on earth; then shall Sul-malla be lonely in the midst of wo!

Macpherson explodes the superstition of these lines with this enlightened footnote:

> It was the opinion of the times, when a person was reduced to a pitch of misery, which could admit of no alleviation, that the ghost of his ancestors *called his soul away.* This supernatural kind of death was called "the voice of the dead," and is believed by the superstitious vulgar to this day. . . . The gloominess of the scenes around [the ancient Scots] was apt to beget that melancholy disposition of mind, which most readily receives impressions of the extraordinary and supernatural kind. Falling asleep in this gloomy mood, and their dreams being disturbed by the noise of the elements around, it is no matter of wonder, that they thought they heard the voice of the dead. This voice of the dead, however, was, perhaps, no more than a shriller whistle of the winds in an old tree, or in the chinks of a neighboring rock. (360; cf. the similarly disenchanting footnotes on 237, 249–50, 269)

Before Radcliffe, Macpherson was apt to rationalize the eerie events he includes in his narrative. In his role of editor he displays the typically ironic temperament of his era: he exploits un-enlightened stances for enlightened ends; he both disapproves of primitive or popular superstitions and compulsively admits them all the same.

While the *Poems of Ossian* thus rationalize the supernatural, they conversely make the marvelousness of mental projection appear commonplace: the ghosts and spirits of the Scottish land-scape may merely be wind in a hollow, but the specters of the mind prove larger than life. Indeed, Ossian's heroes and heroines do not simply apostrophize dead fathers and lovers but hold ghostly converse with the voices of the dead. In contrast to the apostrophic distance maintained by Collins in his sublime Odes, the characters of Ossian summon their absent loved ones in seemingly natural acts of conversation. Sul-malla's address to her father formally anticipates a dramatic monologue such as Ten-nyson's "St Simeon Stylites" or "Rizpah"; but whereas Ten-nyson's monologists are certifiably mad according to Victorian psychopathology, both Ossian's poems and Macpherson's notes take for granted that the ancient Scots should believe in their mental specters more strongly than, and often at the expense of, the sensible world. Macpherson, as enlightened annotator, fails to notice that the supernatural "second sight" of Celtic lore has been domesticated in the ordinary mental experience of Ossian's characters.

An episode of *Cath-Loda* will serve to illustrate the extent to which each of Ossian's characters is obsessed with his or her own private specters. Throughout much of the poem Fingal thinks "of other days, when white-bosomed Agandecca moved like the mu-sic of songs." He is momentarily distracted from these unheard melodies by the song of the maiden Conban-carglas, issuing from the cave where she is held captive. She sings to her father, Torcul-torno, who has been murdered by the Scandinavian king Starno:

"Torcul-torno, of aged locks!" she said, "where now are thy steps, by Lulan? Thou hast failed at thine own dark streams, father of Conban-carglas! But I behold thee, chief of Lulan, sporting by Loda's

hall, when the dark-skirted night is rolled along the sky. Thou sometimes hidest the moon with thy shield. I have seen her dim in
heaven. Thou kindlest thy hair into meteors, and sailest along the
night. Why am I forgot in my cave, king of shaggy boars? Look from
the hall of Loda on thy lonely daughter." (128)

When questioned by Ossian about her captivity, Conban-carglas
lyrically recounts her cruel treatment at the hands of Starno and
concludes with an oddly solipsistic profession of love for Starno's
son, prince Swaran: "But often passes a beam of youth, far distant
from my cave. The son of Starno moves in my sight. He dwells
lonely in my soul" (129). Later, when she mistakenly imagines
that Fingal has killed Swaran, she dies of grief—presumably summoned by the voices of her dead ancestors (130, 140).

Conban-carglas is practically oblivious to the physical presence
of Fingal: the speeches she makes in his presence are addressed to
her dead father, and to the image of her absent—and later sup-
posedly dead—beloved. Her converse with her own mental images occurs, appropriately, in a *cave*, the site chosen by Plato to
allegorize his thesis that what we commonly recognize as reality
is merely a shadow play. The prisoners of Plato's cave "would
have seen nothing of themselves or of one another, except the
shadows thrown by the fire-light on the wall of the cave facing
them." The prisoners, Plato made clear, are "like ourselves" (*Republic* 7.514). Plato's complaint that we know only shadows becomes the preliminary assumption of eighteenth-century skeptical empiricism: from the epistemology of Berkeley and Hume to
the novels of Sterne, all knowledge is understood to derive from
subjective mental impressions. The "commonsense" philosopher
Thomas Reid compares Hume's image of the mind not to a cave
but, similarly, to "an enchanted castle, imposed upon by spectres
and apparitions" (103). Significantly, Reid figures Hume's repre-
sentational theory of knowledge as haunted consciousness in
1764—that is, in the wake of the Ossian poems. Idealist "systems" are thereafter routinely compared to the belief in ghosts;
for example, in Peacock's *Nightmare Abbey* the character Mr.
Flosky (a caricature of Coleridge) pronounces quite flatly, "I live
in a world of ghosts" (235).

Ossian's memoir-epics differ not in kind but only in degree from other eighteenth-century "ghost stories." That is, while the obsessions of Ossian's heroines may be rooted in common epistemological concerns, Macpherson wrings from their fantasies an uncommon violence and disastrousness. Conban-carglas's lonely death points to the related moral that the habit of hearing the dead speak ultimately silences the living. In the Ossian poems, "living among the dead" has an odd way of literalizing itself. Young women who have given themselves to phantoms invariably die of grief; bestowing a voice upon the dead results, paradoxically, in being "called away." This dialectic of projection and privation indeed reflects Macpherson's own achievement—for in the act of reviving an ancient Celtic voice he at once enables and effaces his creative self.

The chiasmic reversal between giving a voice and silencing oneself reappears in *Comala*, the "Dramatic Poem" that follows *Cath-Loda*. Comala, a woman in love with Fingal, awaits his return from war with "Caracul" (according to Macpherson, the Roman emporer Caraculla). While she waits, the weird sisters Malilcoma and Dersegrena interpret various natural portents as signifying Fingal's death in battle; thus, when Fingal indeed returns, Comala believes him to be a ghost, calling her to her own death.

> *Melilcoma.* What sound is that on Ardven? Who is that bright on the vale? Who comes like the strength of rivers, when their crowded waters glitter to the moon?
> *Comala.* Who is it but the foe of Comala, the son of the king of the world [i.e., Caraculla]? Ghost of Fingal! do thou, from thy cloud, direct Comala's bow. Let him fall like the hart of the desert. It is Fingal in the crowd of his ghosts. Why dost thou come, my love, to frighten and please my soul?
> *Fingal.* Raise, ye bards, the song; raise the wars of the streamy Carun! Caracul has fled from our arms along the fields of his pride. . . . I heard a voice, or was it the breeze of my hills? Is it the huntress of Ardven, the white-handed daughter of Sarno? Look from thy rocks, my love; let me hear the voice of Comala!
> *Comala.* Take me to the cave of thy rest, O lovely son of death!

Disconsolate, Comala presumably dies of grief: Melilcoma simply announces, "Pale lies the maid at the rock! Comala is no more!" Fingal replies, "Is the daughter of Sarno dead, the white-bosomed maid of my love? Meet me, Comala, on my heaths, when I sit alone at the streams of my hills!" (144–45). At the outset of the passage, Comala's attributing a voice to the "ghost" of Fingal deafens her to the fact that he indeed lives, and addresses her—even if he appears momentarily uncertain whether it is Comala he addresses or "the breeze of [his] hills." Comala assumes that she hears the voice of the dead calling her away; her abrupt death apparently requires no further explanation or ceremony. Fingal responds with equal haste: after a terse acknowledgment that "the daughter of Sarno [is] dead," he immediately, and with little apparent regret, anticipates conversing with her ghost "when I sit alone at the streams of my hills." Her voice "will remain in [his] ears." It is as if she never died; he may even prove more attentive to her voice when he is alone, no longer mistaking it for the breeze of the hills as he did when she was alive. For Fingal, as for Comala—and for most of the characters who inhabit the Ossian poems—it seems more natural to commune with ghosts than to entertain the living.[13]

But it is Ossian above all who converses with the dead. As an aged poet writing a memoir epic, he takes upon himself the Herculean feat of mourning for every character in the *Poems*. Ossian elegizes; therefore he is. Not surprisingly, he observes no steadfast distinction between reminiscent voices and the sounds of the present. The poem *Conlath and Cuthona* begins on such a dubious note: "Did not Ossian hear a voice? or is it the sound of days that are no more? Often does the memory of former times come, like the evening sun, on my soul. The noise of the chase is renewed. In thought, I lift the spear" (400). What Ossian hears and conveys in the poem are ghostly voices from the past that narrate their parts in the remote tragedy of Conlath and Cuthona: the hero Conlath died in avenging the honor of his beloved Cuthona, and she soon thereafter died of grief. (According to Macpherson's footnote, Cuthona means "the mournful sound of the waves; [it is] a poetical name given her on account of her mourning to the

13. For further examples, see especially "Shirlic and Vinvela," the opening poem of the 1760 *Fragments*; the poem was later incorporated as an episode in the longer Fingalian poem *Carric-Thura* (*Poems* 147–49).

sound of the waves".) But it is a moot point whether these narrat-
ing voices are "heard" or are "the sound of days that are no more."
The distinction has ceased to matter. For Ossian, as for the characters he laments, the past is as likely to speak as the present.[14]

## Mourning (and) the Domestic Woman

Ossian's is, of course, an eighteenth-century predicament. His
sense that ghosts are everywhere is reproduced—and, I would
argue, ultimately rooted—in polite domestic situations such as
that of Anna Seward. Seward was a fervent admirer of Ossian's
"mournful strains" (1:lxvi) who eventually versified a number of
his prose poems; her correspondence of 1764 details a mournful
episode of her own. Following the death of her sister Sarah, Anna
and her mother regularly grieve in "the mulberry shade," "exempt from the intermixture of society with indifferent people"
and hidden from the "cheerful" Mr. Seward, who "has no grati-
fication in recalling the past." The Seward women never tire of
"this eternal looking back to the past, and recalling the image of
the everlasting absent"; indeed, the absent are paradoxically present, as Sarah "seems yet to mix in our conversations. We take
delight in assuring ourselves that her spirit hovers round us."
Anna concludes, regretfully, "I am afraid that men, in general, feel
little of all this" (1:cxxiv–cxxxv).

Seward's correspondence suggests that conversing with the
dead is chiefly the prerogative of domestic female life. Privacy
enables Anna to commune with her dead sister: the "indifferent
people" with whom she need not mingle includes everyone, save
her mother. In turn, her sequestration causes her to focus so in-
tently on the sister she has lost. As Terry Castle argues, our inability to let dead loved ones lie originates in the institution of
the small affective family, better known to us as the "nuclear"

14. Young Werther feels his life, like Ossian's before him, "tremble between
being and not-being" (116); unlike Ossian, however, Werther prefers absolute
states to liminal moments and thus wishes he could "free [Ossian] from the
stabbing agony of a slowly ebbing life with one stroke; and then let my soul follow
the liberated demigod" (111). In place of Ossian's chiasmic tropings, Werther offers
us the clean cut.

family. In the earlier setting of the tribe, clan, or *gens*, an individual's affections were diffused among a large number of relations, making none of them seem quite irreplaceable. By concentrating all our affection from childhood onward on a few irreplaceable loved ones, however, modern familial relationships inspire us with an unprecedented fear of death. That fear is apt to turn into denial: in Castle's words, "The fear of death in the modern era prompts an obsessional return to the world of memory—where the dead continue to 'live'" (244). Thus, the ghosts of modern consciousness ultimately arise from the collapse of the extended family and a broad-based civic life.

It is easy to see why Seward found Ossian so sympathetic. Ossian's clan setting hardly disguises the fact that Macpherson's real interest lies in nuclear dramas. Of all the characters Ossian remembers, two stand out—his dead wife Evirallin, and Fingal, his father. And in recalling Fingal, Ossian chiefly re-creates his father's mourning, first for Comala and finally for Agandecca. Indeed, while all may mourn alike in the Ossianic world, heroes prove hardier mourners than heroines. Men tend to survive. With this observation we return to the second question I posed above: why do so many young women die in the poems of Ossian?

To arrive at a preliminary answer to that question, let me turn to a passage from Mary Wollstonecraft that mirrors the situation of the Ossianic hero. Wollstonecraft here portrays her ideal woman, one who wholly understands and vigorously performs her duties—among them, her duty of mourning her dead husband.

> She is left a widow, perhaps, without a sufficient provision; but she is not desolate! The pang of nature is felt; but after time has softened sorrow into melancholy resignation, her heart turns to her children with redoubled fondness, and anxious to provide for them, affection gives a sacred heroic cast to her maternal duties. She thinks that not only the eye sees her virtuous efforts from whom all her comfort must now flow, and whose approbation is life; but her imagination, a little abstracted and exalted by grief, dwells on the fond hope that the eyes which her trembling hand closed, may still see how she subdues every wayward passion to fulfil the double duty of being the father as well as the mother of her children. (138)

Wollstonecraft's dutiful widow, supervised and chastened by her husband's dead eyes, provides a reverse image of Macpherson's Celtic heroes who find inspiration in the ghostly images of dead wives and lovers. As Macpherson implies that the best woman is a dead woman, so Wollstonecraft suggests the best man is a remembered one.

This strategy serves congruous aims in both authors: it unmoors gender roles from the actual representatives of the opposite sex, distinguishing, as Lacan would say, symbolic others from real others. "Femininity" thus transcends the body of women, while "masculinity"—which Wollstonecraft, like Augustine, equates with rationality—separates itself from the presence of men. Macpherson purifies his text of living women in order to feminize his male heroes, just as Wollstonecraft imagines dead husbands so that women might incorporate masculinity within themselves, becoming "both father and mother." Wollstonecraft's widow has the best of both worlds: she internalizes rational authority and frees herself from adventitious constraints. Mutatis mutandis, this too is Macpherson's fantasy: a dead woman in a man's past infuses him with delicacy of affection or, in Mackenzie's phrase, "natural tenderness of her heart" (*Man of Feeling* 10), while it disencumbers him from any actual restraint. It turns a man into Anna Seward; or rather, it makes a man Ossian.

## Maternal Homes and Ambivalent Sons

Hume asked, "What better school for manners than the company of virtuous women?" and his question elicited responses across the century: Henry Brooke proclaims that women are necessary "to sooth, form and illumine the rudeness of [men's] mass" (quoted in Dwyer, "Enlightened Spectators," 99), and James Fordyce writes that the company of women "cannot fail to soften the temper, enliven the genius, and give an agreeable polish to the whole deportment" (29). But Hume's "school for manners," though modeled on the French salon, was effectively realized in the self-contained, maternally administered family that emerged in Britain during the course of the eighteenth century. The final image of Richard Sheridan's *School for Scandal* is of such a school for manners, as Charles Surface—the man who possesses true *politesse de coeur*, as opposed to the "sentimental French plate" displayed by his brother (5.1.135)—foreswears further "hazard" and falls into the arms of his beloved Maria, saying, "Here shall be my monitor—my gentle guide.—Ah! can I leave the virtuous path those eyes illumine?" (5.3.309–11). Anna Seward indeed contends that "no guard can be substituted for masculine purity, so likely to preserve it from the fatal effects of debauched habits, as a fervid and constant passion for a refined and amiable woman": that passion may be conjugal, filial, or paternal. A "refined and amiable woman" is equally effective as wife, mother, or daughter. Thus, if Seward had a son, she would have him "buried in obscurity" and "dead to wealth and fame, but alive, in every nerve, to domestic comfort and affection" (1:xlix–l).

Thomas Jefferson speaks at times as if he were Seward's son. In 1799, attending Congressional sessions in Philadelphia, Jefferson writes home to his daughter Mary, "Your letter . . . was, as Ossian says, or would say, like the bright beams of the moon on the desolate heath. Environed here in scenes of constant torment, malice and obloquy . . . I feel not that existence is a blessing but when something recalls my mind to family or farm" (quoted in Paul Degategno, "Jefferson Reads the Poems of Ossian," *Ossian Revisited* 94). Jefferson here assumes the role of Fingal, the public leader with a domestic heart; the warrior-citizen whose thoughts are never far from the women at home. Mary's letter arrives "like a beam on the heath": the Fingalian locution Jefferson here recalls is "a beam that was set returns!"—a stock phrase that refers to the feeling a man has when inspired by the image of a dead woman. Though Mary is of course not dead, she resides in Charlottesville, far from the work of realizing the new republic. And it is precisely this work that separates Jefferson from Anna Seward's imagined son, "dead to wealth and fame." Thinking of Mary as an Agandecca figure allows Jefferson to pursue his work softened but uninterrupted, polished but undisturbed. Jefferson sought to be the Solon if not the Demosthenes of the American republic; he aimed to secure ancient fraternal liberties and to revive the scene of eloquence lost since the classical era. As Degategno argues,

Jefferson read Fingal in light of his own aspirations, seeing in the Celtic patriarch an example of "the heroic life which is not incompatible with democracy" (105).

If the increasingly privatized household had come under the surveillance of mother or daughter, it is not surprising that nostalgia for a broader sense of civic community should figure itself as a longing for a heroic father figure. Indeed, we may understand the Country party polemic—from Bolingbroke to John Brown and even to Thomas Jefferson—as based, in part, on an infantile wish for Oedipal resolution; it is not, as Isaac Kramnick contends, a mere Machiavellian excrescence that Bolingbroke concludes his political writings with a call for a great man, a father-king who will reconfirm the social ties between men (*Bolingbroke* 166–68). Nor is it necessarily paradoxical that the father-king could be Queen Elizabeth: as I have shown, gender roles were easily separable from gender. The patriot call, be it for orator, minister, chieftain, queen, or king, is at bottom a plea for a masculine voice to unite us—to tear down, so to speak, the walls between our dividual houses. Thus it is more than a compliment to William Pitt alone when John Brown concludes his sustained attack on the "effeminacy" of modern manners: "Virtue may rise on the ruins of Corruption, and a despairing Nation may yet be saved, by the Wisdom, the Integrity, and unshaken Courage, of SOME GREAT MINISTER" (110). And thus Brown's invocation little differs from Samuel Johnson's wishful assurance to his countrymen upon the accession of George III that "they have at last a king who . . . wishes to be the common father of all his people" (*Political Writings* 344). What is called for is a heroic figure who may save society from "dissolv[ing] into a tumult of individuals" (425), each presumably haunted by his or her own private ghosts.

In light of the controversies that surrounded the rising "feminine" ideal of private life, Macpherson's complex and ambivalent depiction of women and manners could not fail to strike a responsive chord in his readership. The strong governor often imagined by the Opposition was embodied, at least superficially, in Ossian's heroic father, Fingal. Fingal is the patriot king, in a way that neither Frederick, prince of Wales, nor his son, George III, could ever be; in a way that Walter Shandy, for all his eloquence on patriarchal rule, or Prince Rasselas, for all his daydreams of displacing his father, knew they could never be. Unlike these pretenders, Fingal is the benevolent patriarch who unites all his people. Conspicuously, however, his patriarchal world excludes conjugal families and even mature women. Ossian's young heroines die beautifully of heartbreak and only rarely, as in the case of Ossian's wife, Evir-Allen, manage to become mothers before they die. But at the same time the Ossian poems reflect the age's commitment to manners and domesticity: even Fingal, as a stranger among the inhospitable Scandinavians, dreams of hearing the familiar voices of women in his own royal hall. And even Fingal is haunted by the speaking ghosts of women whom he has loved, memorably.

# Epilogue

In sum, the contradiction between the republican ideal of elo-quence and the ideology of politeness is dialectically resolved in the utopia of the *Poems of Ossian*. Like a Sophoclean god, Ossian descends to settle a seemingly insoluble tension that had abided in British society and letters since the ministry of Walpole, the days of Hume's "Of Eloquence" and Pope's late poetry. Macpher-son's achievement is thus of the highest importance for the later eighteenth-century reading public and for us as students of liter-ary and cultural history.

Macpherson cannot, however, resolve the ongoing tension be-tween republican nostalgia and the imperative of politeness that is still in some ways with us in contemporary America. We as students of literature and politics still inhabit a public sphere that generally asks us to write polite prose—an act that carries with it roughly the same ideological import that it did in the age of Hume. Of course, since the deluge in the 1970s of Continental modes of literary criticism and cultural critique, many academics have consciously decided *not* to write in accord with the cadences and presuppositions of the British Enlightenment; the price of such defiance, however, has been that literary critics increasingly address themselves only to a handful of like-minded academics and adopt coolly superior attitudes toward the occasional derision of reviewers in, say, *The New York Times Book Review*, or the dismay of more "public" intellectuals in *The New York Review of Books, The New Republic, The New Yorker, The Atlantic Monthly*, or a quarterly such as *Raritan*. For these latter journals do, for better or for worse, keep alive the ideal (and to a greater or lesser degree the reality) of polite community roughly as Hume envisioned it—that is, a social world of quiet readers that includes professional writers, politicians, university professors, moderate clergy, and members of the other professions and the business community. That this group no longer needs to define itself vocally against "the vulgar" or "the mob" argues as much for its own consolidation as for its peculiarly American commitment to civic equality.

Yet despite the ostensible triumph of politeness, 250 years after Hume's "Of Eloquence" the polite world still at times regrets the loss of eloquence and its passionate communitarian assumptions. Thus during two election years of recent memory, the journalist Henry Fairlie wrote doleful essays in *The New Republic* entitled "The Decline of Oratory" (28 May 1984) and "The Collapse of Oratory" (10 October 1988), both roundly criticizing the presidential candidates of the day for sounding like mere administrators rather than rousing republican orators. This type of complaint is of course compelling to twentieth-century Americans who (probably unlike Fairlie) have not read Hume or Blair for the simple reason that much of our own cultural education still revolves around praise of famous orators who at crucial moments in our history have summoned political community into being. In lieu of Demosthenes or Cicero we have Patrick Henry in the Virginia House of Burgesses; Jefferson drafting the oratorical Declaration of Independence; Lincoln at Gettysburg; King on the steps of the Lincoln Memorial. The tendency to apotheosize orators has deep roots in our republic—to cite only two Americans I have quoted in the course of this book, there is the jubilant oration on the power of eloquence given by John Quincy Adams, first Boylston lecturer on rhetoric and subsequently sixth President of the United States; and there is Jefferson's *Autobiography*, a work that narrates the origins of the American Revolution in terms of an anatomy of political eloquence, ultimately awarding the palm to the "pure, classical and copious" James Madison (43).

In the very heart of politeness, veiled oratory still has her sovereign shrine. The stylistic and political contradiction of eloquence and polite style will not be solved for us, as it was perhaps for Jefferson, by the peculiar utopia of the *Poems of Ossian*. But by understanding both the history and the historicity of that contradiction—as this book has, I hope, enabled us to do—we may better be able to address it anew in terms that speak to our own situation and to our own age.

# Bibliography

Abrams, M. H. *Natural Supernaturalism: Tradition and Revolution in Romantic Literature.* New York: Norton, 1971.

Adair, James. *History of the American Indians* (1775). Ed. Samuel Cole Williams. Johnson City, Tenn.: Watauga Press, 1930.

Adams, John Quincy. *An Inaugural Oration . . . as Boylston Professor of Rhetorick and Oratory at Harvard University.* Boston, 1806.

Addison, Joseph, and Richard Steele. *The Spectator.* 5 vols. Ed. Donald F. Bond. Oxford: Clarendon, 1965.

——. *The Tatler.* 4 vols. Ed. G. A. Aitken. London, 1898–99.

Akenside, Mark. *Poetical Works.* Ed. Alexander Dyce. London, 1834.

Anderson, Robert. *Hume's First Principles.* Lincoln: University of Nebraska Press, 1966.

Andreas Capellanus. *The Art of Courtly Love.* Trans. John Jay Parry. New York: Columbia University Press, 1941.

Arendt, Hannah. *The Human Condition.* Chicago: University of Chicago Press, 1958.

Aristotle. *"The Rhetoric" and "Poetics."* Trans. W. Rhys Roberts (*Rhetoric*) and Ingram Bywater (*Poetics*). Oxford: Clarendon, 1908. Reprint. New York: Modern Library, 1984.

Armstrong, Nancy. *Desire and Domestic Fiction: A Political History of the Novel.* New York: Oxford University Press, 1987.

Baier, Annette. *A Progress of Sentiments: Reflections on Hume's "Treatise."* Cambridge, Mass.: Harvard University Press, 1991.

Baillie, John. *The Interpretation of Religion: An Introductory Study of Theological Principles.* New York: Scribner's, 1928.

Bate, Walter Jackson. *The Burden of the Past and the English Poet.* Cambridge, Mass.: Harvard University Press, 1970.

Barrell, John. *English Literature in History, 1730–1780: An Equal, Wide Survey*. London: Hutchinson, 1983.

Becker, Carl. *The Heavenly City of the Eighteenth-Century Philosophers*. New Haven: Yale University Press, 1932.

Bender, John. *Imagining the Penitentiary: Fiction and the Architecture of Mind in Eighteenth-Century England*. Chicago: University of Chicago Press, 1987.

——. "A New History of the Enlightenment?" In *The Profession of Eighteenth-Century Literature: Reflections on an Institution*, ed. Leo Damrosch, 62–83. Madison: University of Wisconsin Press, 1992.

Bevilacqua, Vincent. "Philosophical Origins of George Campbell's *Philosophy of Rhetoric*." *Speech Monographs* 32 (1965): 1–12.

Bitzer, Lloyd F. "Hume's Philosophy in Campbell." *Philosophy and Rhetoric* 2 (1969): 139–66.

Blackwall, Anthony. *An Introduction to the Classics . . . with an Essay, on the Nature and Use of Those Beautiful and Emphatic Figures which Give Strength and Ornament to Writing*. London, 1719.

Blackwell, Thomas. *Letters concerning Mythology*. London, 1748.

Blair, Hugh. *Lectures on Rhetoric and Belles-Lettres* (1783). 2 vols. Ed. Harold F. Harding. Carbondale: Southern Illinois University Press, 1965.

Bloom, Harold. *The Anxiety of Influence: A Theory of Poetry*. New York: Oxford University Press, 1973.

Bogel, Fredric V. *Literature and Insubstantiality in Later Eighteenth-Century England*. Princeton: Princeton University Press, 1984.

Bolingbroke, Lord. *The Craftsman*. By Caleb D'Anvers (pseud., Bolingbroke et al.). 14 vols. London, 1731–37.

——. *The Idea of a Patriot King*. Ed. Sydney W. Jackman. Indianapolis: Bobbs-Merrill, 1965.

——. *Works*. Ed. David Mallet (1754). Dublin, 1793.

Boswell, James. *Boswell in Search of a Wife, 1766–1769*. Ed. Frank Brady and Frederick A. Pottle. New York: McGraw, 1956.

——. *Life of Johnson*. Ed. R. W. Chapman, with an intro. by Pat Rogers. Oxford: Oxford University Press, 1980.

——. *London Journal 1762–1763*. Ed. Frederick A. Pottle. New Haven: Yale University Press, 1950.

——. *Private Papers of James Boswell from Malahide Castle*. 18 vols. Ed. Geoffrey Scott and Frederick A. Pottle. Mount Vernon, N.Y.: privately printed (W. E. Rudge), 1928–34.

Box, M. A. *The Suasive Art of David Hume*. Princeton: Princeton University Press, 1990.

Brewer, John. *Party Ideology and Popular Politics at the Accession of George III*. Cambridge: Cambridge University Press, 1976.

Bronson, Bertrand. *Facets of the Enlightenment*. Berkeley and Los Angeles: University of California Press, 1968.

Brown, John. *An Estimate of the Manners and Principles of the Times* (1757). London, 1758.

Budgell, Eustace. *A Letter to His Excellency Mr. Ulrick D'Ypres, Chief Minister to the King of Sparta*. London, 1731.

Burke, Edmund. *On Revolution*. Ed. Robert A. Smith. New York: Harper and Row, 1968.

——. *A Philosophical Enquiry into the Origin of Our Ideas of the Sublime and Beautiful* (1757). Ed. J. T. Boulton. New York: Columbia University Press, 1958.

——. *Reflections on the Revolution in France*. Ed. Conor Cruise O'Brien. Harmondsworth, England: Penguin Books, 1968.

Burton, John Hill. *Life and Correspondence of David Hume*. 2 vols. Edinburgh, 1846.

Burtt, Shelley. *Virtue Transformed: Political Argument in England, 1688–1740*. Cambridge: Cambridge University Press, 1992.

Butler, Samuel. *Hudibras*. Ed. John Wilders. Oxford: Clarendon, 1967.

Byrd, Max. *"Tristram Shandy."* London: Allen and Unwin, 1985.

Camic, Charles. *Experience and Enlightenment: Socialization for Cultural Change in Eighteenth-Century Scotland*. Edinburgh: Edinburgh University Press, 1983.

Campbell, George. *The Philosophy of Rhetoric* (1776). Ed. Lloyd F. Bitzer. Carbondale: Southern Illinois University Press, 1988.

Caplan, Harry. *Of Eloquence: Studies in Ancient and Medieval Rhetoric*. Ithaca: Cornell University Press, 1970.

Carretta, Vincent. *The Snarling Muse: Verbal and Visual Satire from Pope to Churchill*. Philadelphia: University of Pennsylvania Press, 1983.

Carson, James P. "Commodification and the Figure of the Castrato in Smollett's *Humphrey Clinker*." *The Eighteenth Century: Theory and Interpretation* 33 (1992): 24–46.

Cash, Arthur. *Laurence Sterne: The Early and Middle Years*. London: Methuen, 1975.

Castle, Terry. "The Spectralization of the Other in *The Mysteries of Udolpho*." In *The New Eighteenth Century: Theory, Politics, English Literature*, ed. Felicity Nussbaum and Laura Brown, 231–53. New York: Methuen, 1987.

Chadwick, Nora. *The Celts*. Harmondsworth: Penguin, 1970.

Chapin, Chester F. *Personification in Eighteenth-Century Poetry*. New York: Columbia University Press, 1955.

Chartier, Roger. *The Cultural Uses of Print in Early Modern France*. Trans. Lydia G. Cochrane. Princeton: Princeton University Press, 1987.

Chase, Cynthia. *Decomposing Figures: Rhetorical Readings in the Romantic Tradition*. Baltimore: Johns Hopkins University Press, 1986.

Chesterfield, fourth earl of. *Characters*. Intro. by Alan T. Mackenzie. Los

Angeles: Williams Andrew Clark Memorial Library (Augustan Reprint nos. 259–60), 1990.

Chitnis, Anand. *The Scottish Enlightenment: A Social History.* Totowa, N.J.: Rowman and Littlefield, 1976.

Christensen, Jerome. *Practicing Enlightenment: Hume and the Formation of a Literary Career.* Madison: University of Wisconsin Press, 1987.

Cicero. *On Oratory and Orators* (1848). Trans. J. S. Watson, with an intro. by Ralph A. Micken. Carbondale: Southern Illinois University Press, 1970.

——. *The Verrine Orations.* 2 vols. Ed. by L. H. G. Greenwood. Loeb Classical Library. Cambridge, Mass.: Harvard University Press, 1959.

[Cicero, erroneous attribution]. *Rhetorica ad Herennium.* Ed. Harry Caplan. Cambridge, Mass.: Harvard University Press, 1954.

Clark, J. C. D. *English Society, 1688–1832: Ideology, Social Structure and Political Practice during the Ancien Regime.* Cambridge: Cambridge University Press, 1985.

Collins, James. *The Emergence of Philosophy of Religion.* New Haven: Yale University Press, 1967.

Condillac, Etienne Bonnot de. *An Essay on the Origin of Human Knowledge* (1746). Trans. Thomas Nugent (London, 1756). Facsimile reprint. Intro. Robert G. Weyant. Gainseville, Fla.: Scholars' Facsimiles, 1971.

——. *Oeuvres Complètes.* 16 vols. Paris, 1821–1822. Reprinted in 8 vols. Geneva: Slatkine, 1971.

[Cooke, Thomas.] *An Ode on the Powers of Eloquence.* London, 1755.

Cox, Stephen D. *"The Stranger within Thee": Concepts of the Self in Late Eighteenth-Century Literature.* Pittsburgh: University of Pittsburgh Press, 1980.

Craig, Cairns, ed. *The History of Scottish Literature.* 4 vols. Aberdeen: Aberdeen University Press, 1987–88.

Crocker, Lester. "The Enlightenment: What and Who?" In *Studies in Eighteenth-Century Culture,* vol. 17, ed. John Yolton and Leslie Ellen Brown, 335–48. East Lansing, Mich.: Colleagues Press, 1987.

Cross, Wilbur L. *The Life and Times of Laurence Sterne.* 3d ed. New Haven: Yale University Press, 1929.

Curtis, Lewis Perry. *The Politicks of Laurence Sterne.* London: Oxford University Press, 1929.

Damrosch, Leo. *Fictions of Reality in the Age of Hume and Johnson.* Madison: University of Wisconsin Press, 1990.

Davies, Edward. *The Claims of Ossian, Examined and Appreciated . . . .* Swansea, 1825.

Davis, Rose Mary. *The Good Lord Lyttelton: A Study in Eighteenth-Century Politics and Culture.* Bethlehem, Pa.: Times Publishing, 1939.

de Man, Paul. *Allegories of Reading: Figural Language in Rousseau, Nietzsche, Rilke, and Proust.* New Haven: Yale University Press, 1979.
——. *The Rhetoric of Romanticism.* New York: Columbia University Press, 1984.
DeMaria, Robert. "The Politics of Johnson's *Dictionary.*" *PMLA* 104 (1989): 64–74.
Demosthenes. *Orations.* Trans. Thomas Leland (1754–61). Intro. by Ephiphanius Wilson. New York: Lamb, 1900.
Derrida, Jacques. "White Mythology: Metaphor in the Text of Philosophy." Trans. F. C. T. Moore. *New Literary History* 6 (1974): 5–74.
Donne, John. *Devotions upon Emergent Occasions* (1624). Ed. Anthony Raspa. Montreal: McGill-Queens University Press, 1975.
Dowling, William C. *The Epistolary Moment: The Verse Epistle in Eighteenth-Century England.* Princeton: Princeton University Press, 1991.
——. "Ideology and the Flight from History in Eighteenth-Century Poetry." In *The Profession of Eighteenth-Century Literature: Reflections on an Institution*, ed. Leo Damrosch, 135–53. Madison: University of Wisconsin Press, 1992.
——. *Jameson, Althusser, Marx: An Introduction to "The Political Unconscious."* Ithaca: Cornell University Press, 1984.
Dryden, John. *Essays.* Ed. W. P. Kerr. Oxford: Clarendon, 1926.
Duff, William. *Critical Observations on the Writing of the Most Celebrated Originial Geniuses in Poetry.* London, 1770.
Dumarsais, César Chesneau. *Traité des Tropes* (1729). 2 vols. Intro. by Gérard Genette. Geneva: Slatkine, 1967.
Dwyer, John. "Enlightened Spectators and Classical Moralists: Sympathetic Relations in Eighteenth-Century Scotland." *Eighteenth-Century Life* 15, nos. 1–2 (1991): 96–118.
——. "The Imperative of Sociability: Moral Culture in the Late Scottish Enlightenment." *British Journal for Eighteenth-Century Studies* 13 (1990): 169–84.
Edwards, Thomas R. *Imagination and Power: A Study of Poetry on Public Themes.* New York: Oxford University Press, 1971.
——. *This Dark Estate: A Reading of Pope.* Berkeley and Los Angeles: University of California Press, 1963.
Empson, William. *Some Versions of Pastoral.* New York: New Directions, 1974.
*Encyclopaedia Britannica; or, a Dictionary of Arts and Sciences, Compiled on a New Plan.* 3 vols. "By a Society of Gentlemen in Edinburgh." Edinburgh, 1771.
Engell, James. "The Modern Revival of Myth: Its Eighteenth-Century Origins." In *Allegory, Myth, and Symbol*, ed. Morton W. Bloomfield, 245–71. Cambridge, Mass.: Harvard University Press, 1981.
Erskine-Hill, Howard. *The Augustan Idea in English Literature.* London: Edward Arnold, 1983.

Erwin, Timothy. "Alexander Pope and the Disappearance of the Beauti-ful." *Eighteenth-Century Life* 16, no. 3 (1992): 46–64.

Fénelon, François de Salignac de La Mothe. *Dialogues sur L'Eloquence* (1717). Paris, 1787.

Ferguson, Adam. *An Essay on the History of Civil Society* (1767). Ed. Duncan Forbes. Edinburgh: Edinburgh University Press, 1966.

Fielding, Henry. *Amelia*. Ed. Martin Battestin. Middletown, Conn.: Wesleyan University Press, 1983.

——. *"Joseph Andrews," "Shamela," and Related Writings*. Ed. Homer Goldberg. New York: Norton, 1987.

——. *Miscellanies*. Vol. 1. Ed. Henry Knight Miller. Middletown, Conn.: Wesleyan University Press, 1972.

——. *Tom Jones*. 2 vols. Ed. Fredson Bowers, with an intro. and commen-tary by Martin Battestin. Oxford: Clarendon, 1974.

Fish, Stanley E. *Doing What Comes Naturally: Change, Rhetoric, and the Practice of Theory in Literary and Legal Studies*. Durham: Duke University Press, 1989.

——. *Surprised by Sin: The Reader in "Paradise Lost."* New York: St. Martin's Press, 1967.

Fisher, Philip. "Thinking about Killing: *Hamlet* and the Path among the Passions." *Raritan Quaterly* 11, no. 1 (1991): 43–77.

[Fleming, Caleb.] "Three Questions Resolved. viz. What Is Religion? What Is the Christian Religion? What Is the Christian Catholic Church? . . . with a Postscript on Mr. Hume's Natural History of Religion." London, 1757.

Flew, Antony. *Hume's Philosophy of Belief: A Study of His First Inquiry*. London: Routledge and Kegan Paul, 1961.

Folkenflik, Robert. "Macpherson, Chatterton, and the Great Age of Liter-ary Forgery." *Centennial Review* 18 (1974): 378–91.

Fontenelle, Bernard. *Oeuvres Complètes*. 3 vols. Ed. G. B. Depping. Paris, 1818. Reprint. Geneva: Slatkine, 1968.

Foote, Samuel. *The Commissary, a Comedy in Three Acts* (1765). Lon-don, 1773.

Forbes, Duncan. *Hume's Philosophical Politics*. Cambridge: Cambridge University Press, 1975.

Fordyce, James. *The Character and Conduct of the Female Sex, and the Advantages to Be Derived by Young Men from the Society of Virtuous Women*. London, 1776.

Foucault, Michel. *The Order of Things: An Archaeology of the Human Sciences*. New York: Vintage, 1973.

France, Peter. *Politeness and Its Discontents: Problems in French Classi-cal Culture*. Cambridge: Cambridge University Press, 1992.

Franklin, Benjamin. *Autobiography*. Ed. J. A. Leo Lemay and P. M. Zall. New York: Norton, 1986.

Fraunce, Abraham. *The Arcadian Rhetoric* (1588). Facsimile reprint. Menston, England: Scolar Press, 1969.

French, David P., ed. *Minor English Poets, 1660–1780: A Selelction of Alexander Chalmers's "The English Poets" [1810].* 10 vols. New York: Benjamin Blom, 1967.

Freud, Sigmund. *The Future of an Illusion.* Trans. James Strachey. New York: Norton, 1961.

——. *Moses and Monotheism.* Trans. Katherine Jones. New York: Vintage, 1967.

Gaskill, Howard, ed. *Ossian Revisited.* Edinburgh: Edinburgh University Press, 1991.

Gay, Peter. *The Enlightenment: An Interpretation.* 2 vols. New York: Knopf, 1966–69.

Gerard, Alexander. *An Essay on Taste* (1759). Intro. by Walter J. Hipple. Facsimile reprint. Gainesville, Fla.: Scholars' Facsimiles, 1963.

Gibbon, Edward. *The History of the Decline and Fall of the Roman Empire.* 7 vols. Ed. J. B. Bury. London: Methuen, 1909.

Gilman, Ernest B. *Iconoclasm and Poetry in the English Reformation: Down Went Dagon.* Chicago: University of Chicago Press, 1986.

Goethe, Johann Wolfgang von. *"The Sorrows of Young Werther" and "Novella."* Trans. Elizabeth Mayer, Louise Bogan, and W. H. Auden. New York: Random House, 1971.

Goldgar, Bertrand A. *Walpole and the Wits: The Relation of Politics to Literature, 1722–1742.* Lincoln: University of Nebraska Press, 1976.

Goldsmith, Oliver. *Collected Works.* 5 vols. Ed. Arthur Friedman. Oxford: Clarendon, 1966.

[Gordon, Thomas, and John Trenchard.] *Cato's Letters; or, Essays on Liberty, Civil and Religious* (1720–23). 4 vols. London, 1748.

Graham, Patrick. *Essay on the Authenticity of the Poems of Ossian.* Edinburgh, 1807.

Gray, Thomas, and William Collins. *Poetical Works.* Ed. Roger Lonsdale. Oxford: Oxford University Press, 1977.

Greenblatt, Stephen. *Renaissance Self-Fashioning: From More to Shakespeare.* Chicago: University of Chicago Press, 1980.

Griffin, Dustin. *Alexander Pope: The Poet in the Poems.* Princeton: Princeton University Press, 1978.

Hagstrum, Jean. *The Sister Arts: The Tradition of Literary Pictorialism and English Poetry from Dryden to Gray.* Chicago: University of Chicago Press, 1958.

Hammond, Brean S. *Pope and Bolingbroke: A Study of Friendship and Influence.* Columbia: University of Missouri Press, 1984.

Havelock, Eric. *The Literate Revolution in Greece and Its Cultural Consequences.* Princeton: Princeton University Press, 1982.

——. *The Muse Learns to Write: Reflections on Orality and Literacy from Antiquity to the Present.* New Haven: Yale University Press, 1986.

Haywood, Ian. *The Making of History: A Study of the Literary Forgeries of James Macpherson and Thomas Chatterton*. Teaneck, N.J.: Fairleigh Dickinson University Press, 1986.

Hedrick, Elizabeth. "Fixing the Language: Johnson, Chesterfield, and *The Plan of a Dictionary*." *ELH* 55 (1988): 421–42.

Henley, John ("Orator"). *The Appeal of the Oratory to the First Ages of Christianity*. London, 1727.

——. *The Art of Speaking in Public: An Essay on the Action of an Orator, as to His Pronunciation and Gesture*. London, 1727.

——. *Milk for Babes . . . No. 5 of Oratory Transactions*. London, 1729.

——. *Oratory Transactions. No. 1*. London, 1728.

——. *Why How Now, Gossip Pope?* London, 1743.

Hertz, Neil. *The End of the Line: Essays on Psychoanalysis and the Sublime*. New York: Columbia University Press, 1985.

Holmes, John. *The Art of Rhetoric Made Easy*. London, 1755.

Homer. *The Iliad*. Trans. Richard Lattimore. Chicago: University of Chicago Press, 1951.

Hope, V. M. *Virtue by Consensus: The Moral Philosophy of Hutcheson, Hume, and Adam Smith*. Oxford: Clarendon, 1989.

Horkheimer, Max, and Theodor Adorno. *Dialectic of Enlightenment*. Trans. John Cumming. New York: Herder and Herder, 1972.

Howell, Wilbur Samuel. *Eighteenth-Century British Logic and Rhetoric*. Princeton: Princeton University Press, 1971.

Hume, David. *Dialogues concerning Natural Religion*. Ed. Norman Kemp Smith. Indianapolis: Bobbs-Merrill, 1947.

——. *An Enquiry concerning Human Understanding*. Ed. Charles Hendel. Indianapolis: Bobbs-Merrill, 1955.

——. *An Enquiry concerning the Principles of Morals*. Ed. J. B. Schneewind. Indianapolis: Hackett, 1983.

——. *Essays Moral, Political and Literary*. Ed. Eugene F. Miller. Indianapolis: Liberty Classics, 1985.

——. *The History of England*. 6 vols. Ed. William B. Todd. Indianapolis: Liberty Classics, 1983.

——. *The Letters of David Hume*. 2 vols. Ed. J. Y. T. Grieg. Oxford: Clarendon, 1932.

——. *The Natural History of Religion*. Ed. H. E. Root. Stanford: Stanford University Press, 1957.

——. *A Treatise of Human Nature*. Ed. L. A. Selby-Bigge. Rev. Peter H. Nidditch. Oxford: Clarendon, 1978.

Hundert, E. J. "The Thread of Language and the Web of Dominion: Mandeville to Rousseau and Back." *Eighteenth-Century Studies* 21 (1987–88): 169–91.

Hurd, Richard. *Letters on Chivalry and Romance* (1762). Ed. Edith J. Morley. London: H. Frowde, 1911.

——. *Works*. 8 vols. London, 1811.

Huxley, T. H. *Hume*. London, 1879.

Ignatieff, Michael. *The Needs of Strangers*. New York: Viking Penguin, 1985.

Jack, Ian. "Gray's *Elegy* Reconsidered." In *From Sensibility to Romanticism: Essays Presented to Frederick A. Pottle*, ed. Frederick W. Hilles and Harold Bloom, 139–69. New York: Oxford University Press, 1965.

Jameson, Fredric. *The Political Unconscious: Narrative as a Socially Symbolic Act*. Ithaca: Cornell University Press, 1981.

Jamieson, Alexander. *A Grammar of Rhetoric, and Polite Literature*. London, 1818.

Jefferson, Thomas. *The Life and Selected Writings*. Ed. Adrienne Koch and William Peden. New York: Random House, 1944.

Johnson, Samuel. *The Lives of the English Poets*. 3 vols. Ed. G. Birbeck Hill. Oxford: Oxford University Press, 1935.

——. *Political Writings*. Ed. Donald Greene. Vol. 10 of the Yale ed. New Haven: Yale University Press, 1977.

——. *"Rasselas" and Other Tales*. Ed. Gwin J. Kolb. Vol. 16 of the Yale ed. New Haven: Yale University Press, 1990.

Jones, Peter. *Hume's Sentiments: Their Ciceronian and French Contexts*. Edinburgh: Edinburgh University Press, 1982.

——. "The Scottish Professoriate and the Polite Academy, 1720–1746." In *Wealth and Virtue: The Shaping of Political Economy in the Scottish Enlightenment*, ed. Ivan Hont and Michael Ignatieff, 89–118. Cambridge: Cambridge University Press, 1983.

Kallich, Martin. *The Association of Ideas and Critical Theory in Eighteenth-Century England*. The Hague: Mouton, 1970.

Kames, Lord, Henry Home. *Elements of Criticism* (1762; rev. 1785). 2 vols. Reprint. New York: Garland, 1972.

——. *Sketches of the History of Man*. 2 vols. London, 1774.

Kay, Carol. *Political Constructions: Defoe, Richardson, and Sterne in Relation to Hobbes, Hume, and Burke*. Ithaca: Cornell University Press, 1988.

Keener, Frederick. "Pope, *The Dunciad*, Virgil, and the New Historicism of Le Bossu." *Eighteenth-Century Life* 15, no. 3 (1991): 35–57.

Klein, Lawrence. "The Third Earl of Shaftesbury and the Progress of Politeness." *Eighteenth-Century Studies* 18 (1984–85): 186–214.

Knapp, Steven. *Personification and the Sublime: Milton to Coleridge*. Cambridge, Mass.: Harvard University Press, 1985.

Knox, Norman N. *The Word "Irony" and Its Context, 1500–1755*. Durham: Duke University Press, 1961.

Kolakowski, Leszek. *The Presence of Myth*. Trans. Adam Czerniawski. Chicago: University of Chicago Press, 1989.

Kramnick, Isaac. *Bolingbroke and His Circle: The Politics of Nostalgia in the Age of Walpole*. Cambridge, Mass.: Harvard University Press, 1968.

——. *Republicanism and Bourgeois Radicalism: Political Ideology in*

*Late Eighteenth-Century England and America.* Ithaca: Cornell University Press, 1990.

Kroll, Richard. *The Material Word: Literate Culture in the Restoration and Early Eighteenth Century.* Baltimore: Johns Hopkins University Press, 1991.

Lamb, Charles. *The Portable Charles Lamb.* Ed. John Mason Brown. New York: Viking Press, 1948.

Landau, Norma. "Eighteenth-Century England: Tales Historians Tell." *Eighteenth-Century Studies* 22 (1988–89): 208–18.

Landes, Joan B. *Women and the Public Sphere in the Age of the French Revolution.* Ithaca: Cornell University Press, 1988.

Langford, Paul. *A Polite and Commercial People: England 1727–1783.* Oxford: Clarendon, 1989.

Lanham, Richard A. *The Motives of Eloquence: Literary Rhetoric in the Renaissance.* New Haven: Yale University Press, 1976.

Laqueur, Thomas. *Making Sex: Body and Gender from the Greeks to Freud.* Cambridge, Mass.: Harvard University Press, 1990.

Leavis, F. R. *Revaluation: Tradition and Development in English Poetry.* London: Chatto and Windus, 1969.

Leland, Thomas. *A Dissertation on the Principles of Human Eloquence.* London, 1764.

Lennox, Charlotte. *The Female Quixote.* Ed. Margaret Dalziel. New York: Oxford University Press, 1989.

Lentricchia, Frank. "Foucault's Legacy: A New Historicism?" In *The New Historicism,* ed. H. Aram Veeser, 231–42. New York: Routledge, 1989.

Livingston, Donald W. *Hume's Philosophy of Common Life.* Chicago: University of Chicago Press, 1984.

Locke, John. *An Essay Concerning Human Understanding.* Ed. Peter H. Nidditch. Oxford: Oxford University Press, 1975.

——. *A Letter concerning Toleration.* Ed. James H. Tully. Indianapolis: Hackett, 1983.

——. *The Second Treatise upon Government.* Ed. Thomas P. Peardon. Indianapolis: Bobbs-Merrill, 1952.

Longinus. "On the Sublime." In *Classical Literary Criticism: Aristotle/Longinus/Horace,* trans. T. S. Dorsch, 99–158. Harmondsworth, England: Penguin, 1965.

Lucas, F. L. *The Art of Living; Four Eighteenth-Century Minds: Hume, Horace Walpole, Burke, Benjamin Franklin.* London: Cassell, 1959.

Lucretius. *On the Nature of the Universe.* Trans. Ronald Latham. Harmondsworth, England: Penguin, 1951.

Lukacs, Georg. *The Theory of the Novel.* Trans. Anna Bostock. Cambridge, Mass.: Harvard University Press, 1971.

Lyttelton, Lord. *Works.* 3 vols. London, 1776.

McIntosh, Carey. *Common and Courtly Language: The Stylistics of So-*

*cial Class in Eighteenth-Century English Literature*. Philadelphia: University of Pennsylvania Press, 1986.

MacIntyre, A. C. "Hume on 'Is' and 'Ought.'" In *Hume: A Collection of Critical Essays*, ed. V. C. Chappell, 240–64. Notre Dame: University of Notre Dame Press, 1968.

Mack, Maynard. *The Garden and the City: Retirement and Politics in the Late Poetry of Pope*. Toronto: University of Toronto Press, 1969.

Mckenzie, Alan T. *Certain Lively Episodes: The Articulation of Passion in Eighteenth-Century Prose*. Athens: University of Georgia Press, 1990.

Mackenzie, George. *An Idea of the Modern Eloquence of the Bar*. Unattributed trans. from Latin. Edinburgh, 1711.

Mackenzie, Henry. *The Man of Feeling*. Ed. Kenneth C. Slagle. New York: Norton, 1958.

——. *Report of the Committee of the Highland Society of Scotland, Appointed to Inquire into the Nature and Authenticity of the Poems of Ossian*. Edinburgh, 1805.

Macpherson, James. *Poems of Ossian*. Philadelphia, 1839.

——. *The Poems of Ossian . . . with Notes and Illustrations by Malcolm Laing, Esq*. Edinburgh, 1805.

Manuel, Frank E. *The Eighteenth Century Confronts the Gods*. Cambridge, Mass.: Harvard University Press, 1959.

Markley, Robert. "Style as Philosophical Structure: The Context of Shaftesbury's *Charactersticks*." In *The Philosopher as Writer: The Eighteenth Century*, ed. Robert Ginsberg, 140–54. Selinsgrove: Susquehanna University Press, 1987.

Meehan, Michael. *Liberty and Poetics in Eighteenth-Century England*. London: Croom Helm, 1986.

Merrill, James. *The Changing Light at Sandover* (incl. *The Book of Ephraim*). New York: Atheneum, 1982.

Middleton, Conyers. *The Life of Marcus Tullius Cicero* (1741). 3 vols. London, 1804.

Midgley, Graham. *The Life of Orator Henley*. Oxford: Clarendon, 1973.

Milton, John. *Complete Poems and Major Prose*. Ed. Merrit Y. Hughes. New York: Odyssey Press, 1957.

[Moir, Andrew.] *The Deist Stretched upon a Death-Bed, or a Lively Portraiture of a Dying Infidel*. Edinburgh, 1755.

Monboddo, Lord, James Burnett. *Of the Origin and Progress of Language* (1773–92). 6 vols. Facsimile reprint. New York: Garland, 1970.

Montaigne. *Essays*. Trans. J. M. Cohen. Harmondsworth, England: Penguin, 1958.

Moore, James. "The Social Background of Hume's Science of Human Nature." In *McGill Hume Studies*, ed. David Fate Norton, Nicholas Capaldi, and Wade L. Robison, 23–41. San Diego: Austin Hill, 1979.

Mossner, Ernest Campbell. *The Life of David Hume.* Austin: University of Texas Press, 1954.

Mullan, John. *Sentiment and Sociability: The Language of Feeling in the Eighteenth Century.* Oxford: Clarendon, 1988.

Ness, Robert. "*The Dunciad* and Italian Opera in England." *Eighteenth-Century Studies* 20 (1986–87): 173–94.

Nietzsche, Friedrich. *Das Philosophenbuch/Le Livre du Philosophe.* French trans. by Angèle K. Marietti. Paris: Aubier-Flammarion, 1969.

Noxon, James. *Hume's Philosophical Development: A Study of His Methods.* Oxford: Clarendon, 1973.

Ong, Walter. *Orality and Literacy: The Technologizing of the Word.* London: Methuen, 1982.

——. "Rhetoric and the Origins of Consciousness." In his *Rhetoric, Romance, and Technology: Studies in the Interaction of Expression and Culture,* 1–15. Ithaca: Cornell University Press, 1971.

Paglia, Camille. *Sexual Personae: Art and Decadence from Nefertiti to Emily Dickinson.* New Haven: Yale University Press, 1990.

Parnell, Thomas. *Collected Poems.* Ed. Claude Rawson and F. P. Lock. Newark: University of Delaware Press, 1989.

Passmore, John. *Hume's Intentions.* London: Duckworth, 1980.

Paulson, Ronald. *Breaking and Re-Making: Aesthetic Practice in England, 1700–1820.* New Brunswick: Rutgers University Press, 1989.

——. *The Fictions of Satire.* Baltimore: Johns Hopkins University Press, 1967.

Peacock, Thomas Love. *Headlong Hall and Nightmare Abbey.* Intro. P. M. Yarker. London: J. M. Dent, 1961.

Petrie, Graham. "Rhetoric as Fictional Technique in *Tristram Shandy.*" *Philological Quaterly* 48 (1969): 479–94.

Phillipson, Nicholas. "Towards a Definition of the Scottish Enlightenment." In *City and Society in the Eighteenth Century,* ed. Paul Fritz and David Williams, 125–47. Toronto: Hakkert, 1973.

Plato. *Gorgias.* Trans. Donald J. Zeyl. Indianapolis: Hackett, 1987.

——. *Phaedrus.* Trans. Harold North Fowler. Cambridge, Mass.: Harvard University Press, 1967.

——. *The Republic.* Trans. Francis Macdonald Conford. New York: Oxford University Press, 1941.

Plumb, J. H. *The First Four Georges.* Glasgow: Collins/Fontana, 1966.

Plutarch. *The Lives of the Noble Grecians and Romans.* Trans. John Dryden et al. Rev. Arthur Hugh Clough. London, 1864.

Pocock, J. G. A. "Cambridge Paradigms and Scotch Philosophers." In *Wealth and Virtue: The Shaping of Political Economy in the Scottish Enlightenment,* ed. Ivan Hont and Michael Ignatieff, 235–52. Cambridge: Cambridge University Press, 1983.

——. *The Machiavellian Moment: Florentine Political Thought and the Atlantic Republican Tradition.* Princeton: Princeton University Press, 1975.

———. *Virtue, Commerce, and History: Essays on Political Thought and History, Chiefly in the Eighteenth Century.* Cambridge: Cambridge University Press, 1985.

Polewhele, Richard. *The English Orator: A Didactic Poem.* 2d ed. Book 1. London, 1786.

Poovey, Mary. *The Proper Lady and the Woman Writer: Ideology as Style in the Works of Mary Wollstonecraft, Mary Shelley, and Jane Austen.* Chicago: University of Chicago Press, 1984.

Pope, Alexander. *Correspondence.* 5 vols. Ed. George Sherburn. Oxford: Clarendon, 1956.

———. *The Poems* (Twickenham ed.). 10 vols. Ed. John Butt. London: Methuen, 1939–69.

———. *Poetry and Prose of Alexander Pope* (for text of *Peri Bathous*). Ed. Aubrey Williams. Boston: Houghton Mifflin, 1969.

Port-Royal, Messieurs du [Bernard Lamy]. *The Art of Speaking.* Unattributed trans. London, 1708.

Porter, Roy. *English Society in the Eighteenth Century.* Rev. ed. Harmondsworth, England: Penguin, 1990.

Potkay, Adam. "Hume's Practice." *Critical Texts* 5, no. 2 (1988): 33–36.

———. "The Spirit of Ending in Johnson and Hume." *Eighteenth-Century Life* 16, no. 3 (1992): 153–66.

[Pratt, Samuel Jackson.] *An Apology, for the Life and Writings of David Hume, Esq. . . .* London, 1777.

Price, John V. *The Ironic Hume.* Austin: University of Texas Press, 1965.

Price, Martin. *To the Palace of Wisdom: Studies in Order and Energy from Dryden to Blake.* Garden City, N.Y.: Doubleday, 1964.

Priestley, Joseph. *A Course of Lectures on Oratory and Criticism* (1777). Ed. Vincent M. Bevilacqua and Richard Murphy. Carbondale: Southern Illinois University Press, 1965.

Puttenham, George. *The Arte of English Poesie* (1588). Facsimile reprint. Intro. by Baxter Hathaway. Kent, Ohio: Kent State University Press, 1970.

Quintilian. *Institutio Oratoria.* 4 vols. Ed. H. E. Butler. Cambridge, Mass.: Harvard University Press, 1920–1922.

Randall, John Herman. *The Career of Philosophy.* 2 vols. New York: Columbia University Press, 1962.

Raynor, David. "Hume on Wilkes and Liberty: Two Possible Contributions to the *London Chronicle.*" *Eighteenth-Century Studies* 13 (1980): 365–76.

Reid, Thomas. *Works.* 2 vols. Ed. William Hamilton. Edinburgh, 1863.

Reiman, Donald H. *Intervals of Inspiration: The Skeptical Tradition and the Psychology of Romanticism.* Greenwood, Fla.: Penkeville, 1988.

Richardson, Samuel. *Pamela.* Ed. T. C. Duncan Eaves and Ben D. Kimpel. Boston: Houghton Mifflin, 1971.

Richetti, John. "Class Struggle without Class: Novelists and Magistrates." *The Eighteenth Century: Theory and Interpretation* 32 (1991): 203–18.

——. *Philosophical Writing: Locke, Berkeley, Hume.* Cambridge, Mass.: Harvard University Press, 1983.

Robbins, Caroline. *The Eighteenth-Century Commonwealthman.* Cambridge, Mass.: Harvard University Press, 1961.

Robertson, William. *The History of the Reign of the Emperor Charles the Fifth.* Continuation by William H. Prescott. Vols. 12–15 of *The Works of William H. Prescott* (22 vols), ed. Wilfred Harold Munro. Philadelphia and London: J. B. Lippincott, 1904.

Rogers, Pat. *Grub Street: Studies in a Subculture.* London: Methuen, 1972.

Rousseau, Jean-Jacques. *Essai sur l'Origine des Langues.* Ed. Charles Porset. Paris: Nizet, 1976.

——. *Julie, ou La Nouvelle Héloïse.* Ed. Michel Launay. Paris: Garnier-Flammarion, 1967.

——. *On the Origin of Language; Two Essays: Rousseau and Herder.* Trans. John H. Moran and Alexander Gode. Chicago: University of Chicago Press, 1966.

Rudé, George. *Wilkes and Liberty: A Social Study of 1763 to 1774.* Oxford: Oxford University Press, 1962.

Rumbold, Valerie. *Women's Place in Pope's World.* Cambridge: Cambridge University Press, 1989.

Schiebinger, Londa. *The Mind Has No Sex? Women in the Origins of Modern Science.* Cambridge, Mass.: Harvard University Press, 1989.

Sekora, John. *Luxury: The Concept in Western Thought, Eden to Smollett.* Baltimore: Johns Hopkins University Press, 1977.

Seward, Anna. *The Poetical Works of Anna Seward, with Extracts from Her Literary Correspondence.* 3 vols. Ed. Walter Scott. Edinburgh, 1810.

Sha, Richard. "Gray's Political *Elegy:* Poetry as the Burial of History." *Philological Quarterly* 69 (1990): 337–57.

Shaftesbury, third earl of, Anthony Ashley Cooper. *Characteristics of Men, Manners, Opinions, Times.* 2 vols. in 1. Ed. John M. Robertson. Intro. by Stanley Grean. Indianapolis: Bobbs-Merrill, 1964.

Shankman, Steven. *Pope's "Iliad": Homer in the Age of Passion.* Princeton: Princeton University Press, 1983.

Shelley, Percy Bysshe. *Shelley's Prose.* Ed. David Lee Clark. Albuquerque: University of New Mexico Press, 1954.

Sher, Richard. *Church and University in the Scottish Enlightenment.* Princeton: Princeton University Press, 1985.

Sheridan, Richard Brinsley. *The School for Scandal.* In *British Dramatists from Dryden to Sheridan,* ed. George H. Nettleton, Arthur E. Case, and George W. Stone, 831–76. Carbondale: Southern Illinois University Press, 1969.

Shuger, Debora. *Sacred Rhetoric: The Christian Grand Style in the English Renaissance.* Princeton: Princeton University Press, 1988.

Siebert, Donald T. *"Bubbled, Bamboozled,* and *Bit:* "Low Bad" Words in Johnson's *Dictionary." Studies in English Literature* 26 (1986): 485–96.

———. *The Moral Animus of David Hume.* Newark: University of Delaware Press, 1990.

Siskin, Clifford. "Personification and Community: Literary Change in the Mid and Late Eighteenth Century." *Eighteenth-Century Studies* 15 (1982): 371–401.

Sitter, John. *Literary Loneliness in Mid–Eighteenth-Century England.* Ithaca: Cornell University Press, 1982.

Smart, J. S. *James Macpherson: An Episode in Literature.* London, 1905. Reprint. New York: AMS Press, 1973.

Smith, Adam. *Lectures on Rhetoric and Belles-Lettres.* Ed. J. C. Bryce. Indianapolis: Liberty Classics, 1985.

Smith, Norman Kemp. *The Philosophy of David Hume: A Critical Study of Its Origins and Central Doctrines.* London: Macmillan, 1949.

Smith, Olivia. *The Politics of Language, 1791–1819.* Oxford: Clarendon, 1984.

Smollett, Tobias. *The Adventures of Peregrine Pickle.* Ed. James L. Clifford. Rev. Paul-Gabriel Boucé. New York: Oxford University Press, 1983.

Speck, W. A. *Stability and Strife: England, 1714–1760.* Cambridge, Mass.: Harvard University Press, 1977.

Sprat, Thomas. *History of the Royal Society.* Ed. Jackson I. Cope and Harold Whitmore Jones. Saint Louis: Washington University Press, 1958.

Stafford, Fiona J. *The Sublime Savage: A Study of James Macpherson and the Poems of Ossian.* Edinburgh: Edinburgh University Press, 1988.

Stephen, Leslie. *English Literature and Society in the Eighteenth Century.* London: Duckworth, 1904.

Sterne, Laurence. *A Sentimental Journey.* Ed. Graham Petrie. Harmondsworth, England: Penguin, 1967.

———. *Tristram Shandy.* Ed. Howard Anderson. New York: Norton, 1980.

Stewart, James B. *The Moral and Political Philosophy of David Hume.* New York: Columbia University Press, 1963.

Swift, Jonathan. *"Gulliver's Travels" and Other Writings.* Ed. Louis A. Landa. Boston: Houghton Mifflin, 1960.

———. *Prose Works.* 4 vols. Ed. Herbert Davis. Oxford: Basil Blackwell, 1939–68.

Terdiman, Richard. "Is There Class in This Class?" In *The New Historicism,* ed. H. Aram Veeser, 225–30. New York: Routledge, 1989.

Thomas, Claudia. "Pope's *Iliad* and the Contemporary Context of His 'Appeal to the Ladies.'" *Eighteenth-Century Life* 14, no. 2 (1990): 1–17.

Thomson, James. *"Liberty"; "the Castle of Indolence"; and Other Poems.* Ed. James Sambrook. Oxford: Oxford University Press, 1986.
——. *The Seasons.* Ed. James Sambrook. Oxford: Oxford University Press, 1981.
Tillotson, Geoffrey. *Augustan Studies.* London: Athlone Press, 1961.
Tolchin, Neil. *Mourning, Gender, and Creativity in the Art of Herman Melville.* New Haven: Yale University Press, 1988.
Traugott, John. *Tristram Shandy's World: Sterne's Philosophical Rhetoric.* Berkeley and Los Angeles: University of California Press, 1954.
Trefman, Simon. *Sam. Foote, Comedian, 1720–1777.* New York: New York University Press, 1971.
Tribby, Jay. "Cooking (with) Clio and Cleo: Eloquence and Experiment in Seventeenth-Century Florence." *Journal of the History of Ideas* 52 (1991): 417–39.
Trilling, Lionel. *Sincerity and Authenticity.* Cambridge, Mass.: Harvard University Press, 1971.
Uphaus, Robert W., and Gretchen M. Foster, eds. *The Other Eighteenth Century: English Women of Letters, 1660–1800.* East Lansing, Mich.: Colleagues Press, 1991.
Utter, Robert Palfrey, and Gwendolyn Bridges Needham. *Pamela's Daughters.* New York: Macmillan, 1936.
Vico, Giambattista. *The New Science.* Trans. Thomas Goddard Bergin and Max Harold Fisch. Ithaca: Cornell University Press, 1968.
Voltaire. *Oeuvres Complètes.* 42 vols. Paris, 1818–20.
Warburton, William. *The Divine Legation of Moses Demonstrated* (1738–41). 2 vols. "To Which Is Prefixed an Account of the Life, Writings, and Character of the Author, by Richard Hurd." London, 1837.
——. *Remarks on Mr. David Hume's Essay on the Natural History of Religion: Addressed to the Rev. Dr. Warburton* (1757). Warburton's marginalia, ed. Richard Hurd. London, 1777.
Ward, John. *A System of Oratory.* 2 vols. London, 1759.
Warner, Michael. "Thoreau's Bottom." *Raritan Quarterly* 11, no. 3 (1992): 53–79.
Warton, Thomas. *Poetical Works.* 2 vols. Ed. Richard Mant. Oxford, 1805.
Weinfield, Henry. *The Poet without a Name: Gray's Elegy and the Problem of History.* Carbondale: Southern Illinois University Press, 1991.
Whitefield, George. *Sermons on Important Subjects.* London: William Tegg, n.d.
Williams, Aubrey. "A Hell for 'Ears Polite': Pope's *Epistle to Burlington.*" *ELH* 51 (1984): 479–503.
Williamson, George. *The Senecan Amble: Prose Form from Bacon to Collier.* London: Faber and Faber, 1951. Reprint. Chicago: University of Chicago Press, 1966.
Wilson, Thomas. *The Arte of Rhetorique* (1553). Facsimile reprint. Intro. by Robert Hood Bowers. Gainseville, Fla.: Scholars' Facsimiles, 1962.

Wind, Edgar. *Hume and the Heroic Portrait: Studies in Eighteenth-Century Imagery*. Ed. Jaynie Anderson. Oxford: Clarendon, 1986.

Witherspoon, John. *Works*. 3 vols. Philadelphia, 1800.

Wollstonecraft, Mary. *Vindication of the Rights of Woman*. Ed. Miriam Brody. London: Penguin Books, 1985.

Womersley, David. *The Transformation of "The Decline and Fall of the Roman Empire."* Cambridge: Cambridge University Press, 1988.

Yandell, Keith E. *Hume's "Inexplicable Mystery": His Views on Religion*. Philadelphia: Temple University Press, 1990.

Young, John. *A Criticism of the Elegy Written in a Country Churchyard*. London, 1783.

Young, William. *The History of Athens, Politically and Philosophically Considered*. London, 1786.

# Index

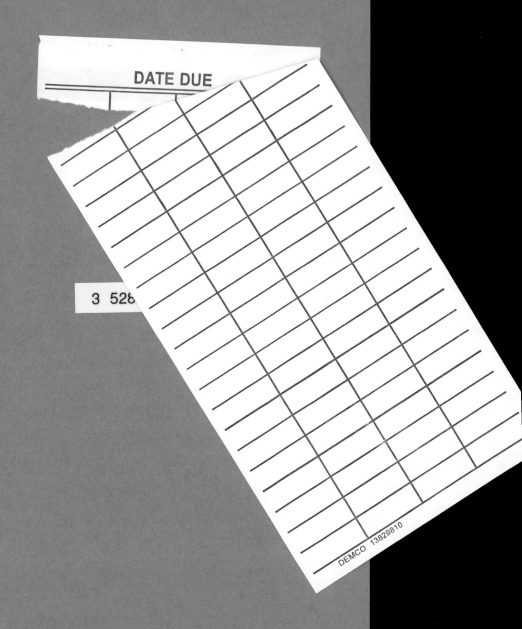

**DATE DUE**

3 528

DEMCO 13829810